USING NEWSROOM

at Home, School, and Work

Gregg Keizer

Part of ABC Consumer Magazines, Inc.
One of the ABC Publishing Companies
Greensboro, North Carolina

To Grandma K., who would have been proud.

Cover: Clip Art reproduced with permission by Springboard Software, Inc.

Printed in the United States of America

10 9 8 7 6 5 4 3 2

ISBN 0-87455-124-2

COMPUTE! Publications, Inc., Post Office Box 5406, Greensboro, NC 27403, (919) 275-9809, is part of ABC Consumer Magazines, Inc., one of the ABC Publishing Companies, and is not associated with any manufacturer of personal computers.

Table of Contents

Foreword

If you use *Newsroom,* the best-selling publishing program for home and personal computers, you've got a lot of company. With over 300,000 copies of *Newsroom* sold, the program has helped create family papers, school newspapers, and business and club newsletters by the millions. Tens of thousands of people like you—budding newspaper publishers—use their Apple II, Commodore 64, or IBM PC personal computer to run *Newsroom* and to turn their dens, classrooms, club houses, and offices into publishing empires.

And most of those *Newsroom* publishers want more from the program—more good writing, more interesting and unique illustrations, more attractive newspaper designs, and more efficient printing.

That's where *Using Newsroom at Home, School, and Work* fits in. This book is the best managing editor you'll ever find. It's packed with tips and tricks that show you how to get the most out of *Newsroom.* It doesn't explain the mechanics—if you've used *Newsroom* for only a short time, you've mastered those—but it describes the ins and outs of the software, and the advanced publishing techniques that you've not yet discovered or you've just barely noticed.

Using Newsroom at Home, School, and Work covers each of *Newsroom*'s six work areas—Copy Desk, Banner, Photo Lab, Wire Service, Layout, and Press—in such detail that you'll find enough ideas to keep you busy for months. Each work area is special, and *Using Newsroom* reflects that. Learn how to write a strong news-story lead, just like a professional journalist, in the Copy Desk. See how to plan in the Banner work area so that your newspaper's nameplate looks its best ever. Follow along as the immense capabilities of the Photo Lab and its clip art are uncovered. Find out why the Wire Service is a valuable addition to *Newsroom* and why you should use it. See effective newspaper design lessons put into practice in Layout. And compare several printing methods—from dittos to lasers—with the Press.

Using Newsroom also shows you how *real* people, not imagined examples, use the program to turn out dynamite newspapers and newsletters (and more) for their friends, classmates, club members, and customers. Four actual *Newsroom* publishers and their work are on display in *Using Newsroom.* They tell you what works and what doesn't. And you'll come away with ideas for your own publication, ideas that will make your paper better read and better looking.

More than just a newspaper-making program, *Newsroom* has undreamed-of abilities that make it the perfect tool to tackle such unusual projects as comic-strip creation, business-form generation, and flash-card writing. Take a fascinating look at what you can do with *Newsroom* besides publish papers as *Using Newsroom* guides you though each step in the process.

Newsroom has made thousands dream of becoming newspaper publishers. *Using Newsroom*—the perfect companion to a great program—helps you realize that dream. Make some news—become a newsmaker—with *Using Newsroom at Home, School, and Work.*

Acknowledgments

No one *really* writes a book alone, and this one wasn't any different. The people at Springboard Software, particularly Kathy Quinby, were uniformly pleasant and eager to help. Springboard's technical support personnel answered all my questions, even when those answers weren't what I wanted to hear. Chapters 8–11 depended on actual Newsroom users, and without Wally Benson, Dolly Bollero, Daniel Roberts, Duncan Teague, and others, those chapters wouldn't have come together as they did. The staff at COMPUTE! Publications worked its professional magic as always, but Janice Fary and Lee Noel, Jr. have always been outstanding members of an outstanding team. Lastly, Lori and Emily Reka managed to do without a husband and father for more weekends and evenings than anyone would have liked. They gave me the time it took to put this thing to bed. Thanks everyone.

Gregg Keizer
July, 1987

Your Own News, Your Own Newspaper

It's unbelievable when you stop to think about it. Produce an entire newspaper, here, with just a personal computer and a single program? A few years ago it would have been impossible.

Then something called *desktop publishing* appeared, and with it a flurry of computer programs that help you do everything from write a fancy letter to publish a book. Desktop publishing may be an overused phrase, but it clearly describes an idea—publishing (and printing) on a desk, not in some huge room that smells of ink and machinery. Publishing for almost everyone.

That's what *Using Newsroom at Home, School, and Work* is all about—showing how anyone can publish a newspaper or newsletter (and much more) and have fun at the same time.

Here's What You Already Know

Newsroom appeared long before the phrase *desktop publishing* became so popular. Released in early 1985 and now available for the most widely used personal and home computers—the Apple II line, the Commodore 64 and 128, and the IBM PC and PC compatibles—*Newsroom* has been used by more people and has produced more newspapers and newsletters than any other program. Over 300,000 copies of *Newsroom* and approximately 50,000 copies of the advanced version of the program, *Newsroom Pro,* are in users' disk drives—more than a third of a million people have bought this elementary publishing program.

In other words, there are a lot of you out there. A lot of people who use *Newsroom* regularly, and a lot who use it once in a while. No matter which group you find yourself in, you probably know a lot about using *Newsroom.* The program is very easy to learn—that's one reason why you bought *Newsroom.* You already know how to type in a story using the Copy Desk. You already know how to look through the clip art and grab a picture in the Photo Lab. And you already know how to lay out your paper and print it. That's the good part—you know a lot about *Newsroom* right now.

But that's not why you picked up this book. You want to know more about the program, things the manual doesn't cover and things you may not have discovered for yourself.

And Here's What You'll Learn

Using Newsroom at Home, School, and Work is packed with information about writing stories, about designing an attractive newspaper, and about printing your publication. You'll find countless *Newsroom* techniques, tips, hints, and tricks. Each will make your work with *Newsroom* easier or more fun or more satisfying.

Take a look at this list—it includes just a few of the things you'll learn how to do with *Using Newsroom.*

- How to write a real newspaper lead that grabs every reader's attention.
- How to create the perfect banner or logo for your newspaper or newsletter, even if you're not an artist.
- How to make great pictures in the Photo Lab with a video digitizer.
- How to use a modem and *Newsroom* to send your paper across town, across the state, or across the country.
- How to design the most attractive newspaper possible.
- How to print your paper in color.

But there's even more to this book. You'll also find out how real people use *Newsroom* in their own home, school, club, or business. You'll see their newspaper and find out how they created that paper. And, in the process, you'll probably learn ways to make your paper better.

Finally, you'll learn what you can do with *Newsroom* besides publish newspapers and newsletters. You'll be surprised at what you can create with this one program and how really simple many of these projects are. Did you ever imagine *Newsroom* could create comic strips? Or simple forms for many small businesses? It can, and in *Using Newsroom,* you'll see exactly how.

Using *Using Newsroom*

You'll be better able to use this book right away, and use it easily, if you know what's in it and where things are.

Using Newsroom is organized so that you can find the information you want and need as quickly as possible.

Part 1. Make News

The first major section of the book covers the six *Newsroom* work areas, as well as takes you through a step-by-step lesson in creating a newspaper. Part 1 is organized along *Newsroom*'s work areas, with each area—Banner, Copy Desk, Photo Lab, Wire Service, Layout, and Press—given a chapter of its own. If you want, you can turn immediately to the chapter which talks about the work area you're most interested in, or most frustrated by.

Chapter 1, Jump Right In, takes you on a guided tutorial through the entire process of creating your first newspaper. If you're new to *Newsroom,* you'll want to read this chapter carefully, and follow each step as you publish a one-page paper. If you're an old hand at *Newsroom,* you'll still find this chapter worth reading, if only as a reminder of the steps you take to write, lay out, and print a paper.

Chapter 2, It All Begins with Words, explores the Copy Desk work area, the part of *Newsroom* where you write and edit your news stories. This chapter contains a wealth of information about writing in general, writing newspaper stories in particular, and the Copy Desk functions. Here you'll find out why it's best to write your story on paper, on a typewriter, or on a computer with a word processor, *before* you start typing in the Copy Desk. You'll also learn how to write a real news lead, answering *Who, What, Where, When, Why,* and *How* questions for your readers. And you'll discover great tips on writing headlines, making columns line up, and using the right type.

Chapter 3, From Extra! to Exceptional, uncovers the ins and outs of the Banner work area. When you're finished with this chapter, you'll know how to make impressive banners and logos for your paper or newsletter. You'll learn how to use shadows and other unusual artistic effects to make your banner stand out. You'll also see how to copy a school emblem, company logo, or almost anything else into a banner.

Chapter 4, A Thousand Words, investigates one of the most powerful parts of *Newsroom,* the Photo Lab. Many *Newsroom*-produced papers live and die by their clip art, and this chapter shows how to make the most of any clip art collection. See how to combine pictures, how to add your own art to them, how to draw great pictures with other software programs, and how to convert those pictures into forms *Newsroom* can understand. There's even information here on how to use *Print Shop*'s clip art collections in *Newsroom.*

Chapter 5, It's a Group Effort, examines the least-used work area of *Newsroom,* the Wire Service. You'll learn how to transfer files across town or across the country, and how to distribute an electronic newspaper to anyone who has *Newsroom,* a computer, and a modem. You'll also see how to save money when you telecommunicate.

Chapter 6, Looks Count, gives you an inside view of one of the most overlooked work areas, Layout. Although *Newsroom* only offers four different page forms, there's a lot you can do to make your paper different and more attractive. Dozens of design tips and sample pages show how to make your paper better looking and easier to read. Specific techniques for school, home, and business newspapers make it simple to add design punch to your publication.

Chapter 7, Start the Presses, explains how to get the most from your printer, and what you can do after printing. You'll learn how to put thin lines, called rules, between your paper's columns; which copying process is best for your paper; and even how to create a two-color (or three- or four-color) newspaper with just a little extra work.

Part 2. Real News

The second part of *Using Newsroom* shows you what real people do with *Newsroom*. Each of the four chapters in Real News puts a *Newsroom* publisher in the spotlight as he or she tells you what they like about the program, what they don't like, why they use it, and even some of the tricks they've discovered. They'll also share some example newspapers with you.

Chapter 8, News from Home, presents a *Newsroom* user who publishes a newspaper for the home and family.

Chapter 9, News from School, shows what someone does who uses *Newsroom* at school.

Chapter 10, News from Clubs, shares experiences of someone who publishes a club or organization newspaper.

Chapter 11, News from Work, examines what one business person does with *Newsroom*.

Part 3. Beyond the News

The last part of *Using Newsroom* is a fascinating look at what you can do with *Newsroom* besides publish newspapers. With a bit of planning and sometimes a few extra steps, you can turn out almost any kind of bulletin, report, brochure, flyer, or advertisement with *Newsroom*.

Chapter 12, Beyond the News at Home and School, presents several *Newsroom* projects for the home and school. You'll learn how to create everything from flyers and flash cards to comic strips and calendars.

Chapter 13, Beyond the News at Work, offers tips on how to make simple business forms, presentation charts, and business letterhead with *Newsroom*.

What You Need to Be a *Newsroom* Publisher

Before you turn to Chapter 1 and learn how to become a publisher with *Using Newsroom*, you'll need a number of things. Other items, though not necessary, can help make *Newsroom* even easier to use. These optional items are also listed here.

Hardware

Hardware means equipment like your computer, printer, and monitor. But it also means smaller, less expensive devices, like a joystick, mouse, or graphics tablet.

To successfully run *Newsroom*, you must have these things.

Must Have

Computer. You must have an Apple II+, IIe, IIc, or IIGS; Commodore 64 or 128; or IBM PC, PC compatible, or PCjr personal computer. If you're using an Apple or IBM PC, it must have at least 64K of RAM.

Disk drive. At least one is required. It must be a 5¼-inch disk drive. If you're using a Commodore computer, it can be either a 1541 or 1571 disk drive.

Monitor or television set. A monitor will generally show a better picture, something that may be important if you're creating a lot of small graphics.

Printer. It doesn't make much sense to write and edit a newspaper if you can't print it. This must be a dot-matrix printer (one that can print graphics and pictures). The Appendix lists all the printers the various versions of *Newsroom* currently support.

Don't overlook cables. You have to have all this equipment connected somehow.

Optional

Another disk drive. Using two disk drives makes working with *Newsroom* faster and easier.

Joystick, mouse, or graphics tablet. Though you can move the cursor and make all your selections with the keyboard, it's not nearly as easy as using a joystick, mouse, or graphics tablet to point for you. If you have an Apple or IBM computer, the mouse is your best bet (if you have a IIGS, the mouse is standard). A joystick works best for the Commodore computers.

Hard disk drive. If you have an IBM PC or PC compatible, a hard disk drive can make disk swapping a thing of the past. A hard disk can store as much information as a stack of floppies, and it can save and load files much faster. Only the IBM version of *Newsroom* can be copied to a hard disk (follow the clear directions in your manual). If you're using an Apple II computer, however, you can also benefit from a hard disk, even if you can't copy the program to the disk. One problem is that *Newsroom* stores its files in DOS 3.3 format, which wasn't created with hard disk drives (and the scores of files and programs which typically are on a hard disk) in mind.

Modem. A modem connected to your computer and a phone line lets you use the Wire Service work area of *Newsroom* to send and receive panels, photos, and even entire pages.

Other things. Maybe you'll use a video digitizer to capture images and pictures (see Chapter 4); or perhaps you'll need your own small copier to create newspapers in color (see Chapter 7). A number of other optional devices are mentioned in this book.

Software

Software means the programs on disk which you use to make the computer hardware do what you want it to.

To successfully run *Newsroom*, you must have this software.

Must Have

Newsroom. You'll need a copy of *Newsroom* which works on your computer. If you have a newspaper staff with several people, you'll need a copy of the program for each computer your staff uses.

Blank disks. Although the manual says you need only one blank disk, have several handy. If you're using an IBM PC or compatible, make sure the disks are formatted before you begin. The Apple and Commodore versions of *Newsroom* let you format disks from within the program.

To format a disk on most PCs or PC compatibles, insert the DOS disk in the drive (in a two-drive system put it in drive A, the one on the left), turn on the computer, and enter the current date and time. When the A> prompt appears, type **FORMAT**, press Enter, and put the blank disk in the drive when the computer asks you to.

If you're using a two-drive system, put the blank disk in drive B (the one on the right); then type **FORMAT B:** and press Enter.

See your computer's manual for more specific instructions.

Optional

Clip Art Collection, Volumes 1–3. These are three collections of clip art from Springboard that you can use just like the art which comes with your copy of *Newsroom*. Volume 1 includes general art, Volume 2 concentrates on clip art for businesses, and Volume 3 offers sports and games clip art.

Conversion software. There are several programs which will convert *Print Shop* (the most popular graphics program for all personal computers) art to *Newsroom* photo format. These programs, some of which are listed in Chapter 4, take a *Print Shop* picture and turn it into something *Newsroom* can use. If you have one of these programs, you'll be able to use the huge *Print Shop* collection of graphics.

Get Ready to Start

By now, you're probably anxious to get going. Before you do, though, just double-check that you have everything you need, from a properly connected printer to blank disks.

Chapter 1, your next stop in *Using Newsroom at Home, School, and Work,* takes you on a guided tour as it shows you how to write, edit, and print a one-page newspaper. If you're brand new to *Newsroom,* make sure you don't skip Chapter 1. If you're a *Newsroom* pro, take the time to read Chapter 1—you'll probably find several new tips and techniques you can use right away.

PART 1

Make News

CHAPTER 1

Jump Right In

Experience is the best teacher.

You've heard that phrase before, haven't you? It just so happens, though, that it's true—especially when you're talking about learning *Newsroom*. You can read about some things—like how to use a computer program—as long as you want, but until you actually *try out* the methods yourself, they just don't seem to make much sense.

That's why *Using Newsroom at Home, School, and Work* starts with this chapter. You'll jump right in and create a one-page newspaper, from start to finish, with every step clearly described. Experience *is* the best teacher.

Your single-sheet paper will contain a news story, a banner, and pictures. You'll type in the story, mix graphics and text to create the paper's banner, and select and compose two *Newsroom* photos. When you've got all the files on disk, you'll lay out the page and then print it. Along the way, you'll discover several tips and techniques that you can use in your own newspaper.

The Perfect Companion

You probably already know a lot about using *Newsroom*. If this is your first attempt at publishing with *Newsroom*, though, take a few minutes to look through the program's manual. Keep the manual handy, because you'll want to refer to it from time to time. *Using Newsroom at Home, School, and Work* is not a replacement for your manual—instead, it's an addition to it. Think of this book as the perfect companion for both *Newsroom* and its manual.

Before you begin, make sure you're familiar with the way you move the *Newsroom* cursor on your computer, and the way you make choices from menus and clip art collections. If you're using a joystick or mouse, it's really easy—just move the joystick or mouse in the direction you want the cursor to go, and press the joystick or mouse button to make a selection.

If you're using the keyboard, though, moving the cursor and selecting an object or feature is harder. With every computer but the Apple II+, you use the arrow or cursor keys to move, and another key (called the *select key* in this book—the open or closed Apple key on the Apple, the Commodore key on the 64 and 128, and the ALT key on the IBM) to select an object or a feature. At times it may seem like you need three hands to do everything. Keep with it—you'll get better the longer you use *Newsroom*.

When you're using the keyboard to move the cursor, don't forget that you can switch between large- and small-sized moves. Change to small moves when you need to carefully and exactly position something, or when you're creating detailed graphics. On the Apple II computers, press Ctrl-S (the Control key and the S key at the same time) to switch back and forth between large and small moves. On the Commodore 64 and 128, press down on the CONTROL key while you press a cursor key. And on the IBM PC, hold down the SHIFT key as you press an arrow key.

When you're ready, put your *Newsroom* program disk (*Disk 1 Master Program*, the side with the label facing up) into your disk drive and turn on the computer.

Writing News

A newspaper is made up of words. Hundreds, thousands of words. Not pictures or graphs or comic strips—though those are all in a newspaper—but words about interesting news and interesting people. Your *Newsroom* newspaper will be mostly words, too, and that's why you should always start an issue by writing news stories. Everything else is secondary and can really be done only when you have the news written.

For this guided tour through publishing, assume you've already written the story (see Chapter 2 for more details on writing news stories in general and writing with *Newsroom* in particular).

Your First News Story

Your first news story is about a school basketball team winning its fifth game in a row. The story itself takes up three complete panels, while a fourth panel shows the points each player scored.

How can you be sure that the story takes up exactly three panels? Well, you can't, not exactly anyway, but you *can* make a good estimate. See Chapter 2 for more information on estimating a story's length *before* you begin typing it in.

- Select the Copy Desk work area from the main menu.
- When the Copy Desk screen appears, select the FONT icon and choose *Serif Small*.
- Move the cursor into the work area (the large white section of the screen) and begin typing. Don't worry about where the cursor is—the text automatically starts at the top left corner. Type the following, pressing the Return or Enter key on your computer only when you see the symbols <> (don't actually type in the less-than and greater-than symbols, though). To indent at the beginning of each paragraph, press the space bar five times. (Unfortunately, there's no Tab key or function in *Newsroom*.)

The Running Lions, East Elementary School's basketball team, won its fifth straight game last Friday against South with a score of 36 to 34.<>

Coach Olsen, in an interview after the game, said, "It was a close one this time, but the players wanted to make it five in a row." He added later, "I guess we'll go for six in a row next."<>

The game was tied with 30 seconds left when Matt Brink made a basket from near the foul line. "I thought it was going to go right in," Matt said after the game. "But it went around the rim a couple of times. That made me nervous."<>

The win set a new record for the Running Lions, who had never before won more than four games in a row.<>

South led in the beginning of the

≡ Your first panel is filled, and should look like Figure 1-1.

Figure 1-1. Panel GAME1

```
The Running Lions, East Elementary
School's basketball team, won its fifth
straight game last Friday against
South with a score of 36 to 34.
    Coach Olsen, in an interview
after the game, said, "It was a close
one this time, but the players wanted
to make it five in a row." He added
later, "I guess we'll go for six in a
row next."
    The game was tied with 30 seconds
left when Matt Brink made a basket
from near the foul line. "I thought it
was going to go right in," Matt said
after the game. "But it went around
the rim a couple of times. That made
me nervous."
    The win set a new record for the
Running Lions, who had never before
won more than four games in a row.
    South led in the beginning of the
```

≡ Take a moment to double-check what's on the screen. Are there any spelling mistakes or typing errors? If you spot some, use the cursor or arrow keys to move the cursor to the incorrect character.

≡ To delete a character, place the cursor on it and press your computer's Delete key. To add a missing character, place the cursor where the character should go and type it in.

≡ When you're satisfied with the panel, move the cursor off the work area and select the Disk icon.

≡ Put your data disk in the drive. If you're using an Apple or a Commodore, and haven't already formatted the disk, do so now by selecting *Format data disk*. You must format your data disks *before* you begin using *Newsroom* if you've got an IBM version of the program.

≡ Choose *Save panel* and name this panel GAME1.
≡ When you return to the work area, the text is still there. Get rid of it by selecting the Eraser icon twice.

Don't confuse the Eraser and Garbage Can icons in the Copy Desk work area. When you select the Eraser icon, it erases only the text in the panel. Choosing the Garbage Can icon, however, erases the text and any pictures.

≡ Follow the same steps to type in the second panel.

game, but by the end of the first quarter, the Running Lions had taken the lead on a free throw by Bailey Walker. The lead changed hands four times before the half, but the two teams went into their locker rooms with the score tied at 19.<>

"Coach Olsen just said that we needed to keep playing like we had," said Terri Carter, the Lions' starting center. "When we started the second half, we knew we could win the game, but then we got into trouble right away."<>

South scored eight points in a row, with the Lions unable to make the simplest shots. Finally, Carter was fouled and made both free throws. That set up a Lions run of ten straight points.<>

Late in the fourth quarter,

It should look like Figure 1-2 before you continue.

Figure 1-2. Panel GAME2

```
game, but by the end of the first
quarter, the Running Lions had
taken the lead on a free throw by
Bailey Walker. The lead changed
hands four times before the half, but
the two teams went into their locker
rooms with the score tied at 19.
    "Coach Olsen just said that we
needed to keep playing like we had,"
said Terri Carter, the Lion's starting
center. "When we started the second
half, we knew we could win the game,
but then we got into trouble right
away."
    South scored eight points in a
row, with the Lions unable to make
the simplest shots. Finally, Carter
was fouled and made both free
throws. That set up a Lions run of
ten straight points.
    Late in the fourth quarter,
```

≡ Choose the Disk icon, select *Save panel,* and name this GAME2.
≡ Type in the third panel.

though, South managed to tie the game again. Solid defense by both South and the Lions kept the game tied at 34 for several minutes.<>

The final play was set up when Bailey Walker stole the ball from South and took it down the court. He was double-teamed right over the ten-second line and passed to Matt Brink.<>

Brink dribbled to his left, then his right, leaving his defender far behind. With seconds left, he made a jump shot from just inside the foul line. It rattled around the rim for a few moments, but went in.<>

South got the ball back, but was unable to get it down the floor in time to take a shot. The buzzer sounded just before the South coach could call for a timeout.

Make sure it's identical with Figure 1-3 before you save it to your data disk.

Figure 1-3. Panel GAME3

```
though, South managed to tie the
game again. Solid defense by both
South and the Lions kept the game
tied at 34 for several minutes.
    The final play was set up when
Bailey Walker stole the ball from
South and took it down the court. He
was double-teamed right over the
ten-second line and passed to Matt
Brink.
    Brink dribbled to his left, then
to his right, leaving his defender far
behind. With seconds left, he made a
jump shot from just inside the foul
line. It rattled around the rim for a
few moments, but went in.
    South got the ball back, but was
unable to get it down the floor in
time to take a shot. The buzzer
sounded just before the South coach
could call for a timeout.
```

≡ Choose the Disk icon, select *Save panel,* and name this GAME3.

Still Text, but Something Different

The fourth panel of this story will still be all text, but it won't look like what you've done so far. Although there are a lot of facts in the basketball story, nowhere did it tell how many points each player scored. That's probably one of the most important things the story could tell its readers.

If you follow basketball, you've seen something like Figure 1-4 in newspapers. It's called a *box score.* You'll include one in your single-page newspaper.

- After erasing the text from the GAME3 panel, select FONT and choose *Serif*.
- Press the Return or Enter key twice. Hit the space bar twice to center the title, and then type **Running Lions Points**.
- Leave the work area again and choose the FONT icon. Select *Serif small* and reenter the work area.
- Make sure the cursor is in the shape of a hand, not a square. If you need to, move the cursor down a bit to turn it into the hand shape.
- Press Return or Enter twice and type **Player**. Type in the rest of the panel, using Figure 1-4 as your guide. Try to line up the columns as best you can, using the space bar to move the cursor over. Press Return or Enter at the end of each line.

Figure 1-4. The Box Score

Running Lions Points

Player	FG	FT	Total
Terri Carter	2	2	6
Matt Brink	3	1	7
Bailey Walker	5	0	10
Brad Clemmon	3	1	7
Eric Houg	1	2	4
Peter Lirse	1	0	2
Paul Frieser	0	0	0
Team Totals	15	6	36

- When you're through, choose the Disk icon, select *Save panel*, and name this GAME4.

Exactly aligned columns are almost impossible in the Copy Desk work area. There is no Tab function, so you must use the space bar to move the cursor to an approximate position. Things don't line up perfectly because the fonts used in *Newsroom* are not *monospaced*. Unlike a typewriter, where every character takes up the same width, letters and numbers in *Newsroom* are of varying widths. An *I*, for instance, doesn't take up as much space as a *W*. It makes the text look much better, more professional, but it makes it hard to create something like Figure 1-4. See Chapter 4 for a technique which uses the Photo Lab to create perfectly aligned columns.

- Choose the MENU icon to return to the main menu.

You're through with the news story and with the Copy Desk work area. Your paper isn't finished, however—it still lacks a headline, some pictures, and a banner. All of these are to come.

Your First Impression

Most people take the banner of a newspaper for granted. The banner—where the name of the newspaper, the issue number, date, and a bit of other information appears—rarely changes. It's one of the few things, along with a newspaper's overall design or look, that stays the same day after day. Perhaps that's why people don't notice it.

Even though a banner is often overlooked, it still provides valuable information to readers. The newspaper's name is most important, of course. When you pick up a newspaper from a newsstand, for instance, you at least glance at its name to be sure you have the right one. Grabbing the reader's attention with an attractive banner is one way to make sure they read your newspaper.

Other elements of a banner might include the issue number, the date of publication (you want to make sure your readers know this is the latest news, don't you?), and other small bits of information. Take a look at your local newspaper, for example, and you might see snippets of information in the upper corners of the banner—perhaps a mention of today's weather or particularly interesting news you can find inside. You, too, can add these kinds of things to your banner.

For now, however, you'll create a simple banner, one that mixes clip art and text, but that doesn't go all out in getting the reader's attention. You'll see how to do that in Chapter 3.

Name the Paper

Let's name the East Elementary School's paper *The Eastern Sun*. It's fairly catchy (*Sun* is an often-used newspaper name), short enough to put in a *Newsroom* banner in large type, and it associates the paper with East Elementary.

- Select the Banner work area from the main menu.
- Choose the Clip Art icon at the top left and insert the Clip Art disk which came with *Newsroom* into the drive. Make sure that side 1 faces up. Press any key.
- Using the cursor or arrow keys, scroll down through the list you see on the screen until BEASTS 6 is highlighted. Press Return or Enter.
- The screen should show four animals, with a lion at the bottom right. Move the cursor onto the page and, when the hand is atop the lion, select it.
- You're back at the banner work screen, with the lion clip art overlaying the white area of the banner itself. It's too large for all of it to fit in the banner, but that's okay.
- Using the cursor or arrow keys, switching to small-sized moves if necessary, position the lion at the left side of the banner. Try to duplicate what you see in Figure 1-5 and then press the select key to drop the lion into place. (The

box around the banner area won't appear on your screen; it's included in most banner figures in this book simply to give you an idea of where in the banner the elements are.)

Figure 1-5. The Running Lion

- Ignore what looks like a double image (no, your eyesight is fine). Move to the icon area and choose the Crayon icon.
- In the Graphics Tools menu, select *Sans Serif* under Large Fonts; then the EXIT box.
- Move the cursor onto the work area until it's about halfway across the banner and lined up with the lion's eyes. Press the select key to begin typing and enter **The**. Hit the Return or Enter key, press the space bar once, and type **Eastern**. Hit Return or Enter again, press the space bar twice, and type **Sun**. So far, the banner should look a lot like Figure 1-6.

Figure 1-6. Add the Name

Fine Details

≡ Choose the Crayon icon again, this time selecting the LINE tool and the smallest pen size before exiting.

≡ Draw two horizontal lines across the banner, from the lion to near the right edge, just below the word *Sun*. Use small-sized moves to position the cursor before you start to draw each line.

It's easy to draw parallel lines—either horizontal or vertical—of the same length. Once you've drawn one line, move the cursor in one direction only—up, down, left, or right—before pressing the select key again to start the second line. For instance, after drawing the first horizontal line from left to right, move the cursor up or down to select the starting point and draw the second line from right to left.

≡ Choose the Crayon icon one more time. Select *Sans Serif* under Small Fonts and exit.

≡ Position the cursor under the double line, just a bit to the left of the *S* in *Sun*. Press the select key to insert the starting point and type **November 16, 1987**. It should just barely fit in the banner.

≡ Compare your completed banner to Figure 1-7. It doesn't have to be identical, but it should be close.

Figure 1-7. The Banner is Finished

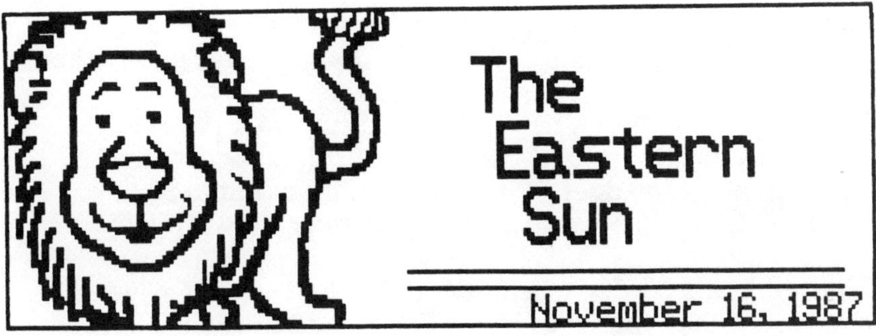

≡ Select the Disk icon, put your data disk in the drive, choose *Save banner,* and name it EASTERN.

≡ Choose the MENU icon to return to the main menu.

One good thing about a banner. If you create one you like, you can use it over and over again, changing only the date and whatever other newslike information you may have placed in it.

Grab Their Attention

Ever see a newspaper without photographs?

There's a very good reason you haven't. Though a picture may not be worth a thousand words (as the saying goes), it does tell a story. And sometimes tells it much more quickly and better than words.

Describing someone in a newspaper story might take several paragraphs, for example. But put that face in a photo and put that photo on the page, and everyone immediately knows what the person looks like.

Showing the effect of a storm, rather than simply telling about it, brings that story to the readers *now*. It almost makes the readers believe they're at the scene right at that moment. Pictures provide the news with something called *immediacy*—as if you're there yourself. It's one reason why television news is so powerful, even when it can't tell as much of a story as a newspaper.

All this has a purpose, of course. Pictures, because they can have such an impact, grab a reader's attention. If you look at your daily paper, for instance, you'll almost always find a dramatic photograph on the front page. Maybe it's a huge fire somewhere. Or the President greeting an important foreign official. It's a calculated method newspapers use to make you look at the news, and so make you think about buying the paper.

As a newspaper editor and publisher yourself, you need to do the same thing. You need to use pictures to help tell a story and to make the reader look at your news.

Not Just Gray Words

Pictures—and other graphics like charts, graphs, or diagrams—have another, just as important, purpose in a newspaper. Not only do they offer information, but they "break up" the newspaper page.

Here's what that means. Find a newspaper and turn to a page that doesn't have any pictures or illustrations, then hold out that page at arm's length. Looks like a mass of gray, doesn't it? It looks boring, uninteresting, when you can't read the individual words. Your eyes aren't drawn to any one spot on the page.

Now find a page that includes several pictures. Hold out the page at arm's length again. Notice that your eyes immediately look at the illustrations. You're more likely to spend more time looking at this page, simply because there's some variety. It's not all text.

This process of mixing pictures and words to create an interesting-looking page is called *lay out*, and it's the subject of an entire work area of *Newsroom* and of a chapter in *Using Newsroom*. But before you can lay out the page, and put your pictures to full use, you have to create them.

- Select the Photo Lab work area from the main menu.
- This looks almost identical to the banner screen, except that the white work area fills most of the picture. Select the Clip Art icon.

≡ Insert the Clip Art disk which came with *Newsroom* into the drive. Make sure that side 2 faces up. Press any key.

≡ Using the cursor or arrow keys, scroll down through the list you see on the screen until SPORTS 5 is highlighted. Press Return or Enter.

≡ Since the story you're illustrating is about basketball, you'll want to use the basketball backboard, hoop, and ball at the top left. Move the hand onto the page so that it's in the middle of the basketball graphic; then select it.

≡ You're back at the Photo Lab work screen, with the basketball clip art at the top left of the white work area. Press the select key and move the cursor into the icon area on the left. Ignore what looks like a double image of the clip art—it's just temporary and disappears as soon as the cursor leaves the work area.

≡ Let's customize the picture just a bit. Select the Crayon icon, choose the black fill pattern (second row, far left), and exit.

≡ Position the crosshairs and press the select key to fill alternating sections of the basketball. Figure 1-8 shows what the clip art should look like.

Figure 1-8. Custom Fills

≡ Move back to the icon area and select the Camera. Return to the work area and position the crosshairs cursor at the top left, press the select key, and move the cursor all the way down to the bottom. Then move the cursor to the right until the box just barely clears the right edge of the clip art. Press the select key again. You've just taken a snapshot of the art (when the selected area of the photo turns black).

≡ Select the Disk icon, put your data disk in the drive, choose *Save photo,* and name it GAME1.

The four kinds of files in *Newsroom*—Panel, Banner, Photo, and Page—are completely different. The program identifies each of the file types with a special two-character prefix or suffix. That means you can safely give a panel and a photo file the same name and store both on the same data disk.

- You need one more piece of art. Clear the work area by selecting the Garbage Can icon and then the Clip Art icon.
- Put your Clip Art disk in the drive, again with side 2 facing up. Press any key. Scroll down through the list you see on the screen until SPORTS 4 is highlighted. Press Return or Enter.
- Move the hand icon atop the basketball players at the far right. Press the select key.
- Use the cursor or arrow keys to move the picture to the left of the Photo Lab work area. Go to the icon area and select the Camera.
- Select the Crayon icon; then choose *LINE* and the pen third from the left. Exit.
- Position the cursor just above the small player's hands and a bit to the right (you'll probably have to use small-sized moves to get it just right). Look at Figure 1-9 for an idea of where to put the line. Press the select key, move the cursor to the right, and press select again. A thick line is drawn. To create the line at the bottom, cursor down, select, move left, and then select again.

Figure 1-9. Readout Lines

To draw parallel lines of equal length, count the number of keypresses it takes to draw the first line. Once the first line is drawn, move the cursor to position the second line and then press the *opposite* cursor key the same number of times.

- Return to the icon area, select the Crayon icon again, and choose *Sans Serif* under Large Fonts. Exit.
- Position the cursor (it should be a large rectangle) right under the left edge of the top line. Use small-sized moves if you have to.

≡ Press the select key to place the insertion point. Type **The final play was set up when Walker stole the ball.** Unlike typing text in the Copy Desk work area, you must break the lines of text yourself when you're in the Photo Lab. When you're done, you'll have a *readout* which looks very much like Figure 1-10.

Figure 1-10. Readout Text

A *readout* is often used to highlight a feature story. When you create a readout, select a phrase or short sentence that will grab the reader's attention and make him or her want to read the entire story.

≡ Move to the icon area and select Camera. Back in the work area, position the crosshairs cursor at the top left, press the select key, and move the cursor all the way down to the bottom. Next, move the cursor to the right until it reaches the right edge of the work area. Press the select key again to take your second snapshot.

≡ Select the Disk icon, put your data disk in the drive, choose *Save photo,* and name it GAME2.

≡ Choose the MENU icon to return to the main menu.

You've now got two pictures in your photo *morgue* (the name often used for a newspaper's photo library, since one of its uses is to store pictures to use in obituary stories).

But in *Newsroom,* photos by themselves are almost unusable (for exceptions see Chapters 12 and 13). You can't place photos in a *Newsroom* page layout unless they've been put into a panel by the Copy Desk. That's why the *Newsroom* manual suggests you work in the Photo Lab before you go to the Copy Desk.

That system—using the Photo Lab to develop your pictures and then the Copy Desk to put them into a panel—works only if you know what your story will be about. After all, the pictures in a newspaper should help the story, not the other way around. Words are still the "meat" of a newspaper. If you follow the suggestions in *Using Newsroom*, you'll have your story written—even know its approximate length—long before you enter it in the Copy Desk. That's the procedure you're following here.

Let's put your two pictures into panels and get them ready for layout.

Pictures into Panels

- Select the Copy Desk work area from the main menu.
- Choose the Disk icon and select *Load photo*. Put your data disk in the drive, press a key, and scroll down the list of filenames until GAME1 is highlighted. Select it.
- You'll return to the Copy Desk work area and should see a line about a third of the way across the white space. That's the photo (or the space the photo will take up). Use the cursor or arrow keys to move the photo to the far right of the panel so that you can add a headline. When it's against the right edge, press the select key and the photo magically appears.
- Select the FONT icon and choose the large *San Serif*. Move onto the panel, press the Return or Enter key twice to shift the cursor two lines down, and then hit the space bar once. Type **Running Lions** and press Return or Enter twice. Hit the space bar and then type **Win Fifth Game**. Press Return or Enter twice more, hit the space bar once, and type **In A Row!** You've just created your first headline, which should look like Figure 1-11.

Figure 1-11. Lions Win!

- Select the Disk icon, insert your data disk, choose *Save panel*, and name this file GAME5 (remember, you saved panels GAME1 through GAME4 earlier when you typed in the news story).
- The screen is still filled with GAME5, so select the Garbage Can icon twice to clear the work area.
- The second photo is easier—it's as large as an entire panel and text has already been added. Choose the Disk icon and select *Load photo*. Put your data

disk in the drive, press a key, and scroll down the list of filenames until GAME2 is highlighted. Select it.

≡ Don't worry—though the screen looks blank, the picture is there. Just press the select key, and it will appear. It should still look just like Figure 1-10.

≡ Select the Disk icon and choose *Save panel*. Name this one GAME6.

≡ Choose MENU to return to the picture menu.

A story, a banner, and photos—you have everything you need to create your first newspaper page. All you have to do is lay it out.

Make a Page

In most newspapers, arranging news stories and photographs to create a page—and so an entire paper—is done by pasting paper onto thin sheets of cardboard.

Stories, headlines, pictures, even advertisements, are photographically printed on paper. That paper is then "waxed" so that its back is sticky. All this paper is then placed on a sheet of thin cardboard a bit larger than the actual size of the final page. The sheet itself is photographed, and a plate is made. The plate is what's put on the printing press.

Wax is used, not glue or paste, so that the stories, headlines, and photos can be moved around. Pick this story up and shift it over there. Get rid of one picture and use another. It can be a time-consuming process, especially when you want to make major changes. Doing the same thing electronically is much simpler. If you need to move a story someplace else, even onto another page, it's a matter of a few keypresses.

Newsroom makes it possible to design newspaper pages electronically. Once you have the necessary parts ready—the panels and perhaps a banner—it takes only a few minutes to lay out a paper. And if you change your mind later, you can easily move stories around before you finally print out the issue.

An Eye for Design

Laying out a page isn't hard with *Newsroom*. What *is* difficult, though, is making the page look attractive, while still clearly telling the news. Newspaper design is an art, one which takes practice and an eye for interesting and appealing pages.

You'll learn about design, and find numerous tips and techniques to make your paper more visual, in Chapter 6, "Looks Count." For now, though, let's put together the six panels and one banner you've created in this guided tour.

≡ Select the Layout work area from the main menu.

≡ Choose *Layout page with banner*. (The other choice, *Layout page without banner*, is used to compose inside pages and other publications.)

≡ Select *Letter size*. That means you'll print the page on normal-sized paper (8½ × 11 inches).
≡ Press the select key when you see the page-layout form on the screen. Place your data disk in the drive and hit any key.
≡ Notice that the banner area, the wide box at the top, has turned dark. Use the cursor or arrow keys to scroll through the list of options. The only banner file on your disk should be EASTERN. Highlight it and press the select key. The word *EASTERN* appears in the banner area.
≡ Use the down-arrow or -cursor key to make the top left panel blink. Select it, scroll through the list until GAME5 is highlighted, and choose that filename. *GAME5* shows in the box.
≡ Select each panel in turn, and choose the appropriate filename as shown in Figure 1-12.

Figure 1-12. Filenames at Layout

EASTERN	
GAME5	GAME3
GAME1	GAME6
GAME2	GAME4

When you select a banner area in layout, only those files created in the Banner work area appear in the list. Select a panel, and only files created in the Copy Desk area show. This simplifies your selection process.

≡ Select *Save* at the bottom of the screen.
≡ Name this page GAME.
≡ At the next screen, choose *Save page layout file to same data disk*.
≡ Choose *Menu* to return to the picture menu.

The time spent at the computer in layout is short compared to other work areas. Even so, it's a vital part of the publishing process with *Newsroom*, for it's here that you take all the parts you've manufactured and create a real page. Don't underestimate it's importance.

Now that you have your first newspaper page, it's time to print it. Time to roll the presses.

Printer's Ink

Every job at a newspaper points towards one thing—the printed paper. Reporters write, editors make changes, photographers take pictures, layout artists wax and paste, all to make the printing possible.

Though electronic newspapers have been promised for years, they've just not come to pass. Perhaps that's a comment on how important the printed word still is, even in an age of television and instant communication.

Or perhaps it's because we like to read our papers in so many places. At the breakfast table, on the train or bus while going to work or school, and in the comfort of a favorite chair. It's hard to imagine taking a computer or some sort of scanner to work, tucked under your arm, just so that you can read a paper.

Newspapers are portable and disposable. Take them anywhere and then throw them away when you're through. After all, there are few things more useless than yesterday's news.

Printing used to mean huge machines filling cavernous rooms, with dozens of people to keep them running and supplied with ink and paper. Today, in an age of desktop publishing, you can turn a computer, printer, and software into a miniature printing press. It takes up space on one desk, doesn't demand scores of employees, and prints efficiently and inexpensively.

That's what you have in front of you—your computer, printer, and copy of *Newsroom* have made you a newspaper publisher. And like all publishers, you have to have a way to print what you write, edit, and lay out.

First Time at the Press

The Press work area of *Newsroom* is straightforward. You'll spend more time here than in layout, but that's only because the actual printing takes awhile.

The first time you print in *Newsroom* you'll have to specify the printer—and on some Apple and all Commodore computers, the interface card—that you're using.

The Appendix lists the printers and interface cards the most current versions of *Newsroom* support.

Choose *Change setup* from the first menu, and make your selections with the cursor or arrow keys and the select key. You'll also have to answer a question about linefeeds. If you're not sure that your printer requires them to print correctly, choose *Default*.

When you select the printer, card, and linefeeds, the information is written to your copy of the *Newsroom* Master disk. You won't have to choose *Change setup* again unless you change printers (or interface cards).

If you have problems printing, look in the *Newsroom* manual or Chapter 7 of this book for information that may be of help.

- Select the Press work area from the main menu.
- Choose *Change setup* as described above if this is your first time printing. If not, or after selecting your printer (and interface card), choose *Print page*.
- Put your data disk in the drive and hit any key. The screen will show a list of the page layout files on the disk (there should only be one, GAME).
- Scroll through the list until GAME is highlighted.
- Make sure your printer is turned on, connected properly to your computer, and is ready to print.
- Align the paper so that the top of the sheet, or the perforation, is just above the printer's printhead.

You can start printing anywhere on a page with *Newsroom*—just manually roll the paper to the starting point you'd like. The program doesn't automatically move the paper to the "top of form" spot. This lets you create some unique publications and documents. You'll find several ideas for using this feature of *Newsroom* printing in Chapters 12 and 13.

- Select the file GAME.
- Double-check that your printer is ready and that the paper is in position before choosing *Ok*.
- After a few seconds, printing should start. *Newsroom* isn't a speed demon when it comes to printing, so be ready to wait up to three minutes for each page to finish.
- If nothing happens, or if the printing looks terrible, you may have entered the wrong information in the *Change setup* step.
- When the page is completed, press the Online or Select button on your printer, and either do a form feed or manually roll up the paper.
- Check to make sure that the page looks right. Does it look like Figure 1-13? If not, maybe you made a mistake in layout.
- Choose *Menu* to return to the picture menu.

You probably won't want to print every copy of each page in an issue on your printer (unless your circulation is *really* small). Instead, you'll usually print just one copy of each page (call it a *master*) and then use a copying machine to make duplicates.

Figure 1-13. The Final Page

Running Lions
Win Fifth Game
In A Row!

The Running Lions, East Elementary School's basketball team, won its fifth straight game last Friday against South with a score of 36 to 34.

Coach Olsen, in an interview after the game, said, "It was a close one this time, but the players wanted to make it five in a row." He added later, "I guess we'll go for six in a row next."

The game was tied with 30 seconds left when Matt Brink made a basket from near the foul line. "I thought it was going to go right in," Matt said after the game. "But it went around the rim a couple of times. That made me nervous."

The win set a new record for the Running Lions, who had never before won more than four games in a row.

South led in the beginning of the game, but by the end of the first quarter, the Running Lions had taken the lead on a free throw by Bailey Walker. The lead changed hands four times before the half, but the two teams went into their locker rooms with the score tied at 19.

"Coach Olsen just said that we needed to keep playing like we had," said Terri Carter, the Lion's starting center. "When we started the second half, we knew we could win the game, but then we got into trouble right away."

South scored eight points in a row, with the Lions unable to make the simplest shots. Finally, Carter was fouled and made both free throws. That set up a Lions run of ten straight points.

Late in the fourth quarter, though, South managed to tie the game again. Solid defense by both South and the Lions kept the game tied at 34 for several minutes.

The final play was set up when Bailey Walker stole the ball from South and took it down the court. He was double-teamed right over the ten-second line and passed to Matt Brink.

Brink dribbled to his left, then to his right, leaving his defender far behind. With seconds left, he made a jump shot from just inside the foul line. It rattled around the rim for a few moments, but went in.

South got the ball back, but was unable to get it down the floor in time to take a shot. The buzzer sounded just before the South coach could call for a timeout.

Running Lions Points

Player	FG	FT	Total
Terri Carter	2	2	6
Matt Brink	3	1	7
Bailey Walker	5	0	10
Brad Clemmon	3	1	7
Eric Houg	1	2	4
Peter Lirse	1	0	2
Paul Frieser	0	0	0
Team Totals	15	6	36

It Takes Longer to Explain

This process of writing, editing, laying out, and printing takes longer to explain than to do. When you use *Newsroom,* you probably won't think of what you're doing in terms of a step-by-step procedure. Instead, you'll quickly fall into a routine that seems very functional and logical.

For the most efficient publishing, especially when you're starting out and haven't had a chance to come up with your own techniques, try to follow these steps when you're using *Newsroom*. Of course, if a different method makes more sense to you—and seems to be working in practice—then use it.

Figure 1-14. A Step at a Time

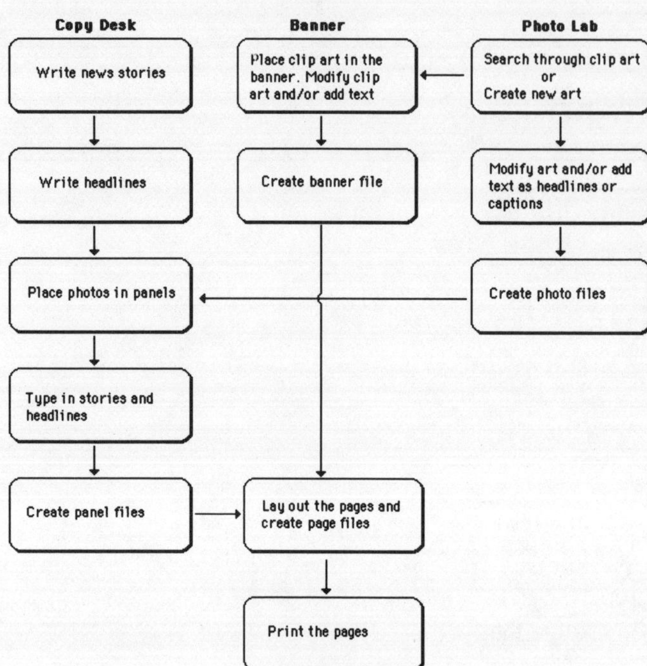

The rest of *Using Newsroom at Home, School, and Work* shows you how to get the most out of the program and your writing, editing, and publishing abilities. In Chapter 2, for instance, you'll learn how to write a real news lead, how to create an attention-grabbing headline, and how to use simple graphics in the Copy Desk work area.

Grab your pencil and notepad (whether real or imagined) and get ready to become a better news reporter and writer with *Newsroom.*

CHAPTER 2

It All Begins with Words

The Copy Desk

The Copy Desk is the most important work area of *Newsroom.*

It's in the Copy Desk that you position the photos you created in the Photo Lab and where you type in your news stories. The files you save here—called *panels*—far outnumber any other kind, for you can use up to ten panels in printing just one page. You'll probably spend more time in the Copy Desk than you will in any other part of the program.

But the Copy Desk can be used for more than just placing photos and typing text. You can use the Copy Desk's own fonts to create interesting effects, add graphics like lines and boxes from the Photo Lab, write attention-grabbing headlines, and more. You'll discover how to use the Copy Desk most effectively and efficiently in this chapter, where words are king.

Writing News

The reason why you bought *Newsroom,* and why you keep using it, is because you like news. Whether you're keeping your club up to date on the latest meeting or telling your school the inside story on everything from athletics to algebra, you like to investigate, write about, edit, and print the news.

But can you tell what's news and what's not? Can you really dig for the stories that are interesting and important to your audience? And can you write so that you get the most information to your readers in the clearest possible way?

If you've had a lot of practice, maybe you know how to do all these things already. But if you're like a lot of *Newsroom* owners, you may be able to use some help as you start your career as a newspaper reporter.

It's Everywhere

News is everywhere. News happens 24 hours a day. It never stops piling up, simply because news is people doing interesting things or interesting things happening to people. That seems to go on constantly, in the smallest town or the largest metropolis.

Your news may not be earthshaking. You probably aren't interested in covering the most recent scandal in government or what the weather was like on the other side of the country. You'll leave that to the large daily newspapers which have dozens of reporters and editors. With a small staff like yours (perhaps it's just one person—you), you can't afford to report all the news you find.

But you *can* report on the news that's of interest to yourself and your audience. If you're creating a school newspaper, that means paying attention to what's going on at school or what's happening to the people who go to your school. If you're publishing a club newsletter, then you'll want to report on things of interest to your club's members. And if you're producing a business news bulletin, you should stick to what your readers will find worth reading, whether that's what the competition is doing or how the new pension plan works.

Just keep this simple formula in mind when you're looking around for news, and you'll quickly see how many things you have to write about.

People + Something Happening + Interesting to Your Readers = News for Your Audience

The first two parts of that equation—*people* and *something that happens*—are easy to understand. But the last element, *interesting to your readers,* can be a bit hazy. What makes one story interesting and worth reading, and another not?

Here are some of the things that can make a news story interesting to people reading your publication.

Neighborly news. The closer something happens to a reader, the more interesting it is. That's just human nature—you're more likely to read a news story if it affects you personally, or at least affects people you know. It doesn't have to be news that physically takes place nearby; if a law is passed hundreds of miles away which says that anyone whose birthday falls on December 25 must always wear a red suit, and your birthday is the twenty-fifth, then it's news you'll want to hear about.

On time. The closer to the present the news happened, and the closer to the time it's read, the more interested readers are. News close to the present is called *timely* news. You're more likely to find a story about a new teacher at your school, for instance, when it's *news*—when the new teacher has been at school only a few days, not several weeks or months. By then, everyone will have heard about the new teacher through other means, and it's no longer newsworthy.

How big? News that's important—news that means something—is always more interesting. You'll want to read about a disaster that injured hundreds and caused millions of dollars in damage much sooner than a story about a storm that blew over one family's storage shed. The bigger the news, the more it's news.

Naming names. Associated with nearby news, this aspect depends on people's desire to see familiar names in print. Some small-town papers thrive on this kind of news, trying to squeeze as many names into an issue as possible. It's done for a good reason—people will read the paper to find names, no matter whether it's their own or just someone they know. Generally, the more names in a story, the more interesting most people will find it. (Don't load up a story with names without reason, though.)

And lots of other unusual things. Some of the other things that make a story interesting (and thus make it news) include humor or comedy, drama, sympathy, and just plain strangeness. The last is particularly effective in making a reader sit up and take notice. Why do you think so many of the supermarket checkout stands' tabloids shout headlines at the reader like "Aliens Took Me on an Interplanetary Vacation" or "New Superstar Diet—Eat Dirt and Lose Weight"?

When you're looking for news stories, or picking one of several possibilities, try to apply some of these news rules. Search out the nearby news that means something to every reader or play up the weird occurrence. See what your readers think.

The Five *W*'s (and One *H*)

So you know what's going to be fascinating reading for everyone who picks up your paper. It's a story about your neighbor and the strange way a small fire started. But how do you get that story into a form that communicates the information in the clearest and quickest fashion?

Keep the word *quick* in mind. It may be a sad fact, but most people just don't have the time to do a lot of reading. There are too many distractions. Like television, outdoor activities, family, work, and so on.

That's why you've got to get as many of the facts of the story to your readers as soon as you can. If your story is longer than a paragraph—many stories written in the Copy Desk won't be much longer than that—put the main facts in the first paragraph if possible. It's almost like a summary of the story.

When you're pressed for time and still want to read the news, just read the headline and first paragraph of any news story you might think interesting. (You can always read on.) Try this same technique with the stories you or your staff write. Can you get the basic idea of the story? If not, perhaps you need to rewrite that first paragraph.

In newspaper jargon, the first paragraph of a news story is called the *lead*. If a lead paragraph is written in the traditional newspaper style, a style which has been perfected over more than 100 years, it should answer a number of questions readers automatically have.

What happened?
Who did it happen to?
When did it happen?
Where did it happen?
Why did it happen?
How did it happen?

These are the five *W*'s and one *H* of newspaper writing. Answering five or six questions in a 25–30 word paragraph isn't always easy and takes practice. A well-written lead, one which answers as many questions as possible, makes readers want to read on.

Practice Lead

Let's take a close look at that neighbor story you'll write and try to create a good lead.

What happened? A house roof caught fire.

Who did it happen to? The Willsons.

When did it happen? Last Saturday.

Where did it happen? At 713 S. Cloudas, three houses away from yours.

Why did it happen? Mr. Willson's gas grill exploded.

How did it happen? The fire department thinks the grill's propane tank was defective, and leaking gas was ignited by a spark from a light switch nearby.

Put what you consider to be the most important fact (or answer) first, then the second most important fact, and so on, until you've got as many included in the lead as possible. Leads are generally between one and three sentences long.

Your story might begin with this lead.

The Willson's roof caught fire last Saturday when a gas grill exploded. The fire department put out the blaze at 713 S. Cloudas, and later said that leaking gas ignited by a spark was the cause.

Or it could read something like this.

A fire almost cost the Willson family their home last Saturday when a defective gas grill suddenly exploded. The fire department believes that a spark from a nearby light switch set off the explosion. Our house wasn't damaged, even though it is only three houses away from the Willson's.

There's obviously more than one way to write a good news story lead. If you have the room, you can add more information, like the second lead, where it's mentioned that your home didn't suffer any damage.

Even the shortest news story can start with a lead. If you're publishing your club's newsletter, for instance, and you're running a story about the next meeting, you'll want to be sure to answer several questions readers automatically have.

The next meeting of the Southern Railroaders Association will be held Tuesday, December 14, at 907 Tremont Dr. beginning at 7:30 p.m.

That one sentence answered the questions What? (next meeting), Who? (Southern Railroaders Association), When? (December 14 at 7:30), and Where? (907 Tremont Dr.). Notice that the Why? and How? aren't answered. Not all questions have to be answered all the time, especially if you can assume that those answers are obvious to the readers. Your fellow club members, for example, take for granted the fact that there will be a next meeting. There's *always* a next meeting.

Upside-Down Egyptians

Once you've written the lead paragraph, and you're sure you'll have the reader's attention, you can finish the rest of the story.

Newspaper stories have a very particular organization. The most important information is always at the *beginning* of the story, right after the lead. The next-most important information is in the next paragraph, and so on, until the last paragraph, which contains the least important facts of the story. That's different from a lot of other kinds of writing, where you'll often put the most important things—such as the outcome of a short story—at the end of the piece.

This pattern is usually called an *inverted pyramid.* If you drew a thick line for each paragraph, and drew the longest lines for those having the most important information, it would look like Figure 2-1.

Figure 2-1. The Inverted Pyramid Look

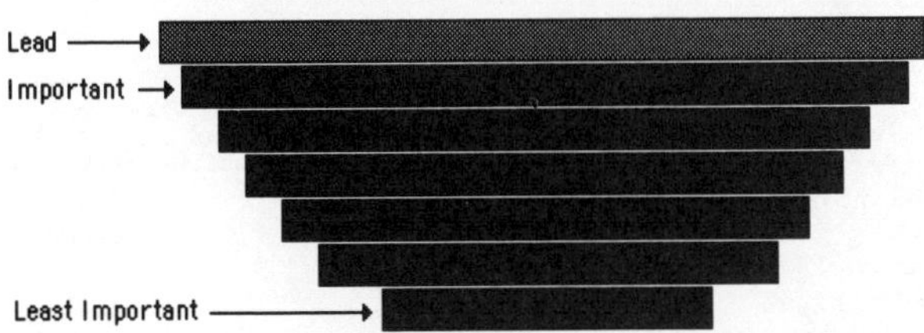

When you represent a story's organization this way, it looks like an upside-down pyramid.

There are several reasons for using the inverted-pyramid structure when writing news stories. Some of them even apply specifically to *Newsroom.*

Reader interest. As you've already learned from the discussion about leads, readers generally expect news in this order. They're used to reading the most important facts first. One thing this does is make it easy for a newspaper reader (you, too) to quickly decide if the story is interesting enough to finish.

Say you're reading a paper and have the time to read only five of the ten stories. You can read a story's lead and if that sparks your interest, you can continue. In fact, you can keep reading the story until you finish, or until you have all the facts you're looking for.

Easy to cut. Stories organized in this style are easy to trim if they're too long. If you have a news story that runs four panels, for instance, but you have only three available, you can quickly cut it by just chopping off the last quarter of the story. Assuming you wrote in an inverted pyramid, the least important facts are dropped.

Get the Scissors Ready

This ability to cut the last parts of the story, and still keep the important parts, is really useful in *Newsroom*. Because the Copy Desk forces you to work in panels, you'll often find that your story is just a bit too long to fit in the space you'd planned. It can be aggravating when you have only a small amount of text to carry over onto the next panel.

What happens, for example, if you have a short news story that you had estimated would take up just one panel? When you typed it in the Copy Desk, however, you found out different.

Figure 2-2. Too Long

A fire almost cost the Willson family their home last Saturday when a defective gas grill suddenly exploded. The fire department believes that a spark from a nearby light switch set off the explosion. Our house wasn't damaged, even though it is only three houses away from the Willson's.

No one was hurt in the fire and though the back of the house was blackened and some parts burned, damage was light.

A neighbor, Kathy Parker, used her garden hose to fight the fire, but by the time she arrived, the fire had leaped from the porch to the roof.

An unknown person called in the alarm and the first fire truck arrived within ten minutes of the explosion. Five minutes later, the fire was under control, and then out within another five minutes.

"It could have been really bad," said one of the firefighters. "But the roof was wet from the recent rains."

The family's insurance will pay for the damage.

The two short paragraphs at the end of the story (the shaded text) run over onto the next panel, but take up only a few lines. You don't want that space to go to waste. What are you going to do with the rest of the panel?

You could use it for clip art. Or if you had a *filler*—a short news item—you could use that instead. Or you could start the next story there.

It's a good idea to have a number of *fillers* on hand for those times when you have a small space to fill in a panel. An example for a company's newsletter might be something like "Mary Beth Kelly, an accountant in the Finance Department, celebrated her thirty-third year with the company last Friday." Look for such short (and relatively unimportant) news items and then enter them in the Copy Desk.

Save the filler panels with filenames such as FILLER1, FILLER2, and so on. When you need a filler, scan the FILLER panel files, locate the one you want, and then print only that panel so you know exactly what it says. Then retype the filler into the panel that ran short.

Chances are, though, that you already have plans for that second panel. Perhaps you need the space for a full-panel picture or you must have the entire panel for the next story.

Don't worry. Since you wrote the story in an inverted-pyramid style, you can afford to drop the last two paragraphs. Leave them out by stopping after you've typed in the sentence *Five minutes later, the fire was under control, and then out within another five minutes.* Or if you've already entered the two paragraphs in the second panel, delete the text by selecting the Eraser icon.

The only facts in the last two paragraphs are that the roof was wet and that the insurance will pay for the damages. Neither of these facts is vital to the story. Both add to the story, of course, but it still stands without them.

Without those paragraphs, the story fits in your planned space. Your job as newspaper editor has suddenly become easier, because you don't have to scramble to figure out how to fit two panels of copy in only one.

As a *Newsroom* user, you need to know what's news and how to find it. Once you have the news, you need to know how to write it. By now, you have a good idea of what makes news—something interesting happening to people your readers can identify with. You've also seen what makes news interesting. And you've learned that writing a lead paragraph and putting the rest of the story in an inverted-pyramid form can help keep your readers interested and make your job as editor simpler. But now you want to know how to apply those things to *Newsroom*.

Not a Word Processor

The Copy Desk in *Newsroom* is not a *word processor,* even though it may look and act like one sometimes.

A word processor is a computer program that makes writing, editing, and printing text much easier than using pencils, pens, or typewriters. Word processors are often loaded with features that do many of the mechanical chores you may associate with writing.

With a word processor loaded and running on your personal computer, you can easily make changes and correct mistakes, move text from one place to another by pressing a few keys, and quickly delete entire words, sentences, and paragraphs. You can make sure your letter or report or novel is just the way you want it, before you print it. And when you print it, you can create as many copies as you want. In other words, you have control over almost every aspect of writing and editing.

The Copy Desk isn't a word processor—it's too primitive to be called that. Instead, it's a *text editor,* a term used for programs (or parts of programs as in *Newsroom*) with fewer features, but which still let you type in text and make simple changes and corrections.

Because the Copy Desk doesn't have all the functions and features of a word processor, you may find it more efficient if you use something else to write your news stories. Once you've written the stories, you use the Copy Desk to retype them into *Newsroom.* In the long run, it's the best way to handle words with *Newsroom.*

What the Copy Desk Offers

The Copy Desk work area has a limited number of features, some of which seem to make it hard to enter and change your words and stories. Load *Newsroom,* select the Copy Desk from the main menu, and you'll see a screen like the one in Figure 2-3.

Figure 2-3. The Copy Desk Screen

As you probably already know, the icons on the left of the screen offer various functions of the work area. Selecting an icon either does something immediately or presents more choices.

FONT

FONT lets you pick the type face and size of the text you'll type in. You can choose between sans serif, serif, and English typefaces. Within the sans serif and serif type, you can select either small (for text) or large (for headlines).

Eraser deletes all text on the screen.

OOPS lets you change your mind. If you altered something and then decide you want it back the way it was, OOPS allows you to undo your latest change.

Garbage Can erases all text and all graphics from the screen.

Disk makes it possible to load photos and panels from disk and to save panels to disk. The Commodore and Apple versions of *Newsroom* also let you format a data disk here.

MENU

MENU returns you to the main menu.

A lot of what you can do in the Copy Desk area, however, doesn't show on the screen.

Enter text. After you've chosen the typeface and size from FONT, all you need to do is move the hand-shaped cursor into the white work space and begin typing. The text automatically starts at the upper left of the work space or of whatever's left after adding a piece of clip art.

Adding text. You're always in what's called *insert mode* when you add new text to what already shows in the work space. That means when you place the cursor in the middle of existing text, anything you type is added at the cursor spot. The existing text is always pushed to the right and down.

Deleting text. To erase one letter at a time, you must place the cursor on the character and press the Delete key. Text to the right is pulled left when a character is deleted.

Block operations. You can erase or copy a section of the work space and then put that section elsewhere in the same work space. To mark the block of text, press the select key when the cursor is on the first (or last) character of the block; then move the cursor to the last (or first) character and hit the select key again. The section turns white against a black background. Press Delete to erase the block or press Control-C to copy it. If you want to move that section elsewhere, shift the cursor to the desired spot and press Control-W.

These are the basic things you can do with text in the Copy Desk work area (adding graphics is an entirely different subject and will be covered later in this chapter).

When you're using the Copy Desk to type in your stories—even if you originally wrote them with something else (more on that later, too)—you can avoid some of the typing and editing frustration if you keep the following techniques in mind.

Entering Text

- In a fresh panel, just move the cursor into the work space and start typing.
- In a panel which already includes text, move the cursor into the work space and then move it until it turns into a hand. Whatever you type is added onto the end of the existing text.
- If the cursor appears as a black rectangle, text is entered wherever the cursor is placed.
- Because *Newsroom* automatically starts new lines for you, long words are often dropped to the next line. These unsightly gaps at the ends of lines can be avoided if you use a hyphen to break up long words. Use a dictionary to locate the hyphenation points. You can hyphenate words while you type them or after they're entered.
- If you're close to the end of the story, and you need to squeeze a few more words in the current panel, look for hyphenation possibilities. *Newsroom* automatically reformats the text when hyphens are inserted. Usually, this frees up some more room at the bottom of the work space.

Figure 2-4. Text-Entering Pointers

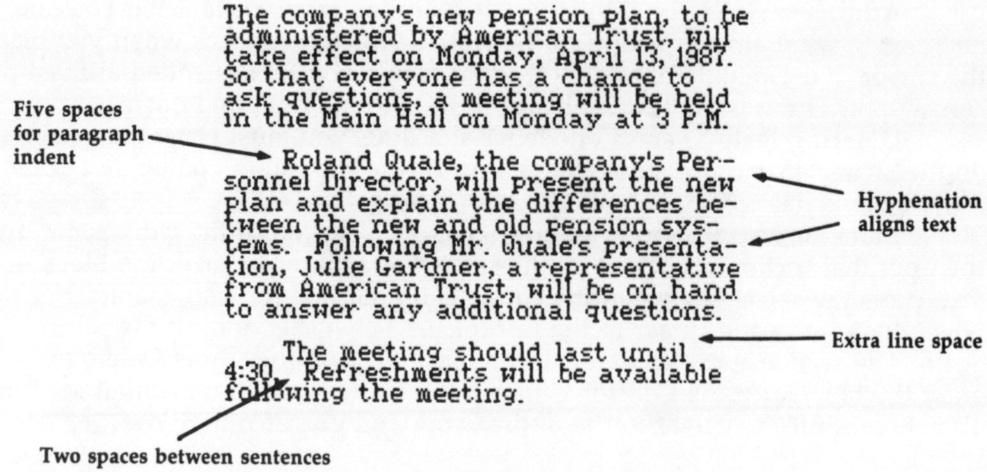

- Insert two spaces between the end of one sentence and the beginning of another. The extra space makes the text easier to read.
- For additional readability, press the Return or Enter key twice after ending a paragraph.
- The Copy Desk has no Tab function. To indent a paragraph, insert five spaces before typing.

Inserting Text

- *Newsroom*'s Copy Desk is always in *insert mode*. In other words, anything added at the cursor pushes existing text to the right.
- Since there's no way to turn off the insert mode, you can't simply type over a mistake. To correct the misspelled word *rihgt*, for instance, you have to delete the *h*, move the cursor atop the *t*, and type an **h**.
- When you're adding new text to a nearly full panel, there's a danger you'll lose some of the old text as it's pushed off the bottom of the work space. It's not gone—not yet. To retrieve it—if only to see what it is—delete enough of the newly entered text so that the old text is pulled back onto the work space.
- A major problem with the Copy Desk's text editor is that there is no way to transfer text from one panel to another. You cannot, for example, take the text that will be pushed off the work space (when you insert new text) and put it in another panel without retyping.
- If you *must* insert a significant amount of new text in a full panel, first print that panel so you have it for reference. When you're finished inserting your new sentences, retype in a new panel the text that was shoved off the old one.

Deleting Text

- Press the Delete key when the cursor is atop the character you wish to erase.
- As you press the Delete key, existing text moves to the left (and up from lines below).
- Don't hold down the Delete key; the computer may think you've pressed the key a great number of times. You may erase more than you want to. Instead, count the number of characters you're going to erase and press the Delete key that number of times. Or pause briefly between each keypress so that you're sure not to delete more than you planned on.
- When deleting more than a few characters, position the cursor on the unwanted character that's the farthest to the left and closest to the top of the work space. You can delete multiple characters as they shift to the left and appear under the cursor. You won't have to waste time moving the cursor.

Block Deleting, Copying, and Writing

≡ You mark a block of text for deleting or copying by pressing the select key at both ends of the block. The marked text is highlighted, as in Figure 2-5.

Figure 2-5. Marked Words

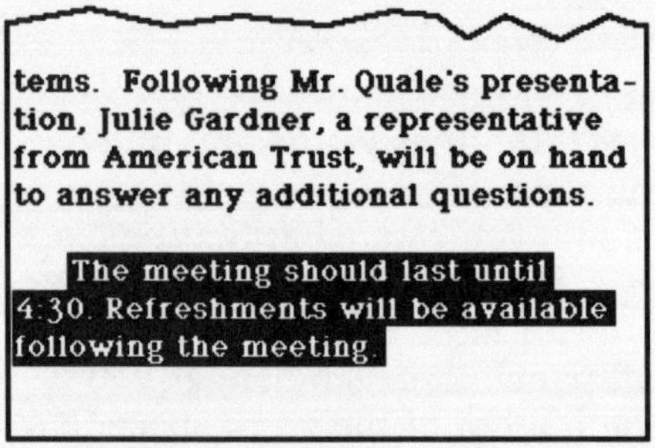

tems. Following Mr. Quale's presentation, Julie Gardner, a representative from American Trust, will be on hand to answer any additional questions.

The meeting should last until 4:30. Refreshments will be available following the meeting.

≡ It doesn't matter which end of the block you mark first. If the cursor is near the bottom of the block, for example, mark the end first; then move the cursor to the beginning of the block and mark that.

≡ Text deleted in a block is not lost—it's still in memory. It can be retrieved either by selecting the OOPS icon or by pressing Control-W (Write the block).

≡ Text deleted or copied in a block remains in memory until another block is deleted or copied, or until any icon other than OOPS is selected.

≡ When writing a block to the work space, put the cursor where you want the block to start before pressing Control-W.

≡ You can write a copied or deleted block as many times as you want in a single panel.

≡ Remember that you can only carry out copying and writing block operations in the current panel. There's no way to transfer text from one panel to another.

Saving the Panel

≡ Save the panel before you erase the current work space with the Eraser or Garbage Can icons, load another panel from disk, or return to the main menu.

≡ Make sure you save the panel to the same floppy disk, or to the same directory on hard disk, as all other panels for that page.

≡ Also make sure to save to the same disk any photo files which were used to construct the panel.

≡ Name the panel appropriately. A good method is Issue#/Page#/Panel#. The fourth panel on page 1 of issue #32, for instance, would be named 32/01/4. Drop the issue number if you keep each issue on a different disk.

Writing Outside *Newsroom*

If you've used the Copy Desk for any length of time, you're aware of its greatest failing, which is (and which can't be stressed too much)

Though stories may be made up of more than one panel, text cannot be transferred from one panel to another.

The following has probably happened to you at least once.

You're typing in the Copy Desk, and you've already saved two panels of the story to disk. You're working on the third, and suddenly discover you left out a paragraph—or maybe you realize you have to add one—in the first panel.

To add the paragraph, you have to load the first panel from disk and insert the new text. But that pushes old text off the screen, and when you save the panel, that text is gone. Okay, you load the second panel, and type at its top the words which were shoved off the first panel. But that bumps off text from this panel.... If this is a long story, you're in for some serious retyping.

Newsroom only recognizes the parts of a story—the various panels—and doesn't recognize the story as a single, whole document. *If you want to change anything more than a few characters in a story, you'll end up retyping everything which comes after the location where you added text.* There's just no way around that fact if you use *Newsroom* to write your news stories.

That's why you should really consider using something else—whether it's a pencil, typewriter, or word processing program—to write your news stories. If you use another writing tool, the Copy Desk is used only to *retype* what you've written. Then there are no surprises and there's no need to retype panel after panel.

Write in a Ribbon

Think of your news story as a ribbon—it has a beginning, a middle, and an end—cut to the right length. You can draw a line from start to finish on that ribbon without a break. That's what your story is like if you write it on paper or with a word processor.

Now imagine that ribbon cut into several pieces. Each piece is a panel created by the Copy Desk. There's no way to trace that line through the entire story. That's your story in *Newsroom*.

You want to be able to easily add more, take some away, and generally make changes to your stories. With alternative methods, you can.

Pencil and paper. This is the simplest and the most common way to write. It's inexpensive, won't break down at the worst possible time, and can be used by almost anyone, regardless of age or experience.

Changes are easy—just scratch out what you don't want and add what you do. Arrows can be drawn from new paragraphs written at the bottoms of pages to their new positions, and entire sentences can be eliminated with a single line.

When you use pencil and paper, remember that someone (maybe it will be you) must decipher what you wrote when it's eventually in final form and ready to be typed into the Copy Desk work area. Be as neat as your penmanship allows and try to make your intentions clear. If you have a staff of several people, however, it may be a good idea to standardize the kinds of marks you'll use to indicate such things as insertions, deletions, and capitalizations.

Figure 2-6 shows a few of the symbols you may want to use.

Figure 2-6. Editing Symbols

pet,

Before

Happy, our ~~tabby~~ cat, was found safe and sound
in the Humane Society's animal Shelter yesterday.
She was a bit thinner but healthy. ~~The people at~~
~~the shelter had~~ She was well looked after by
the people at the shelter.

Becomes

After

Happy, our pet cat, was found safe and sound
in the Humane Society's Animal Shelter yesterday.
She was a bit thinner, but healthy. She was well
looked after by the people at the shelter.

Typewriter. A typewriter shares some of the same advantages as pencil and paper—many people know how to use one, and changes can be made with editing marks. It can also give you a good idea of how many panels a particular story will take up once you put it into the Copy Desk (see the next section, "How Long?").

Typing stories also makes them easier to read. That's important if your paper or newsletter has a large staff, where stories must be passed back and forth for editing before they're entered in *Newsroom.*

If you're using a typewriter, set it at double space, so there's extra room between lines for editing marks, corrections, and additions.

Word processing program. You're already using a computer to publish your newspaper or newsletter. Why not use the machine to write it, too?

A word processing program lets you enter text, erase characters or entire sections at will, shift words and sentences around, and much more—all before you print out a single copy. Only when the story is just as you want it do you have to turn on the printer.

Some word processors aren't much more complicated than the Copy Desk text editor, while others are full of features. The important thing all word processing programs share is the ability to make changes to the whole story, not just to one panel. You won't need to retype the entire story to make the smallest changes.

The Commodore, Apple, and IBM personal computers have an almost endless array of word processing programs for you to choose from. Which one you decide to use may depend on such things as its price, features, and ease of use. *Using Newsroom* isn't large enough to describe all the available word processing programs for these computers, but here's a place to start.

Commodore 64	**Apple II**	**IBM PC**
SpeedScript	*Magic Slate*	*PC Write*
Paper Clip	*AppleWriter*	*WordPerfect*
WordPro	*AppleWorks*	Microsoft *Word*

A word processing program is the best tool you can have for writing of any kind. That's true whether you're writing a short news story before typing it into *Newsroom*, or writing a massive novel. Once you use a word processor, you'll never go back to a typewriter or pencil and paper.

How Long?

One of the disadvantages of writing with something other than the Copy Desk is that it's difficult to tell how long the story will be. Remember, *Newsroom* always counts in panels. However, you may think of your story in terms of pages if you're using a pencil or a typewriter, or in characters if you're using a word processor. When you don't know the length of your stories, planning pages becomes impossible. Will this story take up three panels, or four? How many pages will this issue be?

It's not hard to estimate the length of your story, though. In fact, you can become quite accurate if you're using a typewriter or word processor.

Before you see how to estimate story length, you need to know how much text a typical *Newsroom* Copy Desk panel holds.

Figure 2-7. How Much Text?

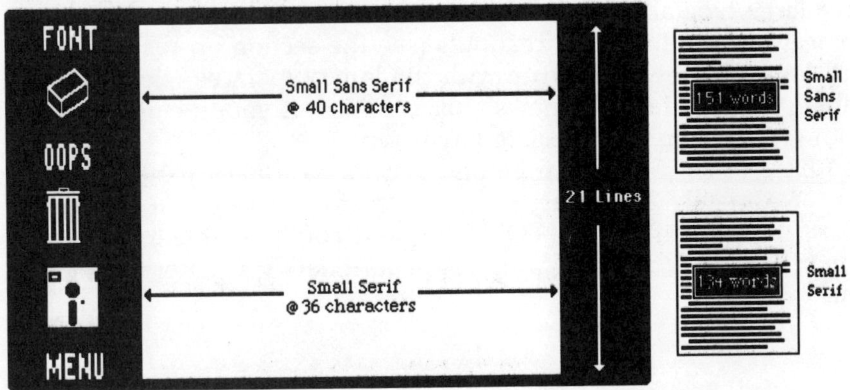

Using one of the small type sizes for your story gives you exactly 21 lines of text. Depending on which typeface you select—serif or sans serif—the line length ranges from approximately 36 to about 40 characters. That all translates into the average number of words which will fit in a panel.

The approximate number of characters per line is important when you're writing and fitting headlines, and when you're writing captions for photos.

Normally, you'll use words as your measuring unit when estimating story length. Words are easy to count, and they give an accurate estimate—two requirements for page planning.

With the sans serif typeface, you should be able to fit about 151 words in a single panel. The serif typeface, however, takes up more room, and so you can squeeze only about 134 words in a panel when using that typeface. Note that these numbers are correct only if the entire panel is text and in a small type size.

You can get a bit more in a panel by selecting the sans serif font. If you've already entered text in the serif font, just choose the FONT icon and select *Small Sans Serif*. The text appears to shrink somewhat, freeing up room at the bottom of the panel.

When you include a picture in the panel, estimate what percentage of the panel is occupied by the graphic and then reduce the word counts above by that same percentage. For instance, if the panel has a photo which appears to take up 50 percent of the panel, you should be able to enter about 75 words in the sans serif face, or 66 words in the serif face.

The three large typefaces aren't normally used for story copy, but instead are most-often seen in headlines and readouts (see the section on readouts later in this chapter). You can, however, write with the large typefaces when you need very legible print. Perhaps the newsletter is aimed at young children or the elderly. Both groups would appreciate larger type.

Only ten lines of large type can be placed on a *Newsroom* panel. Each line can hold approximately 23 characters, no matter which face you choose.

Select *Serif* or *English* from the FONT list, and you'll be able to put about 38 words in a panel; *Sans Serif*, being a narrower font, lets you enter around 42 words per panel.

Figure 2-8. How Much Large Text

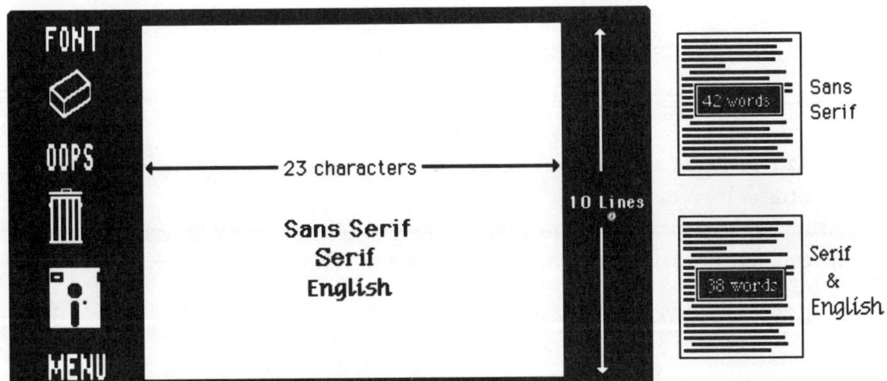

There's more than one way to estimate the length of your news stories before you type them into *Newsroom*. Use the method that's appropriate for your writing tools.

Pencil and paper. Count the number of words in the story, either by manually counting them all (if the story is short), or by doing this:

- Count 100 words and place a mark.
- Count the number of written lines the 100-word block occupies.
- Count the total number of lines in the story.
- Divide the total by the number of lines 100 words requires.
- Multiply that result by 100 for the total number of words.

To determine the number of panels:

- Divide the total number of words by the average number of words per panel for the typeface and size you'll use in *Newsroom*.
- The result is the number of panels it will take to run the story in your newspaper or newsletter.

Note that this method produces a *very* rough estimate.

Typewriter or word processor. This technique provides a much more accurate word count.

- Set your typewriter or word processing software margins to match those of the type size and face you'll use for your *Newsroom* stories. If you're going to use the small serif font, set the left margin on 0 and the right margin on 36. Slide the right margin over to 40 when you intend to use the small sans serif font.

Figure 2-9. Margin Settings

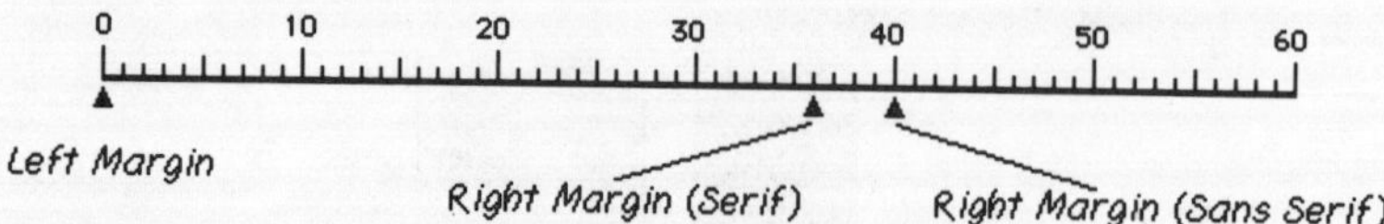

- Type as close to the right margin as possible, hyphenating words only if you intend to hyphenate in *Newsroom*.
- Don't let characters extend over the right margin. That's easy if you're using a word processor, which will automatically "wrap" the words to the next line, just like the Copy Desk text editor.
- When the story is complete, count the lines in groups of 21 and mark the end of each group.
- The number of 21-line groups is equal to the number of panels this story requires in your newspaper or newsletter.

With either method, remember to take graphics into account. Check your clip art collections, make your tentative choices, and estimate how many panels those pictures will need. Add that to the number of text panels and you should have the story's total length.

When you have an accurate idea of the space requirements of all your stories, you'll be in a much better position at layout time.

Read All About It

When you look at a newspaper, what's the first thing you see and read? Things like:

Killer Gets Life Plus 50	and	**Spring Rainstorms Deluge State**

You see *headlines*—the two- or three-line phrases and short sentences set in large type. Take a look at any paper; even when you hold it at a distance, you can read the headlines.

Headlines must quickly tell the main point of the story so that if time is short, readers can skim the headlines and still get some news. And since your readers may not want to read every story, headlines must get their attention and get them to read on. Where there's a boring headline there's probably a boring story. At least that's what your readers will think.

Like those you see in a daily paper, your headlines should summarize and advertise. Both are easier to do when you remember these things about writing headlines.

- Look for key words in the story that express its main point.

- Use short words. You can often say more with several short words than with just a few long words.
- Leave out words like *a, and, the, be, is,* and *are.*
- Use action verbs whenever possible.
- Avoid verbs in the past tense (those which end with *ed*).
- Make sure that the headline has both a subject and verb.

Although you can create custom headlines in the Photo Lab and insert them as graphics into a panel, you'll probably type most of your headlines in the Copy Desk work area.

Pick Your Headline Style

Like many other things which have to do with newspapers and newsletters, consistency in your headlines' appearance can make your entire publication look more professional. Decide on a headline style and stick with it.

Number of lines. This can vary between one and three lines. Not all headlines on a page have to be the same number of lines. In fact, it's best if they're not.

Other publications determine a story's importance by the size of the headline type. You don't have that luxury with *Newsroom,* where you can really use just one type size—large.

You can still tell your readers which stories are more important, though, by the number of lines in a headline. The more lines, the larger the headline will look, and thus the more important the story will seem to your readers. Take a look at Figure 2-10; the most important story on this front page is the one beneath the three-line head in the right column.

Figure 2-10. How Important Is It?

When you create your headlines in *Newsroom,* keep this in mind: Pick the most important story on every page and write a three-line head for it. Less important stories get a two-line headline, and the least important story has a single-line head. You don't have to stick to this formula all the time, but it's a good place to start.

Font. Consistency in the typeface you use will really make your publication appear more professional. Choose a typeface and use another only in *rare* cases.

Your newspaper or newsletter will look best if you use a typeface that's different from the normal *body copy,* the basic text of your stories. Since the English typeface is not very readable, and thus should not be used for headlines, your choice is made for you.

If you use small sans serif type for the body copy, use large serif type for your headlines. It's the opposite if you use small serif type for the body copy—select the large sans serif type for the heads.

This difference in typefaces makes headlines stand out even more from the stories they accompany.

Many newspapers use a serif typeface for their body copy, and a sans serif typeface for their headlines. That's because serif type is generally considered more readable when it's grouped in large chunks, as in a newspaper story's body copy.

Figure 2-11 demonstrates this idea with two side-by-side panels. The story on the left has both its headline and body copy set in serif type, while the one on the right uses the sans serif type for the headline. The panel on the right has the more noticeable headline.

Figure 2-11. Headlines in Different Font

Fire Alarm False, 18 Hurt In Snowstorm and Cold

A false fire alarm sent students and teachers alike into a blinding snowstorm on Wednesday, April 6. Although it was quickly known that the alarm was false, and everyone returned to the building within ten minutes, 18 people were treated for injuries suffered in the cold temperatures.

Both the police and Mrs. Themyer, school Principal, have vowed to find the person or persons who pulled the alarm.

"It was dangerous out there,", Mrs. Themyer said, "but we had to assume the fire was real. Whoever did this was acting very stupid."

Fire Alarm False, 18 Hurt In Snowstorm and Cold

A false fire alarm sent students and teachers alike into a blinding snowstorm on Wednesday, April 6. Although it was quickly known that the alarm was false, and everyone returned to the building within ten minutes, 18 people were treated for injuries suffered in the cold temperatures.

Both the police and Mrs. Themyer, school Principal, have vowed to find the person or persons who pulled the alarm.

"It was dangerous out there,", Mrs. Themyer said, "but we had to assume the fire was real. Whoever did this was acting very stupid."

Length. Headlines which include short lines (less than half of the available line length is used) are less effective than headlines which use longer lines. A headline with short lines look thin and incomplete and doesn't attract the reader's attention. Headlines with extremely uneven line lengths also look odd.

Figure 2-12. Use the Line Length

New Sales Record Set
By Company In March

The company's biggest sales month ever ended with a flurry of last-minute orders as buyers rushed to beat the tariff increases which take effect April 1.

New Sales Record
Set By
Company In March

The company's biggest sales month ever ended with a flurry of last-minute orders as buyers rushed to beat the tariff increases which take effect April 1.

Establish a minimum and maximum number of characters that you'll use in each line of a headline. Since you can put an average of 23 characters of a large typeface on one line, you can use that as your maximum. The minimum number of characters is up to you, but it's best if it's at least three-fourths of the maximum. That would be about 17 characters.

Try to write each line of a headline so that it falls between those two numbers—between 17 and 23 characters if you're using the formula above.

Capitalization. You also need to decide how your headlines will use capital (also called *uppercase*) letters. Here are your choices:

- All capitals
- Capitalize the first letter of each word
- Capitalize only the first word of the headline and all proper nouns (people's names, place names, and so on)

Some *Newsroom* users prefer the first choice. It has the advantage of making the headline most noticeable, but all uppercase text is hard to read. The second option is probably the most traditional way of capitalizing headlines and is found in many professional publications. The third choice is much more informal and is used by a number of newspapers. It's readable, but the uppercase characters at the start of each word attract the reader's eye. Because many *Newsroom* newspapers are much more "relaxed" in their news and the way that news is written, the third method may be just what you're looking for.

Experiment with capitalizing your headlines until you decide which form is best for your paper and then stick with it.

Placing Headlines

Write your headlines *before* you enter the Copy Desk work area. This precaution will pay off later, for if you know what headlines you're using before you begin typing in *Newsroom*, there's less chance that you'll have to change something later.

Although headlines are distinct from the body copy, and even though they're treated as separate items in professional newspapers and newsletters, *Newsroom* thinks of headlines as just words in a large type size. That means if you have a headline at the top of the panel and body copy filling the rest of the panel, and you decide to lengthen or shorten the headline, it's going to affect the text set in small type. Lengthen the headline, and some of the existing text vanishes off the bottom. Shorten it, and you have a sudden hole in your story.

Once you've got your stories and their headlines written, you're ready to begin.

Entire panel headlines. You can use an entire panel for a headline if you want. When you're including a large piece of clip art as an illustration, and you want it to share the panel with the headline, you'll need the whole panel anyway. Chapter 1's Figure 1-11 used a complete panel for a picture and a three-line headline.

Figure 2-13. Room to Breathe

Though it takes up one-sixth or one-eighth of your page, you can dedicate a whole panel to just the headline. This lets you position the headline where you want in the panel—perhaps in the middle—so that the *white space,* the empty areas without text, makes the head stand out even more dramatically. A headline crowded against body copy always is less effective in advertising its story than one which has room to "breathe." It's just less noticeable.

In Figure 2-13, the page on the left uses an entire panel for a headline, and offers an open look. Type isn't jammed together. The page on the right, however, shows a more traditional headline-body copy relationship. The headline sits atop the text, with no room between the two elements. Remember that at many times, *less is more* when it comes to a newspaper's appearance.

When typing headlines, you probably won't want the Copy Desk text editor to wrap the words to the next line for you. Instead, break the head into its individual lines manually by pressing Return or Enter at the end of each line. If you really want to spread out the headline, press the Return or Enter key twice after each line to double-space.

Shared-panel headlines. Most of the time you won't want to use entire panels for headlines. The most common location for headlines in *Newsroom* is alongside or above graphics or above body copy.

Headlines which will appear with a piece of clip art can be entered in either the Copy Desk or the Photo Lab. If you want the two elements—headline and art—to be inseparable so that they can be positioned and moved together, type the headline in the Photo Lab. But since the Photo Lab isn't the easiest place to enter text, you'll probably create your headline in the Copy Desk most of the time.

When placing a headline in the same panel as a photo or other text, there are some things to keep in mind.

- Write your headline *before* you select and crop the photo. The width of the photo will determine how long the lines in your headline can be. Once the headline is written, you can choose a photo of the right dimensions and crop it so that there's enough room for the headline to one side.

Figure 2-14. Photo Width Affects Headlines

Rock Climbing
Classes Now
Offered At
Town's New
Sports Store

Rock
Climbing
Classes
Now
Offered
At
Town's
New
Sports Store

The photo on the left was cropped tightly, and so there was plenty of space for an attractive headline. On the right, however, the photo was cropped much too wide. There was only a narrow area left for the headline, with the unfortunate results shown in Figure 2-14.

> If you want to place the headline below or above the photo, and want to make sure that *no* text can appear beside the picture, crop the photo so that it extends the entire width of the panel.

- Press the Return or Enter key once or twice to put some space between the clip art and headline if you're positioning the headline below the photo.
- When a headline shares a panel with body copy, you have fewer restrictions on line length since the headline can run the whole width of the panel.
- Use the Return or Enter key to end headline lines at the right spot when they share a panel with text.
- Insert space before the body copy begins by pressing Return or Enter twice at the end of the headline. In many cases this can substitute for using an entire panel. It doesn't provide as much white space, but for most purposes it works well. For a thinner band of white space, select a small type size from the FONT icon after typing in the headline, but *before* pressing Return or Enter.

Graphics and the Copy Desk

Newsroom's Copy Desk actually has two major functions. The first lets you enter text to create news stories. The second is just as important.

Only in the Copy Desk can you use the files you create in the Photo Lab. Clip art cannot be placed in a *Newsroom* layout in the photo file form—you must load a photo file from within the Copy Desk and place it in a panel to include it as part of a newspaper page.

Selecting, cropping, and modifying clip art is easy, even if you're just starting with *Newsroom.* For that reason, and because the more advanced techniques of the Photo Lab are covered in Chapter 4, you won't find much information here about placing pictures in panels.

But there's a lot more than clip art which you can create in the Photo Lab and use in the Copy Desk to enhance your stories. The Photo Lab is the only place in *Newsroom* where you can produce simple graphics—things like lines, boxes, inset letters, sidebars—for use with text.

Take a look at almost any newspaper and you'll see evidence of simple graphics. Perhaps it's a box in one corner which acts as a table of contents, or maybe it's a *rule,* a thin line that separates one short news story from another in the same column. It may be that the first letter of a story is larger than the others, or you may find an outlined mini-story that adds more information to the main article.

You can add this kind of graphics punch to your own newspapers with just a little extra time and work. All of the techniques which follow use both the Copy Desk and Photo Lab work areas. Remember, though, that the Copy Desk is the place you'll always end up—you must save your graphics to disk in the form of a panel file.

Lines and Boxes

Lines are the easiest graphic elements to create. They're also among the most useful. With a thin or thick line (called a *rule* in newspaper terminology), you can separate short news stories, show your readers that there is more than one section of a story, or simply break up a page.

Here are some places you might find lines worth using.

- To separate short news items that are grouped together under one logical headline.
- To set off text which really isn't part of the main story and is of great interest, but that can't really be considered a separate story. This kind of information is usually called an *insert.*
- To indicate the end of every story.
- To set off a photo from text above and below it.
- To separate the end of a story from the message *Continues on page xx.*
- To draw the reader's eye to that spot on the page (perhaps because right below it is a brief description of an important news story on an inside page).

Use lines for a reason, not just because you can create them. If you throw a handful on a page, your readers will have trouble following the news. As with any graphic, make sure there's not a simpler, cleaner way of accomplishing your goal. You can often use white space instead of a line, for example, and still tell the reader that there are two stories, not one.

To create a line and place it within a story, try this.

- Select the Photo Lab from the main menu.
- Choose the Crayon icon and select *Line* and the appropriate pen. Stick to the two leftmost pens when creating rules.
- Draw a horizontal line which stretches from just inside the left edge of the work space to near the right edge. If you draw it from edge to edge, it's hard to crop.
- Choose the Camera icon and crop the line as closely as you can. In other words, don't include a lot of extra space above or below the line within the cropping box. Stretch the cropping box clear across the work space, though.
- Select the Disk icon, choose *Save photo*, and name it something simple like LINEHOR.
- Return to the main menu and choose Copy Desk.
- Type in whatever part of your story will include the line graphic. When you come to the spot where the line is needed, choose the Disk icon and load LINEHOR.
- Here's where it gets tricky: With the outline of the line (it should be a narrow rectangle) on the screen, the text you entered is invisible. You'll have to estimate where to put the line. Press the select key to place the line.
- If you're off, just press the select key again and re-position the line.
- Once the line is in the right place, continue entering text by selecting FONT and the appropriate type size and face.

Figure 2-15. Lines

Grade 1 -- The newest project under construction in the class art center is a model of an early American town. The model town is huge, measuring four feet by three, and includes a town hall, a bank, several businesses, a smithy, a church, and numerous houses. The town, still unnamed, is to be finished by Thanksgiving.

Grade 2 -- Mr. Flander's class is studying several kinds of musical instruments in the Music Center. Each student is examining three instruments and giving a short oral report on his or her favorite.

If you want, you can create lines of various lengths and then use them in different situations. Save them with filenames which make it easy for you to remember the lengths, such as LINE1 for a line as wide as the panel, LINE12 for one-half the width, and so on.

You can also produce vertical lines in the Photo Lab, though you won't find as many uses for them as for horizontal lines. Place vertical rules in pairs, one on each side of the panel, for the best effect. Most of the time, it will work best if you position them before entering text.

Vertical rules can set off small news briefs, and they work especially well when they've been placed some distance inside the edges of the panel. Since all text starts to the *right* of a photo, the vertical rules force a narrower margin for the text. This narrow margin alone will make the text stand out on the page.

Figure 2-16. Vertical Rules

Kay Ellen Darwin has been named the Outstanding Employee of the Month, according to Ann Otick, Director of Personnel.
Kay has been with the company three years and has received the award before.
A check for $50 will be presented to Kay on Friday.

Boxes. Boxes are more quickly noticed by a reader, so they are used to provide more important information. Some of the places you'll see boxes used in a newspaper or newsletter—which you can duplicate in your publication—include

- The paper's contents.
- News briefs, where important stories are summarized.
- The masthead, where the staff names and titles are listed.
- An important story.
- A story that may not belong on that page, but is still important. For instance, an important sports story that appears on the front page, where more general news is usually located.
- Advertisements.
- Sidebars (see below for more information on sidebars).

Boxes can be produced and filled with text in one of two ways. The first, which is discussed here, involves the Copy Desk. The second method, which is covered in Chapter 4, uses the Photo Lab almost exclusively.

There are two methods, but there are advantages and disadvantages to both. With the Copy Desk, it's easy to enter and change the text in the box, but hard to create the box itself. The Photo Lab is just the opposite; the box can be drawn in a moment, but typing text takes much longer. Choose the method you think best for your purposes.

You'll need some patience, but you can create a text-filled box within the Copy Desk.

- Write the text you intend to box and estimate its length. Add another ten percent for good measure (and to account for the box's edges).

- Go to the Photo Lab and create two lines, one horizontal and one vertical, to form the box. It will be much easier if the box is about as wide as the panel. Crop each line very closely and then save them as separate files.
- Enter the Copy Desk and choose the Disk icon. Load the horizontal-line photo file.
- Position the line to form the top of the box.
- Return to the Disk icon and load the vertical line file.
- Position the line to form the right side of the box. You may have to reposition the line several times to place it exactly in the right spot. Here's where the close cropping pays off; there should be just the smallest gap at the corner of the two lines. It's almost impossible to eliminate that gap entirely—look at Figure 2-17, for instance. Even though great care was taken in creating the box, the results were less than perfect.
- Place the bottom and left side of the box by loading the same horizontal and vertical photo files and positioning them.
- Choose the typeface and size from the FONT list, move the cursor into the work space, and begin typing. If the box is at the top left of the area, the first character will appear inside the upper left corner of the box. You may have to use the Return or Enter key, and the space bar to position the cursor if the box is in a different part of the panel.
- Boxes narrower than the panel width present special problems. You'll have to use the Return or Enter key and the space bar constantly to keep the text within the box's outline.

Figure 2-17. A Box

In This Issue

Ask Allen	Page 2
Comics	Page 2
Editorials	Page 3
Sports	Page 4
Weather	Page 4

Shadowed Boxes. Sometimes called *drop-shadowed* boxes, these are simply boxes which seem to have a shadow beneath them. The purpose is the same, but the look is different. Creating a shadowed box isn't much harder than making a standard box.

Instead of two line photo files, you'll need four—a normal vertical and horizontal line, and a vertical and horizontal line in the next largest pen size. Position the thick horizontal line first, as the bottom of the box. Next, place the thick vertical line as the right side of the box.

Put the normal-width horizontal and vertical lines in the panel as the top and left sides, respectively. Enter the text as you would with any box.

Figure 2-18. Drop-Shadowed Box

Sidebars

A *sidebar* is a short but separate mini–news story connected with another, more important story. As the term implies, a sidebar is usually placed alongside the main story and is often boxed or shaded to show that it's not part of the more important story.

You can use sidebars in your newspapers and newsletters for the same purpose. Because of the space available on a page, however, your sidebars will likely be short—a panel at the most. If they're longer than a panel (more than 1/6 or 1/8 page), they should be considered stories in their own right.

Sidebars make sense when you have a complicated story that has many angles or viewpoints. Let's say you're editing your company's newsletter. You'd devote most of an issue to a major story about a possible merger with a large corporation. The main story would tell the straight news, but sidebars could be included to provide information on the corporation's financial state or on the recent increase in your company's stock.

As with boxes, you can create a sidebar in either the Copy Desk or the Photo Lab. Since a sidebar should be nearly a panel long, though, it's best to make one in the Copy Desk work area, where typing and changing text is much easier.

Although a sidebar can have its own headline and lead, you'll want something more to call attention to it; the readers have to know the sidebar isn't just another story.

- You can use different type for the sidebar to make it stand out. If your body copy is normally serif, for instance, select *Sans Serif Small* from the FONT list for the sidebar's text.
- Edge the sidebar with two vertical lines which stretch from the panel's top to its bottom.
- Create a box as large as the panel to hold the sidebar.

Figure 2-19. Alongside Sidebars

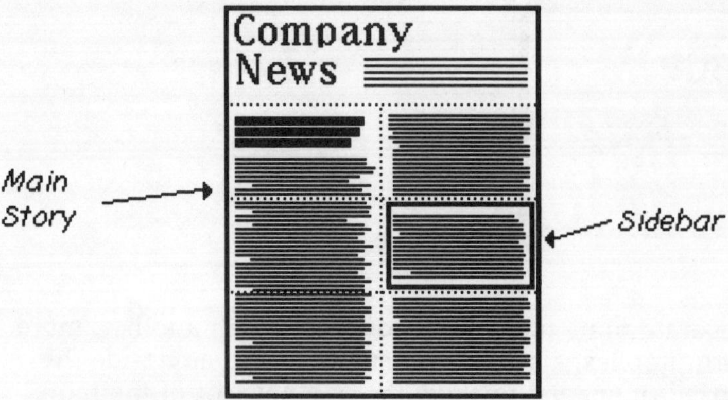

Don't forget to place the sidebar panel next to the main story when you enter the Layout work area.

Inset Caps

Another graphic device you can use in your publication is the *inset cap,* where the first character of the first word of a story is set larger than the rest of the type. You don't often see inset caps in straight news stories; magazine articles and newspaper features and human interest stories do make use of them, though.

This is an example of an inset cap. Normally, only the first letter is larger, but a whole word or even a short phrase can be set in large type for greater emphasis.

Here's the simple way to create an inset cap.

- Select a large type size, say *Serif,* from the FONT list.
- Enter the first character and then choose FONT again.
- Select the small size of the same typeface. If you used Serif before, choose *Serif Small.* Type in the rest of the text.

It's hard to pick out the inset cap among the other, smaller letters in Figure 2-20, however. Much of the inset cap's effect has been lost.

By using the Photo Lab to create the inset cap, you can make the character much more visible, both because of some special effects you can create and also because there will be more white space around the letter. Try this technique when you have a little more time.

- Enter the Photo Lab work area and select the Crayon icon. Select *Large Serif* and exit.

Figure 2-20. Inset Cap the Easy Way

Under the bridge--that's where the
Malin family lives.
    Five people--Bob and Margaret
Malin and their three children--live
in the shelter of a concrete highway
bridge that's part of Interstate 85.
    "We didn't have anyplace to stay,"
Bob Malin said. "I lost my job and we
didn't want to split up the family,
you know?"
    The Malins prefer the underside
of their bridge to some of the
shelters for the homeless that
they've stayed in.
    "Some of the places we've been,"
Margaret Malin said, "were so dirty
that this is even cleaner." She
pointed to the bare concrete her
three children played on.

≡ Position the cursor anywhere in the work space and press the select key. Type in the letter(s) for the inset cap.

≡ At this point, you can do one of two things: crop the letter and save it to disk as a photo file, or add some special effects. Let's add something to this character.

≡ Choose the Crayon icon again and pick *Box* and the thinnest pen. Draw a box around the letter you typed.

≡ Select the Magnifying Glass icon and zoom in on the letter and its box.

≡ Paint the squares around the edges of the letter black and turn the squares which were black to white.

≡ Exit the magnifying view, choose the Crayon icon, select the black fill pattern, and exit. Fill the inside of the box with black. The letter is *inverted,* or white against black. Figure 2-21 shows before and after versions of the letter.

Figure 2-21. Before and After *U*

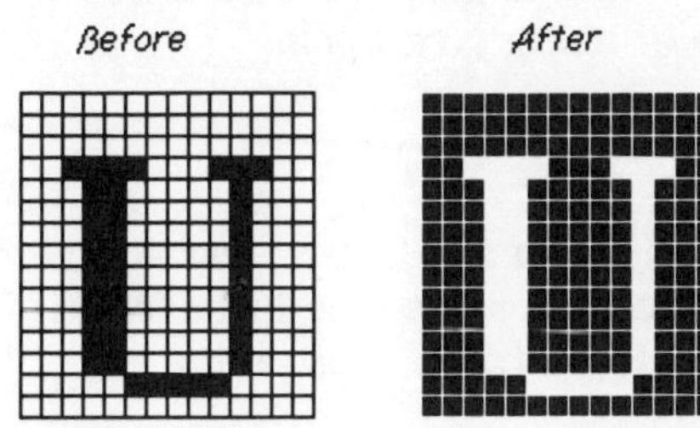

≡ Choose the Camera icon and closely crop the box. Select the Disk icon and pick *Save photo.*
≡ Return to the main menu and enter the Copy Desk.
≡ Activate the Disk icon and choose *Load photo.* Load the inset cap photo file and position it in the upper left corner of the work space.
≡ Select *Serif Small* from the FONT icon list, move the cursor into the work space, and start typing. The first letter you type should appear to the right of the inset cap, with some space between the two. As you enter more text, it should wrap around the inset cap, and will look something like Figure 2-22.

If you want more white space around the inset cap—to the side or below—just crop the letter in the Photo Lab a bit wider or deeper.

Figure 2-22. Inset Cap More Noticeable

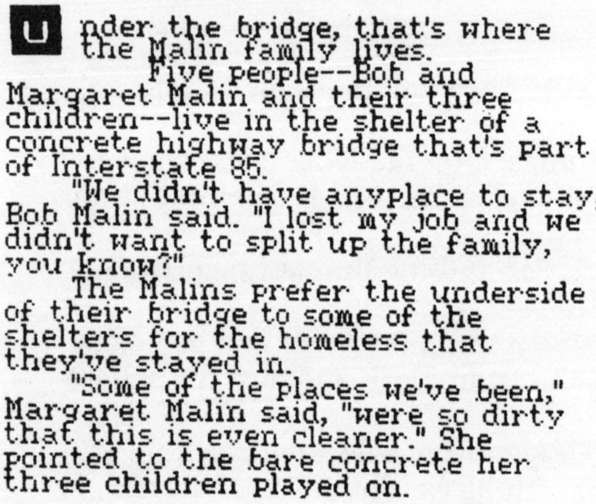

U nder the bridge, that's where
the Malin family lives.
Five people--Bob and
Margaret Malin and their three
children--live in the shelter of a
concrete highway bridge that's part
of Interstate 85.
"We didn't have anyplace to stay,"
Bob Malin said. "I lost my job and we
didn't want to split up the family,
you know?"
The Malins prefer the underside
of their bridge to some of the
shelters for the homeless that
they've stayed in.
"Some of the places we've been,"
Margaret Malin said, "were so dirty
that this is even cleaner." She
pointed to the bare concrete her
three children played on.

There are dozens more graphic elements that you can use in the Copy Desk to make your newspaper more attractive, more informative, and easier to read. As you publish more with *Newsroom,* you'll discover graphic techniques that aren't mentioned here. That's part of the fun of using *Newsroom.*

Odds and Ends

There's almost a limitless number of things you can do in the Copy Desk to make your newspaper or newsletter more professional looking. The last section of this chapter is simply a short collection of Copy Desk tricks, tips, and techniques.

Tabs

Newsroom doesn't have a Tab function, even if your computer keyboard does. Tabs are valuable when you're putting things in columns or indenting the first line of a paragraph. Even though you don't have a Tab key while entering text in the Copy Desk, you can duplicate its effect with the space bar.

Indenting. Paragraphs are normally indented five spaces from the left margin. Simply press the space bar five times at the start of every new paragraph.

An alternative to indenting is to insert a blank line between paragraphs by pressing the Return or Enter key an extra time. This uses up more space, of course, but can make your stories more readable.

Columns. If you've tried to line up columns in the Copy Desk, you already know how hard the job is. You can come close to straight columns, but as long as you're using the Copy Desk, that's as good as you can do. For a more exact, but more time-consuming method of entering things in columns, see Chapter 4.

Things don't line up in the Copy Desk because not every letter is the same width. Unlike a typewriter, where every letter takes up the same amount of space horizontally, in *Newsroom* each letter varies in width. An *I*, for instance, is much narrower than a *W*.

The space bar is your only tool for positioning the cursor. All you can do is press the space bar until the cursor is closely aligned with the column. The edge of your columns will be a bit ragged, but most readers won't notice.

Page Numbers

If your paper is longer than two pages, you'll probably want to include page numbers. Adding them is easy.

You can place them at the top or the bottom of the page. Readers are used to seeing them in either spot.

Top of page. If the page is a left hand page (even numbers: 2, 4, 6, and so on), type *Page X* in the upper left corner of the panel which will be laid out in the upper left corner of the page. If the page is a right-hand page (odd numbers: 3, 5, 7, and so on), place the page number in the panel which will be laid out in the upper right of the page. Press the space bar until the cursor is close to the right edge of the work space; then type *Page X*. If it wraps to the next line, move the cursor back and delete enough spaces to bring the page number back up to the top line. Press Return or Enter twice to insert a blank line and then type in the text.

Make sure that the text in the panel on the other side of the page lines up. Press the Return or Enter key twice before entering any text in the panel which will appear across the page.

Bottom of page. Position the page number as above, but at the end of the appropriate panel. You'll need to stop entering the body copy two lines before the end of the panel and then press Return or Enter twice to get to the final line.

Again, make sure that the text across the page lines up. You'll need to leave the bottom two lines of the opposite panel blank when you put the page number at the bottom.

The FONT Icon

- You can have only one large and one small type size in any one Copy Desk work space. The two sizes can be different faces—you can mix the small sans serif with the large serif, for instance.
- Use large text only for headlines or other limited special effects.
- Use small text for the body text (the words which make up the story).
- It's often very effective to use one face for the headlines (say large sans serif) and the other face for the body text (small serif).
- Pick the face you'll use for the headlines and the one you'll use for the body text, then stick with them throughout your entire publication. Using too many different typefaces (and sizes) in one newspaper or newsletter is the quickest way to confuse your readers. More on this in Chapter 6.
- Don't mix large and small size text throughout a work space. The results, as you can see from Figure 2-23, can be strange. Notice how the large text *Mr. Burrel* pushes down the entire line, creating a large gap at the beginning of the line (above *his cage*) and end of the line (above *science*).

Figure 2-23. Nix on Mixed Type Sizes

A small disturbance in the science class yesterday forced the evacuation of the West Wing for two hours.

Cause of the trouble was the disappearance of "Rocky," the science class pet. Rocky, a rare flying squirrel from South America, escaped from his cage. **Mr. Burrel, the** science teacher, asked that all classes be excused from their rooms until Rocky was located. He was afraid Rocky might bite one of the students.

≡ Here's how to quickly change the typeface of any text you've already entered in the work space. Return to the icon area, choose FONT, and make another selection in the same size as the text you want to change. For example, if you have large sans serif and small sans serif in the work space, but want to change the large sans serif to serif, select *Serif* from the FONT list and all that was large sans serif becomes large serif.

≡ Be aware that changing the typeface like this can dramatically change the way the final panel will look. Figure 2-24, which is based on Figure 2-23, changed all the large sans serif text to large serif characters. It looks even more disturbed than Figure 2-23.

Figure 2-24. More Confusion

A small disturbance in the science class yesterday forced the evacuation of the West Wing for two hours.

Cause of the trouble was the disappearance of "Rocky," the science class pet. Rocky, a rare flying squirrel from South America, escaped from his cage. **Mr. Burrel, the** science teacher, asked that all classes be excused from their rooms until Rocky was located. He was afraid Rocky might bite one of the students.

≡ The two sizes of the serif typeface take up more room, character by character, than do the sans serif typefaces. If you select *Small Sans Serif* from the FONT list, for instance, you can type approximately 40 characters in one line. Using small serif, however, means you can only squeeze about 36 characters on a line.

≡ The English typeface is difficult to read. Don't use it except in very small amounts.

Words, Words, Words

From this chapter's length alone, you now realize how important the Copy Desk work area is to *Newsroom* and to successful newspaper publishing. Words—putting them together in the right form, entering them efficiently, and displaying them attractively—are important to any publication, yours included.

There's a lot of information here, some which you may have known already, but much you didn't. That's going to be true of the rest of *Using Newsroom at Home, School, and Work*. The title of the book says a lot, though, for all the information helps you *use* the program.

For the moment, put aside your pen, typewriter, or word processor and get ready to explore another work area of *Newsroom*, the often-overlooked Banner.

CHAPTER 3

From Extra! to Extraordinary

The Banner

If the Copy Desk is the most important work area of *Newsroom,* then the Banner is the one most taken for granted.

If you're like most *Newsroom* users, you quickly put together a banner for your paper or newsletter the first time you used the program and let it go at that. You wanted to get to the "real work" of the Copy Desk, Photo Lab, Layout, and Press work areas. The banner, you probably thought, was just the name of the paper. No one looks at it anyway. Right?

Not quite. The banner, called the *nameplate* in newspaper terminology, is the most prominent element on the most prominent page of your paper. Its text (the name of your publication) and the way that text is displayed make an impression on your readers. If the banner contains a name like *Watertown Tattler,* your readers know two things—the paper is from a city (or perhaps school) named *Watertown* and that the news will be somewhat gossipy. But if that name is the *Watertown Tribune,* your readers know that the publication is likely to present straight, hard news.

The name of the publication isn't the only information the banner can provide. Whether it's an eye-catching piece of art, a slogan which summarizes the publication's news philosophy, or small advertisements for terrific stories inside the issue, the text and graphics of a banner can tell your readers much about your newspaper.

This chapter shows you how to create the most informative and appealing banner possible by mixing graphics and text in the Banner work area. Put these techniques to work, and your banners won't be taken for granted any longer.

Naming Names

The first step to a powerful banner is the right name for your paper or newsletter.

This may not be something you can decide yourself. The name may already be set and not open for change. If your school, club, or company newspaper has been around for years, it's unlikely you'll want to change the name.

Readers become used to names of newspapers, look for that name, and expect to find it. Don't change a paper's name without good reason, and then only after some careful thought.

But if you're creating a new publication for home, school, or work, you (and perhaps your staff) get to pick a name.

Start with Two Parts

Take a look at the names of newspapers you see in your community. Most names can be divided into two parts.

- Word(s) which describe where the paper is from, or what group, organization, or institution it is associated with.
- A descriptive word which makes the readers think of *news.*

You can create your paper's name by following this same pattern. Select a word that describes who or what produces the paper or newsletter. It doesn't have to be exact, but it should make readers think of your group, organization, or institution. Consider your choices carefully; if you want your publication to be taken seriously, make sure your selection isn't too cute or an obscure pun that only insiders understand. It's hard to be *too* clear when choosing a name for your paper.

On the other hand, if your newspaper is intended to be funny, and you want your readers to share in the fun, don't worry about using a traditional name.

Here are some starting places for finding the first part of your paper's name.

Starting Place	Example
Family/school/company name	The *Hatfield* Times
Nickname or school mascot	The *Warriors* Wire
Company product or service	*Landscaping* News
Specialized subject	The *HO Railroad* Herald
City or town	*Madison* Weekly News

The second part of your publication's name should make readers think of news. One way to do this is to use a word that, through tradition if not in meaning, has come to be thought of as a "news" name. Here are a few such names.

Bulletin	Journal	Post	Telegraph
Courier	Journalist	Press	Times
Dispatch	Monitor	Star	Wire
Gazette	News	Sun	World
Herald			

Of course, this isn't a complete list. And since these are traditional newspaper words, you may reject them because you're looking for something that sounds more modern.

Above all, choose a name which will invite people to read your newspaper. Come up with your own name through any method that works for you—the suggestions here are only offered to get you started. If you want to call your paper *Bubba Talks,* and think that will make your readers read your newspaper, then by all means use it.

Name Length

There are limits to the number of characters that can be placed on one line in the Banner work space.

Most names will be entered in the Banner using one of the three large type sizes. (You want to make the name noticeable, don't you?) Approximately 23 characters can be typed in one line when a large-size type has been selected. There's room for five lines in the banner, though you certainly won't be filling banners with text.

It's unlikely you'll use the two small type sizes for the name, but you will use them for such things as the date, other information in the banner, or a slogan. You can get an average of 36 characters on a line with the small serif type, or approximately 40 characters with small sans serif. There's enough room for ten lines of small-sized text in the banner.

Want a Slogan?

Before you actually enter the Banner work area and start putting your nameplate together, decide if you want to include a slogan or saying. Not all papers have one, but of those that do, the slogans range from the traditional (All the News That's Fit to Print) to the informative (The Long Island Newspaper) to the proud (One of America's Greatest Newspapers).

You might want to use a slogan as a kind of subtitle for the name of your paper or newsletter. If you're don't include the name of your school or company in the name of the publication, for instance, you can put it in the slogan. You could use your school's motto (Learning Is Good) or your company's trademark phrase (We're Third—We Try Hardest) for the same purpose, to link the newspaper with the organization it covers.

You might use a slogan to tell the readers a bit more about your newspaper. Something like "All the News from Around the Block," "Nothing Is Like Sailing," or "The Latest News in the Construction Industry" provides more information about what a reader can expect to find inside.

Or you might just want a slogan because it's fun. Try one like "Printed by Fossner Family Publications, Inc." or "Only Good News Inside."

Whatever your slogan, you'll want to print it in a small-size type. The name of the newspaper is the most important element of the banner, and you don't want to confuse the reader into believing that "All the News I Like" is the name of your home newspaper.

With the name and slogan (if any) chosen and jotted down, you can move to the Banner area of *Newsroom*.

A Mixture of Words and Pictures

The Banner work area is tailor-made for merging graphics and text. It's much like the Photo Lab—in fact, with two exceptions, the icons are identical. Clip art can be selected from the Banner and then put into the work space on the screen. Text can be added and graphics created with *Newsroom*'s Graphics Tools. You can even fine-tune anything on the screen with a zoom feature.

Load *Newsroom*, select the Banner work area, and you'll see a screen similar to Figure 3-1.

Figure 3-1. The Banner Screen

Some of the icons at the left edge are identical to ones you've used in the Copy Desk. The new icons are:

Clip Art lets you access *Newsroom* clip art disks, select clip art files, and choose specific pictures. These pictures then can be placed in the Banner work space.

Flip reverses any piece of clip art horizontally. Whatever pointed right before flipping points left after flipping. Only clip art can be flipped—anything created with the Graphics Tools cannot be flipped.

Crayon displays the powerful Graphics Tools menu. From here, you can pick the typeface and type size of any text you'll enter, specify a fill pattern, choose a drawing mode (line, lines, circles, box, freehand draw, and erase), and select a pen size. This is the most valuable icon in the Banner area.

Magnifying Glass zooms in on any area you want, revealing each pixel, or dot, on the screen. You can make the finest adjustments to any graphic, character, or drawing with this feature.

Half Screen, Doubled When Printed

The work space itself is a white rectangle twice as wide as it is tall. There's a reason for this shape. When printed, a banner stretches across most of a page; twice as wide as a Copy Desk panel. A banner, however, is the same height as a panel. To keep the dimensions correct (twice as wide as tall) and keep the entire work space visible, it had to be shrunk vertically on the screen. (It still appears normally when printed, however.)

This has an interesting side effect. Since the screen shows the banner half the height of a panel, anything on the Banner screen prints out twice the size of the same thing shown on the Copy Desk screen (or on the Photo Lab screen, which has the same dimensions as a panel). Small-sized text in a banner, for instance, prints out twice the size of small-sized text in a panel. The same goes for large text, clip art, and graphics.

That's why you can only enter 5 lines of large text in a banner, compared to 10 in a panel; or only 10 lines of small text, compared to 21 in a panel.

By now you're probably asking, *so what?*

This doubling is important because it affects how things look on the printed page. When you're looking at the Banner work-space screen, you must remember that what you see will be much larger than what you would see if you were looking at the same thing on the Copy Desk or Photo Lab screen. That may be hard, since you spend far more of your *Newsroom* time in the Copy Desk and Photo Lab work areas than in the Banner work area. Draw a box in the Photo Lab and it prints one size; draw a box that *looks* the same—on the Banner screen, anyway—and it prints twice that size. Small text which seems like it might get lost in the banner actually appears large when you print. Even thin lines look thick when your page comes out of the printer.

And a small mistake on the screen—a line a bit too long or lines that don't seem to quite meet—grows in size when you print your page.

Your selection of clip art is restricted, too. The doubling-when-printed problem prevents you from using many pieces of clip art, or at least from printing them in their entirety. Clip art that takes up the entire Photo Lab screen, and which can be placed in a Copy Desk panel, doesn't fit in the narrower work space of the Banner. Stick to the smaller pieces of clip art if you want them to print completely within a banner. Large clip art will always look like it's been cut off in a banner.

In other words, plan ahead. Plan for the larger sized text, graphics, and clip art. Turn the problem to your advantage by creating correctly sized graphics, by choosing appropriate clip art, and by remembering that small text looks large and large text looks huge.

Plan Your Banner

Just as it pays to plan news stories before typing them into the Copy Desk, it's also more efficient if you plan your banner before you spend a lot of time in the Banner work area.

Here's why. With the exception of clip art that you bring into the Banner, nothing can be moved once you put it down on the screen. Text, lines, even patterns cannot be moved once they've been entered, drawn, or filled. If you fill a piece of clip art and then later decide it should go somewhere else, the fill pattern stays where it is. The effect may be interesting, but it's probably not what you had in mind. It's also hard to change a letter or two of text without things looking out of line. Take a look at Figure 3-2, which shows examples of both of these banner problems.

Figure 3-2. Wrong Moves

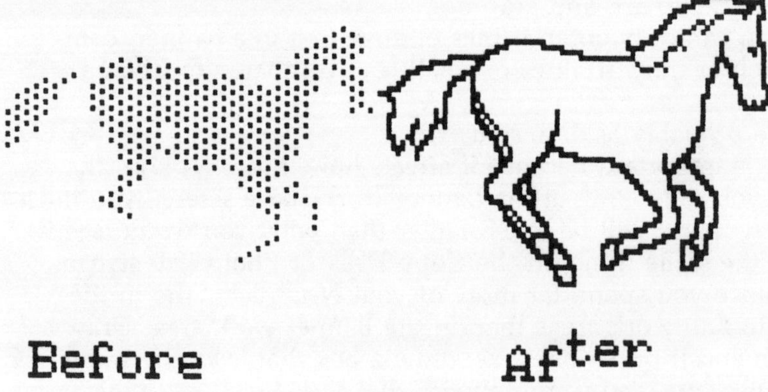

The best way to avoid mistakes like these is to design your banner on paper before you go to the computer. Designing a banner isn't difficult and shouldn't take you too long.

Box an area twice as wide as it is tall on a sheet of paper. Within that rectangle, sketch out the major parts of a banner, such as the name, clip art, slogans, the date, issue number, and other elements. You don't have to make the design look finished; it's only going to give you a general idea of what the banner will look like when it appears on the page. Make several such sketches (called *thumbnails* in publication design terms) and choose the one you like best.

Figure 3-3. Banner Sketches

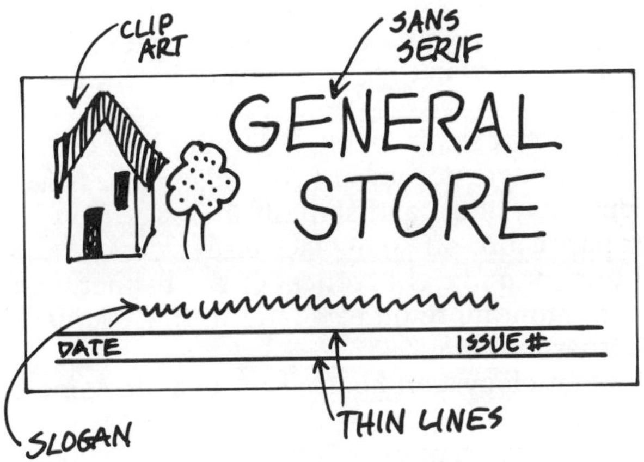

When you look at the thumbnail and see something you don't like, just draw another quick design and see if that's better. Keep doing this until you're satisfied. The completed thumbnail now serves as a miniature blueprint for your banner. Of course, you still can change the banner, tweak it here and there, as you put it together.

Some design tips can be helpful when you're sketching a banner thumbnail. None of the following are hard and fast rules—few things in publication design are—but you'll find that many of them will fit your own situation.

- Don't crowd the banner with text, art, and graphics. Leave some room at the edges so things don't appear packed together. It's an even better idea to leave some white space at the bottom of the banner so that it doesn't crowd the text which follows in the top two panels.

≡ A box surrounding the entire banner can be an effective design. Try a box with a shadow on the bottom and one side for a different look.

≡ Try to balance the banner—don't pack everything on the right-hand side and leave the left completely blank. This doesn't mean a banner has to be symmetrical or centered, however.

≡ Graphics should "look into" the page. Art that's facing a definite way should point toward the middle of the page, not toward the edges; otherwise the reader's eyes will follow the direction of art and skip off the page. You want your readers to look *at* your paper, not off someplace else.

≡ *Ears,* small boxes or areas at the top left and right corners of the banner, can be used to display interesting information (more on ears later in this chapter). If you use ears, put one in each corner for balance.

≡ Lines, called *rules* in newspaper terminology, can be used to separate some of the banner elements for the reader.

≡ Centered names look more traditional than names set off-center. Set your newspaper's name to one side, even slightly, for a more attractive banner. (This also opens up room for a medium-sized piece of clip art, something not usually possible if the name is centered.)

≡ The most important design rule you can remember is: **Do what looks good to you.** Your first instinct will, many times, be the best choice.

Figure 3-4 shows two banner designs—one for a school, another for a family newspaper—which follow several of the design rules listed above.

Figure 3-4. Good-Looking Banners

Building Your Banner

With several things in hand—a name, slogan, and overall design—you can get started on your banner.

The accepted manner of composing a banner is with these four steps.

1. Place clip art.
2. Modify the clip art or use the Graphics Tools to create your own art.
3. Position and type text.
4. Save the banner to disk.

If you've predesigned your banner, though, the order in which you build the banner isn't that important. As long as you leave enough room for the clip art you're planning on using, for example, you can enter the name and other text first and then fit everything else around that.

With a design as a blueprint, it actually makes more sense to group your work around the different icons, and within the Graphics Tools menu, around similar tools. Concentrating your work like this has two effects—it cuts down on some disk swapping and saves some of the time you'd spend waiting for the Graphics Tools menu to appear.

Here's what that means.

Select and place all the clip art you're using before choosing another icon to cut down on disk swapping. If necessary, copy a piece of clip art before grabbing another. Wait until all the clip art is in the banner before doing any flipping.

Enter at one time all text of the same typeface and size. Type in all the large serif text before entering any small serif text. Select and completely use each drawing tool and pen size before choosing another tool and/or size. For example, draw all thin lines before drawing any thick lines. Move all clip art (with the Hand) at one time.

Don't worry about cleaning up small mistakes until you've got the banner elements in place. Then select the Magnifying Glass icon and make your changes.

It's a good idea to save the banner to disk several times while you work. That way, if there's a power surge or a power outage, or you trip over the power cord, you won't have lost everything. Save the banner each time with the same name. All this means more disk swapping, not less, but the alternative—losing your work—is worse.

The rest of this section offers Banner tips and techniques to make your job easier or your banners better looking and more informative.

Banner Art

Although *art* can both mean clip art and the art you create with the Graphics Tools, let's look at just clip art for the moment.

Most banners will include at least one piece of clip art. With the basic *Newsroom* package you have more than 600 pieces of clip art to choose from, though not all fit in a banner (see below). Three volumes of *Clip Art Collection* are available from Springboard, each with at least another 600 pieces of art. The more clip art you have at your disposal, the more likely you'll find just the right piece of clip art for your banner.

The right size. Make sure that the clip art is the right size. As you look through the Clip Art Directory, remember that the Banner work space is not as high as a full panel. Much of the taller clip art won't entirely fit in a banner, though you can use just part of a piece of clip art if you want.

To quickly tell which clip art will completely fit in a banner, make yourself at *template* representing the size of the banner.

Get a piece of paper, or better yet, a 3 × 5 inch index card. Draw a rectangle exactly 1-1/2 inches wide by 9/16 inch high. Cut out that rectangle, leaving a hole in the paper or card.

Figure 3-5. Sizing Template

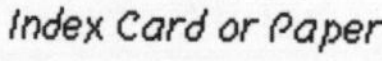

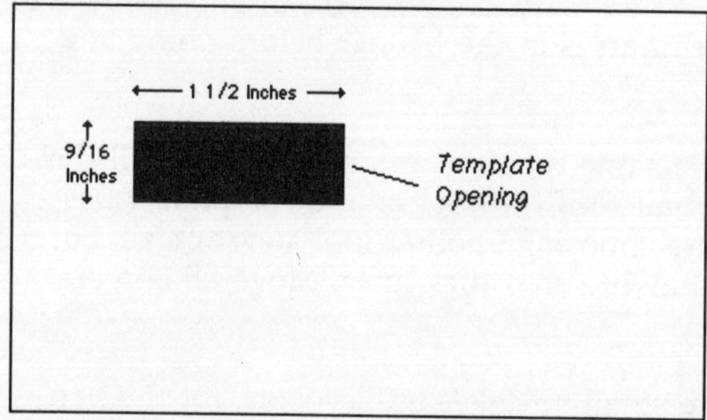

Place the opening over the clip art as it's shown in the Clip Art Directory in your *Newsroom* manual, or in any of the *Clip Art Collection* manuals. If the entire piece of art can be seen through the template opening, it will fit in the banner.

Figure 3-6. Through the Opening

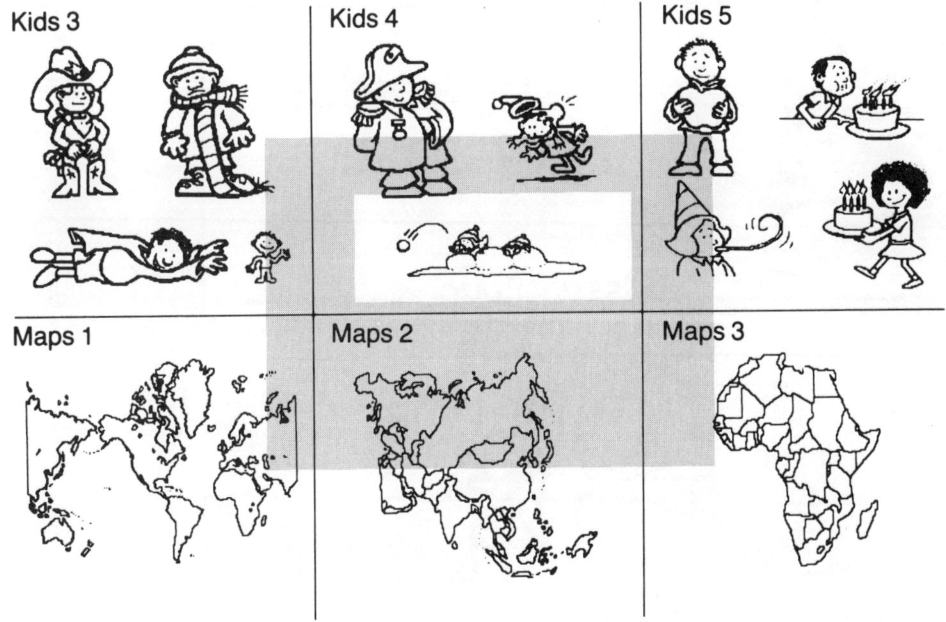

You can use this template opening to gauge how much of the banner the clip art will occupy. If you choose the sluglike alien from ALIENS2 on the clip art disk which comes with *Newsroom*, for example, it would fit vertically within the banner, but would leave little room for anything else.

The right message. Select your clip art carefully. Don't choose just any piece of art, but pick one that goes with the name of your paper or the subject it covers. Let's say your school mascot is a ferocious bulldog; unfortunately, you won't find a bulldog on the clip art disks. Amongst the dogs pictured in the files DOGS1–DOGS4, there's only one that would be a good substitute—the snarling dog at the bottom left of DOGS1. All the other dog art wouldn't get the message across that your school's mascot (and thus each of your school's teams) is something to watch out for.

Placing the art. When you're using just one piece of clip art, don't center it in the banner, but put it to one side. Not only does that make your banner more attractive, but it gives you more room for text or other graphics. Figure 3-7 shows two banners; the top one puts the clip art at the left side so there's space at the right for the name. The bottom one, however, has the art in the center, so the name must be crowded into a much smaller area.

Figure 3-7. Better on the Side

When you use two pieces of clip art, and they're about the same size, the banner will look best if they're placed on either side. The center is left open for the name and other information.

Banner Graphics

Graphics differ from clip art in that they're created with the drawing tools, pens, and fill patterns found in the Graphics Tools. Custom graphics are the easiest way to build a terrific banner—you can change the clip art you put in the banner, quickly draw lines, boxes, and other shapes, and fill areas with interesting patterns. Here are some of the things you can do with the Graphics Tools in *Newsroom.*

Borders. Most professional newspapers and newsletters use a rule, border, or box to separate their banner from the rest of the page. Sometimes this is just a thin rule, other times it's more complex, like a drop-shadowed box. Many *Newsroom* users do much the same thing with their publications. It lets readers know where the banner ends and the news begins.

Clip Art Collection Volume 1 and *Volume 2* both include custom designs that you can select, place, and duplicate to make special-looking lines and borders. But you may not have anything more than the basic *Newsroom* package. Don't worry—there's plenty of great effects you can create on your own.

- Simple lines and boxes are the easiest to produce. Draw lines so that they run the entire width of the work space. Draw boxes as close to the edges of the work space as possible.
- Double lines of unequal thickness can be very effective. Draw one line with the smallest pen, for example, and a parallel line with a pen two or three times thicker.
- Boxes with shadows are easy to make and nicely set off a banner. Make one by choosing one of the diagonal pen sizes (second and third from the right in the pens list) and the Lines tool. If you choose the left-facing diagonal (\ ), draw the right and bottom sides. If you choose the right-facing diagonal (/), draw the left and bottom sides. Now go back to the Graphic Tools and select a normal pen (thinnest or next larger is best) to draw the remaining two sides. A drop-shadowed box is a bit different, but just as simple to create. Choose the square pen shape and draw two lines—one at the top, another at the left side. Change to a thin pen and draw the rest of the box so that it appears below and to the right of the black shadow. Figure 3-8 shows all three kinds of boxes.

Figure 3-8. Shadow Boxing

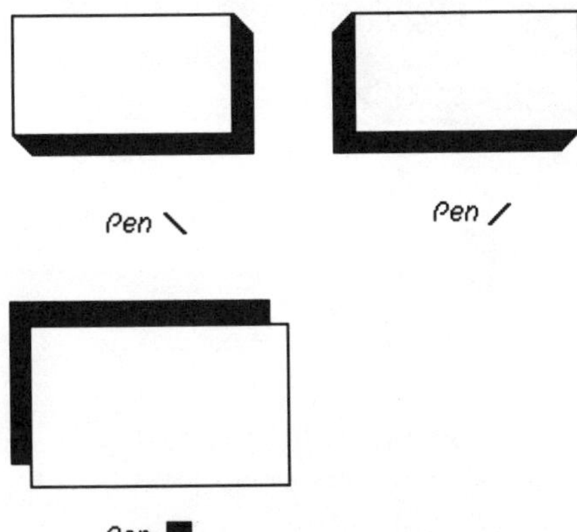

- Instead of a box, consider lines at the top and bottom of the banner, but not on the sides.
- Banner lines don't have to be straight and black. Even without additional clip art, you can create custom borders. Look at the Clip Art Directory in your manual for very small pieces of clip art. You can find such tiny art in files like ALIENS3, BEASTS1, CATS5, MISC4, SCARY4, TREES2, VEHICLE2, and more. Pick up the clip art and set it down in the banner. Move the shadow to the side (it needs to be moved up two small moves as well) and lay that one down. Continue to duplicate the art. Take a look at Figure 3-9, which includes three such lines of clip art. Notice that black lines have been added to the first and second examples.

Figure 3-9. Custom Lines

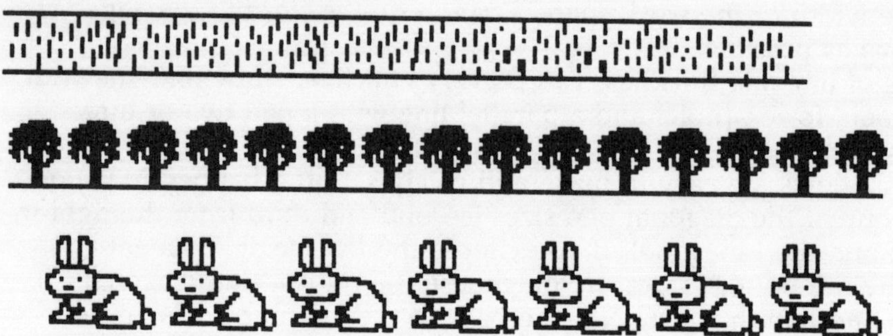

Silhouettes. Any clip art can be turned into a silhouette simply by filling it with the black fill pattern. Silhouettes can be a striking addition to a banner and look especially good in businesslike newsletters.

Figure 3-10. Silhouette Art

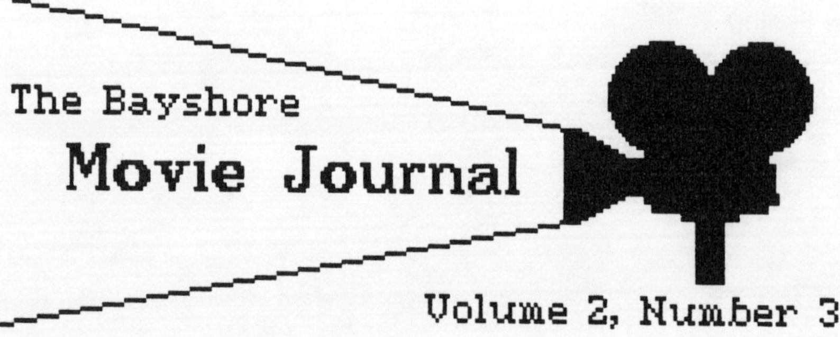

To create a silhouette, place the art and select the black fill pattern. Fill the art as much as you can—some parts won't fill because they're so small and because you can't place the crosshairs cursor accurately enough.

Make sure there's no way for the pattern to "escape" from the art and fill the entire screen. If there is, close it off by drawing a line or blackening pixels with the Magnifying Glass icon.

Clean up the artwork with the Magnifying Glass option.

Ears. *Ears,* small boxes found in the upper corners of many newspaper banners, are used for such bits of information as today's weather and to mention extraordinary stories inside. Newspaper ears, just like real ones, usually come in pairs. Place one in either upper corner.

Depending on your banner design, you may or may not have room for ears. If you have a complicated banner already, ears will only clutter up things. Figure 3-11, an example of ears, is a plain banner, without any clip art. There's not much room for anything else once the ears are in place. Note, too, how the ears give the banner a formal, traditional look.

Small shadowed boxes or drop-shadowed boxes look better than simple line boxes. Choose a small typeface for an ear's text; remember that sans serif is slightly narrower than serif, and so lets you squeeze an extra character on each line in a typical ear.

Figure 3-11. Two Ears

Banner Words

Text is the most important element in a banner—you create the name of your newspaper with it.

Enter the name in a large type size and display it prominently in the banner. Imagine your readers seeing your paper for the first time. Is the name the first thing in the banner that they notice?

> We read from left to right—putting the name of the paper on the left side of the banner and clip art on the right makes good sense when you remember that.

All three typefaces are acceptable for a name. *Serif* gives a traditional look, good for business newsletters, school papers, and other formal publications. *Sans serif* seems more modern and informal and fits in best with home newspapers and school publications. The *English* typeface is similar to that used by some old and established newspapers. It's an interesting typeface for newspaper names and can be used for almost any kind of publication. (Since it's doubled in size, it's much easier to read in a banner than in a headline.)

Other text in the banner—a slogan, issue number, date, and other information—should be entered with a small-sized type. For this smaller text, stick with the same typeface as the name (unless you used English). The fewer changes of typeface in the banner, the less jarring it will be to your readers. There are exceptions to this suggestion, of course, such as when you want to pack a little more in a pair of ears.

Use graphics to set off the name and other text within the banner. A box around the newspaper name will protect it from a fill pattern used throughout most of the banner (see Figure 3-11 for an example). Lines can be used to separate the main body of the banner from the area used to display the volume/ issue number and the publication date.

As you've probably found out, entering text in the Banner (and the Photo Lab) is much different than typing in the Copy Desk.

- There's no Delete key. To erase a character, move the cursor with the right and left cursor or arrow keys—they're the only ones that work here—and retype or space across the mistake. You may have to retype everything from that point on to make it look right.
- You can return to previous text only with the right or left cursor or arrow keys. The Return or Enter key moves the cursor one line down.
- There is no word-wrap feature as in the Copy Desk. A new line is started whenever the right edge of the screen is reached, which can make for some peculiar word breaks.
- Once you press the select key to exit from that section of text, changing anything in it will be difficult. To change or retype something, you must position the cursor exactly. Prevent this by proofreading everything in a text section before pressing the select key.
- Text typed across any art—whether created with the Graphics Tools or clip art—erases the art. Text in the Banner is actually printed across a band of white. Transparent clip art laid over text, however, lets that text show through.

There are numerous techniques and tricks you can apply to text entry in the Banner—far more than could be mentioned here. What follows are two suggestions which most *Newsroom* publishers will find useful.

Text over graphics. You can create some interesting effects, especially with the name, when you lay text on graphics. Figure 3-12 shows a simple example of this. It took only a few minutes to create this classy-looking banner for a home newspaper.

Figure 3-12. Text Across Graphics

The Masons

- Draw three lines of varying thicknesses across the work space. From top to bottom, the pen sizes were the first, third, and fifth from the left of the pens list.
- Select the *English* typeface and position the cursor so that its bottom edge rests just above the thickest line.
- Type the name.
- Select the Magnifying Glass icon and erase some of the lines to the left of the first character. You'll often need to do this to match the space created in the graphics at the right of the text.

An even more dramatic effect can be produced by typing over a fill pattern. Fill a box, or the entire banner, with a pattern. Choose a typeface and size and position the cursor. Type in your text—the fill pattern is erased as the text is entered. Figure 3-13 shows two examples.

Figure 3-13. White Holes

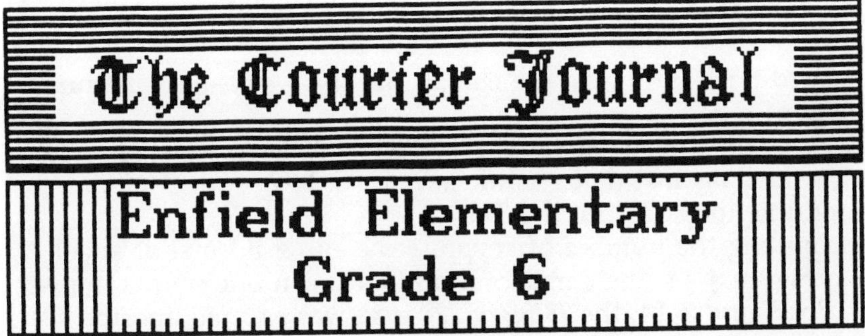

The top box needed some cleanup to the left of *The*. The box on the bottom used the space bar to center the second line. The text was erased and retyped several times before it appeared centered.

Dates and issues. You'll probably want to include a publication date in the banner so that your readers know this is the latest news. Many newspapers or newsletters also display the issue number, sometimes even the volume number. This is more important when your newspaper comes out at irregular intervals; by looking at the issue number, the reader can tell if he or she has missed any papers.

Both a publication date and an issue number are easy to add to a banner. The most common location is at the bottom of the banner, with the date on one side (usually the left) and the issue number on the other.

It's a good idea to define the date and issue area with a rule or box, so that they don't get lost in the banner. If you do use a rule or box to set off the date and issue, make sure there's enough white space above, below, and to the sides of the text.

Remember that once you finish your banner, you'll use that banner again and again—for every issue of your newspaper. The only thing that should regularly change is the date and issue number. That's why you want plenty of room around the date/issue text; it makes it much easier to insert the new date and issue number without disturbing anything else in the banner.

Here's a technique to use for exact placement of the date and issue number. Figure 3-14 includes a publication date and issue number, and demonstrates the technique. (It takes longer to describe the technique than to carry it out.)

Figure 3-14. Date and Number Placement

- Select a small-sized type and move the cursor into the work space. (Figure 3-14 used small serif type.)
- Pick a graphic—line, box edge, part of a piece of clip art—and position the cursor so that it's flush against that graphic. (Figure 3-14 used the hanging end of the second line to the left of the *The.*)
- Cursor down, counting the number of keypresses—either normal or small-sized moves. (In Figure 3-14, the cursor was shifted down one normal move.)
- Enter the text. (In Figure 3-14, the *January 22, 1988* was entered and the select key pressed. The graphic mark for *Issue #14* was the second line to the right of *Masons.*)
- Create the rule or box which will set off or surround the date and issue number. (Figure 3-14 used a thin-ruled box.)

Jot down this information and save it for the next issue. When you change the date and number, just follow the same process to exactly position the cursor.

Save the Banner file. When you're satisfied that the banner is done, save it to disk using a name like MASBANNR, for *master banner*. For each issue, load this file into *Newsroom*, make your date and issue-number changes, and then save it to disk again. This time, use a filename associated with that particular issue, such as BANNER14 for issue #14.

Advanced Banner Techniques

Sometimes the commonplace methods of building a banner just won't do. If your publication's banner needs things like special art, an exact reproduction of a school emblem or company logo, or a hand-crafted typeface, you'll need some unusual skills.

Such advanced techniques aren't for everyone. They require more time and effort on your part. But the results can be just what you're looking for—a distinctive banner that's perfect for your newspaper.

The advanced banner techniques you'll find below are just three of many. Undoubtedly, you'll discover some on your own as you work with *Newsroom*; you may have done so already if you're a *Newsroom* pro.

Copying an Emblem or a Logo

If you're publishing your school, business, or club newspaper, you may want something more than clip art or simple lines and boxes in the banner. The school's emblem, the business's logo, or the club's design can add a lot to a banner.

First of all, your readers will instantly recognize the emblem, logo, or design. They've seen it dozens of times on school book covers, in yearbooks, and on tee-shirts. Businesses use logos on everything from letterhead and stationary to company products. Prominently displaying the same design in your newspaper's banner says one thing—that the paper is part of that school, business, or club.

Secondly, a lot of the hard work has been done for you. The art has already been designed and created. All you have to do is copy it into your banner.

That's all? It may be simple if you're artistic, but if you're like most people, drawing anything but lines, boxes, circles, and other geometric shapes is as far as you can go with *Newsroom*. Anything else comes out looking like worms on the screen.

Don't worry. Here's how to copy even the most intricate design to your banner.

≡ Find or make a copy of the emblem, logo, or design in approximately the same size as it will appear on the screen in the Banner work area. If you have a small design, use a copying machine that makes enlargements to create a copy.

- Buy several sheets of *plastic transparency*. This is the material that you place on an overhead projector and then write on with a marker or grease pencil. You can find transparencies in almost any office supply store.
- Replace the paper in a copying machine with several transparencies. Make a copy of your design to a transparency. The design should print to the plastic just as it would to paper. You can enlarge or shrink the design if the copier has those features. When you're finished, the design should have crisp black lines or filled areas.
- Tape the transparency to your computer monitor screen, positioning it so that the design is where you want it.
- Select the Crayon icon; choose *Draw* and the thinnest pen.
- Trace the design. A mouse or joystick may help here. Another method, slow but sure, is to use small-sized cursor movements to draw accurately.
- Rough out the design, ignoring minor mistakes. When you're through, use the Magnifying Glass option to clean up the design.
- Save the design to disk; then build the rest of the banner.

The result should be a faithful reproduction of the emblem, logo, or design.

> Another method of duplicating a logo or emblem—one that requires some additional equipment—is discussed in Chapter 4. Look for the information concerning digitizers and digitizing art for *Newsroom* in that chapter.

Creating Your Own Art

Let's assume you're not an artist. At least not a Van Gogh or a Rembrandt.

You can still create your own customized art for a banner. The several tricks and tips listed below should help as you try your hand in the Graphics Tools area of the Banner. More are offered in Chapter 4, which discusses the Photo Lab. Remember that these two work areas are identical in features and function.

- Build the banner—without the art—first. Save it to disk, and only draw on a copy of that file which you've loaded into the Banner work area. This way you can easily erase what's on the screen with the Garbage Can icon and then load a fresh original and start again.
- If a piece of clip art is close to what you want, start with that. A face can be loaded from a clip art disk, for instance, and everything but the outline erased. At least you won't have to draw that part.
- You may be able "build" all or part of the art from lines, circles, and boxes. An arc or semicircle, for instance, can be created by drawing a circle and then erasing sections of it.

- The freehand *Draw* in the Graphics Tools menu is difficult to control. A mouse or a joystick can help somewhat. Most precise, however, are the cursor keys when you're in the small-move mode. The Commodore 64/128 and IBM-PC versions of *Newsroom* require that you constantly press two keys for small cursor moves—this demands some finger gymnastics. The Apple, version, however, which lets you toggle the small-move option on and off, is much easier to use for fine drawing.
- Other drawing programs are much easier to use and produce much more impressive-looking art and graphics. If you're using the Apple and Commodore versions of *Newsroom*, there are conversion programs that allow you to create art with a drawing program and then transfer the results into something *Newsroom* can use. See Chapter 4 for details.

New Type

Another way to build that perfect banner is to customize the type. If you're really ambitious, you can even create letters from scratch.

Newsroom's Graphics Tools doesn't pretend to be a font editor, a program that lets you design and make new typefaces. But with some careful dot-by-dot work, you can create new and unusual characters.

The simplest way to modify the name of your newspaper is to use existing letters and then change them to fit your design. Figure 3-15 is a banner that uses altered text for the publication's name, *Trans*.

Figure 3-15. ***Trans*** **Transformed**

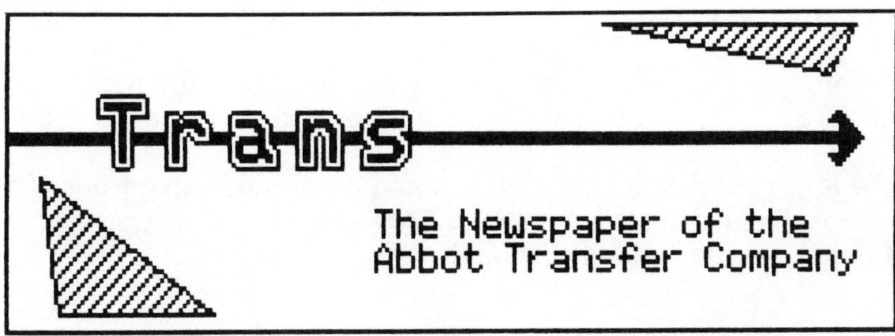

The process is straightforward, though somewhat tedious. Here's how *Trans* was done.

- Letters were typed in large sans serif, with a space between each character.
- The Magnifying Glass icon was selected several times, and the outlines drawn one pixel from the characters.

Figure 3-16. Dot-to-Dot

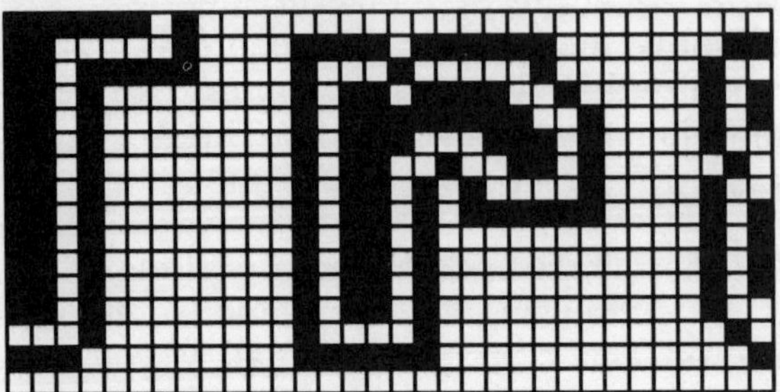

- The Magnifying Glass icon was also used to draw the three-pixel-wide line between the characters. (There is no three-pixel-wide pen size.)
- To extend the line to the edges of the banner, the second pen size was chosen, and overlapping two-pixel-wide lines were drawn.
- Other text and some filled graphics shapes (drawn with the Lines tool) were added.

This is a simple example. You can alter letters by making them slant forward, adding serifs (small horizontal lines) to sans serif characters, thickening letters, and more. Experiment as much as you want.

If you're thinking of creating entirely new characters, keep these hints in mind.

- Draw rectangles to represent the largest size of a character. It's easier to "stay in the lines" this way, and it insures that the characters are all the same size.
- A small mark alongside the rectangles can serve as a guide for the height of lowercase letters like *a, s, w, e, r, c,* and of the body of such letters as *p, b, d, h, k.*
- *Descenders*—the lower parts of letters *y, p, g, j,* and *q*—should extend out of the bottom of the rectangle. *Ascenders*—the top parts of letters *t, f, b, h, k,* and *l*—should remain in the rectangle, though.

A Banner Day

There's a lot more to putting together an effective banner than most *Newsroom* users realize. Merging graphics and text doesn't have to be as plain as pulling clip art into the Banner work area and slapping down some text to create a forgettable name.

With thought and care, you can start your newspaper right—with the right banner. By now, your banner should be exactly the way you want it. Its name should be a memorable one and its art should be appealing and eye-catching.

The next chapter sends you into the darkroom of the Photo Lab, the area most like the Banner, and after the Copy Desk, the most vital part of *Newsroom*.

CHAPTER 4

A Thousand Words

The Photo Lab

The Photo Lab is the most powerful work area in *Newsroom*.

No other part of *Newsroom* puts both the artist's brush and the writer's pen in your hands. The Photo Lab combines pictures and words to create impressive graphics, graphics that are vital to almost every *Newsroom*-produced newspaper or newsletter.

The Photo Lab's capabilities run from grabbing clip art to generating hand-drawn illustrations, and everything in between. *Every picture tells a story*, the saying goes, and it's a phrase worth remembering, for Photo Lab–created art exists to help tell your stories.

The majority of your *Newsroom* time will be spent in either this work area or the Copy Desk. The two are the heart of your newspaper publishing process, and perfectly complement each other. One deals with words, the other with pictures. Those two elements placed in a pleasing design make a newspaper.

In this chapter, you'll learn how to get the most out of the Photo Lab. Not just a guide to using clip art, "A Thousand Words" shows how to create new art by combining pictures, how to draw your own art from scratch, and how to use other software to produce dazzling *Newsroom* art. You'll even see advanced Photo Lab techniques demonstrated, like computerized scanning and digitizing. This chapter makes possible that extra-special graphic, that superb photo, that just-right piece of clip art.

Art the Easy Way

The simplest and most common way of adding pictures to your newspaper is with *clip art*, the predrawn *Newsroom* art. Over 600 pieces of clip art are on the disk which came with *Newsroom*. Another 2000 pictures can be found on the three *Clip Art Collection* disks available from Springboard.

The process of capturing and placing clip art in the Photo Lab work space is pretty simple. Once it's there on the Photo Lab screen, you can change it to your heart's content. Small changes, large modifications—it doesn't matter. You can turn a piece of clip art into the exact picture you need with some time, a smattering of artistic talent, and a knowledge of the Photo Lab's tools.

The Photo Lab Look

If you've been reading *Using Newsroom*'s chapters in order, you've already seen what the Banner work area offers. The Photo Lab screen is almost identical to the Banner screen, showing all of that work area's icons as well as one new icon.

Load *Newsroom*, select the Photo Lab work area, and you'll see a screen like Figure 4-1. (You won't see the OOPS icon until you draw or place something in the work space; you won't see the Flip icon until you grab and position a piece of clip art.)

Figure 4-1. The Photo Lab Screen

Here are the nine icons on the left side of the Photo Lab screen:

Clip Art lets you view *Newsroom* clip art disk directories, choose clip art files, and grab individual pictures.

Flip horizontally flips any piece of clip art that's placed in the work space. Only clip art can be flipped. Art created with the Graphics Tools cannot be flipped.

Crayon shows the powerful Graphics Tools menu. You can select the typeface and size of text, specify a fill pattern, and choose a drawing mode (line, lines, circles, box, freehand draw, and erase) and pen size. This is the most valuable icon of the nine.

Magnifying Glass reveals each pixel within the boxed area. This option lets you make fine adjustments to anything on the screen.

OOPS lets you undo your latest action or change.

Camera crops the picture before it's saved as a photo file. In effect, it acts as scissors, cutting out just the right part of the graphic for you.

Garbage Can erases all text and graphics from the work space.

Disk makes it possible to load photo files from disk and to save photo files to disk. The Apple version of *Newsroom* lets you convert a standard Apple hi-res screen file to *Newsroom* photo format. Both the Commodore and Apple versions of *Newsroom* also let you format a data disk from this menu.

MENU returns you to the main menu.

The Photo Lab's white work space is the same size as that of the Copy Desk's, and twice the size of the Banner's. This is important, for it means two things:

- Even full-screen Photo Lab creations will fit within a panel when you later load them into the Copy Desk.
- There's no single piece of clip art too big to fit within the Photo Lab (you can't say the same about the Banner work area).

In other words, the Photo Lab offers a tremendous amount of flexibility—you can build and draw panel-sized graphics without worrying about which piece of clip art will fit and which one won't.

> Remember that for almost all purposes (some of the most notable exceptions are in Chapters 12 and 13), the Photo Lab is *not* the last step in the graphic process. To place your clip art and custom creations in panels, you have to use the Copy Desk. Only there can you add photos to panels with text, or make full-panel graphics. Without the Copy Desk, you can't include Photo Lab graphics or art in a layout file for printing as part of a page.

Clipping Collections

Instant art is only as far away as the next *Clip Art Collection* disk. Together, the four disks from Springboard contain almost 3000 pieces of clip art for you to browse through, select, and use in your publications.

***Newsroom Clip Art* disk.** This disk comes with every copy of *Newsroom*, and it includes over 600 pieces of clip art organized in more than 100 files and divided into 28 categories. With a few exceptions, the clip art is quite cartoonlike and most suitable for home and elementary-school newspapers.

Figure 4-2. ***Newsroom Clip Art*** **Disk Files**

Category	Files	# Pieces	Category	Files	# Pieces
Aliens	3	22	Misc	7	75
Bears	1	4	Penguin	2	13
Beasts	8	40	People	2	14
Birds	5	37	Pigs	3	10
Bugs	2	19	Rabbits	3	16
Cats	5	32	Reptile	1	8
Cattle	1	4	Rodents	3	15
Dinos	3	13	Scary	4	23
Dogs	4	24	Sports	6	31
Frogs	3	14	Trees	2	25
Holiday	1	6	Vehicle	3	31
Kids	5	19	Women	7	41
Maps	12	12	Words	2	28
Men	5	27	Workers	5	15

Best Category: Maps
Worst Category: Frogs
Price: Free with Newsroom

Clip Art Collection Volume 1 provides over 600 additional pieces of *Newsroom* clip art in a wide variety of categories. The artwork is generally more realistic, although there's a number of cartoonlike drawings. Several new categories are introduced on this disk. The art found in *Volume 1* is useful to almost any *Newsroom* publisher, though it's still predominantly home and school oriented. The clip art is arranged in 93 files and grouped into 38 categories.

Figure 4-3. ***Clip Art Collection, Volume 1*** **Files**

Category	Files	# Pieces	Category	Files	# Pieces
Aerial	2	9	Kids	3	22
Auto	2	22	Letters	3	28
Beasts	3	12	Men	6	27
Birds	3	12	Misc	3	19
Birthday	1	10	Music	3	25
Boats	1	4	Office	1	6
Borders	3	78	Places	2	6
Castles	1	3	Scenery	3	35
Compute	1	4	School	1	7
Dance	2	5	Space	2	12
Faces	1	30	Sports	6	17
Fantasy	7	21	Symbols	1	15
Flags	2	12	Time	2	18
Flowers	2	12	Tools	2	8
Food	1	17	Vehicle	1	4
Fun	6	59	Wedding	1	4
History	3	11	Women	3	11
Holiday	2	17	Words	1	12
House	2	10	Workers	4	14

Best Category: Borders
Worst Category: Fantasy
Price: $29.95

Clip Art Collection Volume 2 is the largest clip art disk, holding over 800 individual pieces. All the clip art is business-oriented, with a number of specialized businesses represented, like florists, health care, and travel. Cartoonlike art is in the distinct minority. Most of the clip art is realistic and perfectly suitable for almost any kind of business newsletter. Of particular note are the three CHART files and the one BALLOONS file (see Chapters 12 and

13 for special uses of these files). *Volume 2* is organized into 51 categories and includes 85 clip art files; it's a virtual necessity for all business users of *Newsroom*.

Figure 4-4. ***Clip Art Collection, Volume 2*** **Files**

Category	Files	# Pieces	Category	Files	# Pieces
Account	1	3	Legal	1	8
Ads	1	5	Measure	1	4
Appliances	1	8	Medical	3	31
Arts	1	6	Misc	4	36
Audio	1	9	Money	3	38
Auto	1	15	Office	4	28
Balloons	1	14	Optics	1	7
Beauty	1	7	People	4	18
Borders	3	75	Petshop	1	5
Build	2	28	Phones	1	7
Chart	3	50	Photo	1	7
Cliches	5	29	Politics	1	9
Compute	2	18	Realty	1	14
Daycare	2	10	Seals	1	23
Dentist	1	11	Shopping	1	5
Dining	2	23	Skylines	1	5
Drawing	1	9	Spirits	1	12
Farming	1	10	Stocks	1	7
Film	1	7	Symbols	2	45
Florist	2	6	Tailor	1	5
Furnish	2	13	Time	1	16
Hands	2	16	Travel	1	5
Health	2	8	Vehicles	1	4
Holiday	2	15	Words	4	39
Industry	1	8	Yardwork	1	6
Jeweler	1	25			

Best Category: Chart
Worst Category: Measure
Price: $39.95

Figure 4-5. ***Clip Art Collection, Volume 3*** **Files**

Category	Files	# Pieces	Category	Files	# Pieces
Aerial	1	3	Gym	4	19
Archery	1	8	Hockey	3	18
Badminton	1	7	Horse	2	8
Baseball	6	33	Horseshoes	1	7
Basketball	4	20	Hunting	2	11
Bike	2	9	Iceskating	2	10
Billiard	1	9	Karate	1	4
Boats	3	10	Misc	7	49
Bodybuild	1	5	Play	2	10
Bowling	2	11	Raquetball	1	4
Camping	2	24	Rollerskate	1	3
Cars	1	5	Skydiving	1	3
Cheer	1	5	Snow	1	4
Climb	2	14	Skiing	3	12
Cricket	1	6	Soccer	2	15
Crowd	2	13	Surf	1	4
Dance	3	12	Swim	2	9
Fencing	1	6	Tennis	3	16
Fight	2	9	Track	4	29
Fishing	4	30	Trophy	1	14
Fitness	2	9	Umpire	2	32
Football	4	25	Volleyball	2	15
Games	2	17	Waterski	1	5
Golf	4	21	Words	4	25

Best Category: Baseball
Worst Category: None
Price: $29.95

Clip Art Collection Volume 3 specializes in sports and recreation clip art. Over 600 pieces of art in 48 categories are grouped into 106 files. The quality of the clip art is uniformly outstanding, with many examples of top-notch realistic art. Almost every sport is represented, either by entire files or by individual pieces of art (check out the lacrosse players and the scuba divers in the MISC files). This disk is a must for any school newspaper; it has much to offer the home user, too.

Grabbing Clip Art

Taking clip art from disk, placing it in the Photo Lab work space, and saving it to disk is an easy-to-learn five-step process.

1. Grab the clip art from a clip art disk and position it in the work space.
2. Use the Graphics Tools to modify the clip art or to add your own handmade art.
3. Type in any text accompanying the art.
4. Crop the part of the work space you want to include in the photo.
5. Save the photo as a file to disk.

Though the process is quite simple, there are a number of things you need to keep in mind as you're composing even the plainest photos.

- Position clip art exactly where you want it *before* you begin to modify it. Only the original clip art, not any changes, can be moved.
- Erased sections of clip art reappear when the clip art is moved.
- Grab and place all required clip art in the work space before altering any of it.
- If necessary, flip the clip art before changing it with the Graphics Tools.
- When selecting multiple pieces of clip art, the last-accessed clip art file is marked in the file list.
- Draw your handmade art (boxes, circles, lines) after you're sure the clip art is in the correct position.
- Text entered in the Photo Lab does not automatically wrap when it reaches the right edge of the work space. Use the Return or Enter key to move the cursor down to the next line.
- Text typed across any art—clip art or handmade art—erases part of the artwork.

Much of Chapter 3—the parts about clip art and the Graphics Tools—also pertains to the Photo Lab.

Editing Clip Art

Even the youngest user of *Newsroom* can be grabbing and positioning clip art in a matter of moments. Like so much of *Newsroom*, it's easy.

But once you have the clip art in the Photo Lab work space, what else can you do with it? Make it different, of course.

For many people, this is much of the fun in using *Newsroom*. You don't have to be an artist, since the art is already drawn for you. But you can customize it so that it looks completely different. It's now *your* art, not *Newsroom*'s.

There are almost as many ways to change clip art as there are *Newsroom* publishers. Let's take a look at just three ways to modify clip art, the three that are used most often and change clip art most dramatically.

Fills. There are ten Graphics Tools fill patterns. Depending on the quality of the monitor or television set connected to your computer, it may be difficult to tell exactly how each pattern will look when it's printed. Figure 4-6 shows examples of each of the ten patterns (printed on an Apple ImageWriter).

Figure 4-6. The Ten Patterns

You can fill any enclosed space with any of the ten patterns. Before you do, make sure the clip art is in exactly the right spot. Once you add a pattern, you can't move the clip art and expect the pattern to follow along.

In Figure 4-7, for instance, the scenery clip art was placed at the top, and a copy was set down again in the middle and then filled with three patterns. The clip art was then picked up with the Hand and moved down, leaving the patterns floating in midair.

Figure 4-7. Moving Clip Art After Filling

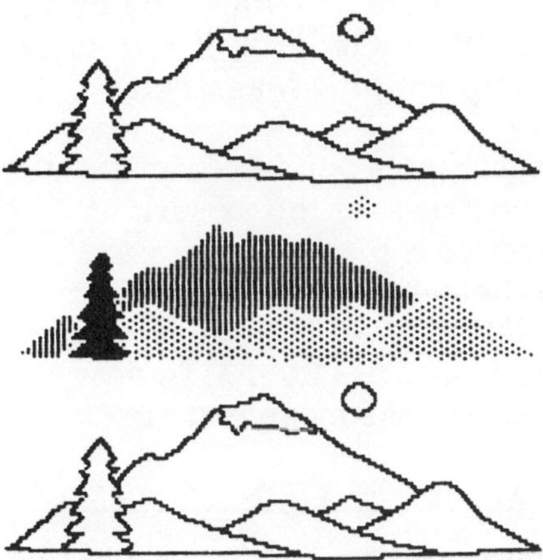

To use a pattern, select one from the Graphics Tools and move the crosshairs cursor so that it's *inside* the space you want to fill. Make sure that there are no gaps in the lines enclosing the space; you can accidentally fill the entire work space if there are. When that happens, select the OOPS icon *before doing anything else.* That will undo the photo-wide fill and give you another chance.

At times, spaces within clip art are too small to fill. This is especially true of the wider-spaced patterns, such as the patterns at the far right on the top row and second from the right on the bottom row. Other spaces, though able to be filled, are small enough that the pattern is distorted when it's used. In the trombone's slide (Figure 4-8), notice that the pattern puts dots in single file horizontally.

Figure 4-8. Distorted Patterns

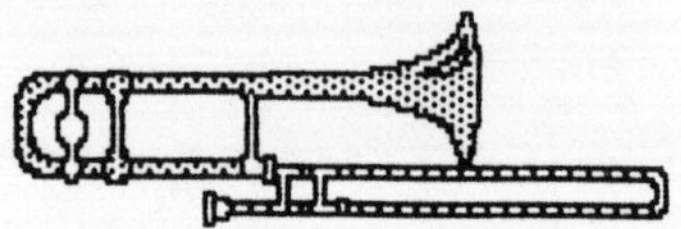

The black fill pattern, however, can fill even the smallest areas if you're patient (see Figure 4-9).

Figure 4-9. Black Fills Anywhere

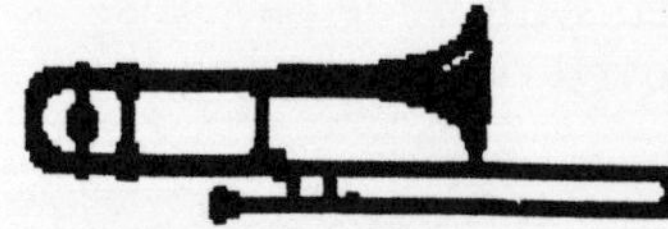

To fill the tiny spaces, position the crosshairs carefully, perhaps by using the cursor keys set to small moves. Be ready to use the OOPS icon if you make a major mistake. Smaller mistakes can be cleaned up with the Magnifying Glass.

Magnifying Glass. The Magnifying Glass icon puts you in command of every pixel on the screen. Using the cursor or arrow keys, or the joystick or mouse, you can turn on or off any dot in any piece of clip art.

Select the icon and move the rectangle to the desired location. The Photo Lab screen is replaced by a 28 × 16 grid. Filled boxes indicate the dark pixels and open boxes show white pixels. Below the grid are the EXIT and CANCEL selections, as well as a window which shows the magnified area in actual Photo Lab size.

EXIT the grid when you're done to record the changes. CANCEL will undo *all* modifications, so use it with caution. Watch the window to see the effect of your work.

Turn pixels on and off by pressing the select key (the joystick or mouse button works, too) at the blinking box location. Hold down the select key and move the cursor for wide-ranging changes. When the first pixel changed is from open to filled, all the boxes are filled; if the first pixel is changed from filled to open, all the boxes the cursor moves across are left open.

Figure 4-10. Magnifying Glass Grid

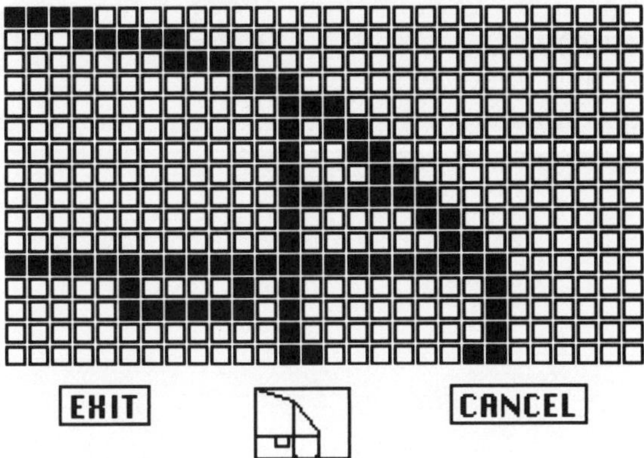

Use the Magnifying Glass for really fine work, such as this:

- Minor alterations to small sections of clip art, such as changing smiles to frowns on kid clip art.
- Filling tiny spaces with black where a pattern won't easily reach.
- Adding details to both clip art and handmade art; shading a circle to make it look spherical is a good example.

Figure 4-11. Using the Glass

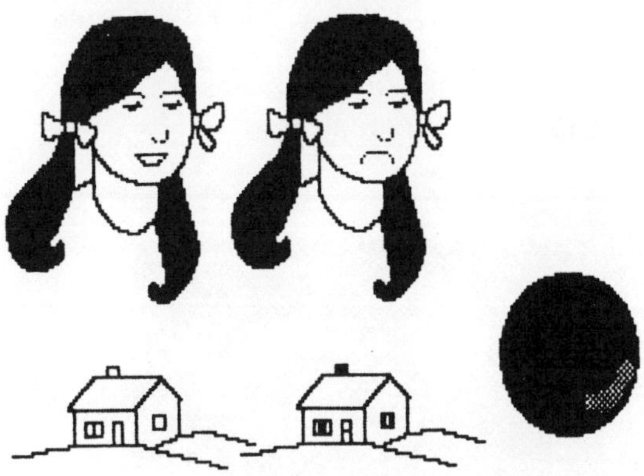

Silhouettes and white on black. Creating silhouettes is as easy as filling clip art with the black fill pattern. Position the art (remember, you can't move the clip art and the pattern together) and fill as much as you can. You'll probably have to use the Magnifying Glass at some point to fill every pixel.

For a striking effect, completely fill the clip art as if you were creating a standard silhouette; then go to the Graphics Tools and choose the Hand. Pick up the clip art and throw it away by moving it out of the work space. What remains is the now-filled interior of the clip art. You've thrown out only the outline of the art. In other words, what you have is a negative of the clip art—what was originally white is now black, and vice versa.

Figure 4-12 shows two silhouettes—one standard, the other the slimmed down version.

Figure 4-12. Thick and Thin

It takes just a few moments to reverse a piece of clip art by placing it against a black background. The result is white clip art on black.

≡ Draw a box larger than the clip art you'll reverse. Fill the box with black.

Or

≡ Use the large, square pen and the Draw tool to paint wide black brush strokes on the screen.
≡ Grab the clip art.
≡ Set it down inside the black box or on the black brush strokes.

Figure 4-13. White on Black

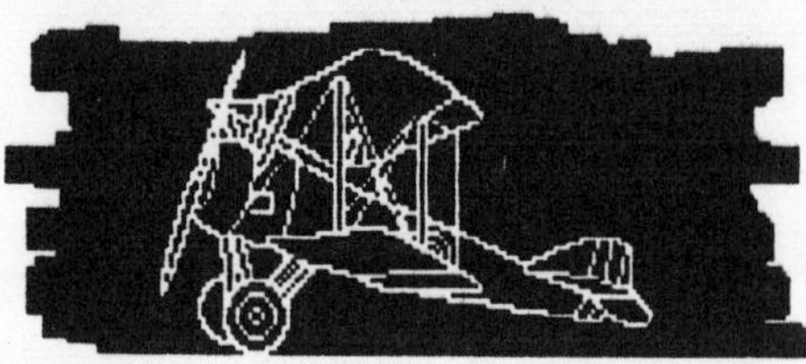

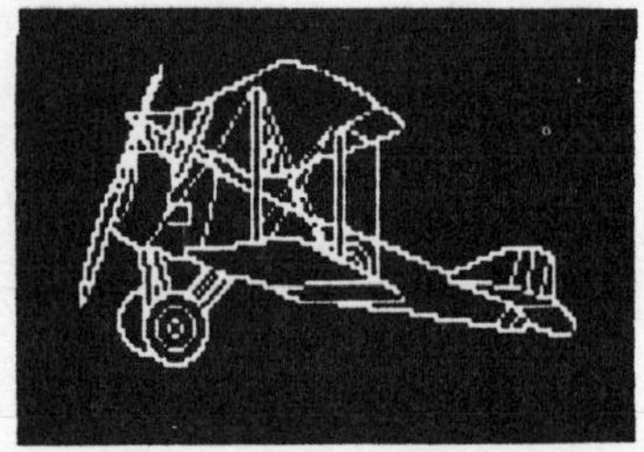

Parts Into Photos

Another way to create new and different artwork is to combine several pieces of clip art into one picture.

Some of the files on the *Clip Art Collection* disks are expressly set up for making combination pictures. They include pieces which are intended to fit together, sometimes in lots of ways. One of the best examples is the FACES1 file on the *Clip Art Collection, Volume 1* disk.

Figure 4-14. Faces In Pieces

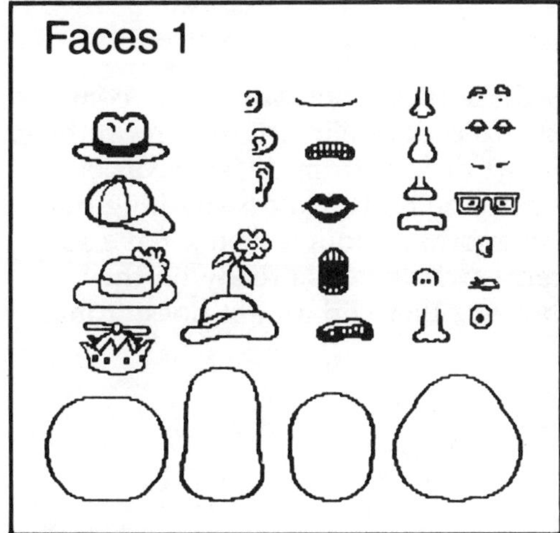

By repeatedly grabbing and placing, you can build almost any face. It's sort of like using an electronic Mr. Potato Head set.

Figure 4-15. Build-a-Face

Some of the other files which lend themselves to this kind of building-block approach include:

Volume 1	**Volume 2**	**Volume 3**
AUTO1	AUTO1	CAMPING1–2
BIRTHDAY	BORDERS1	CROWD1–3
BORDERS1–3	CHARTS1–3	FISHING2–3
FANTASY1	JEWELER1	GAMES2
FUN1–4, FUN6	REALTY1	MISC2–3
KIDS3	SEALS1	TRACK3
SCENERY1–3		TROPHY
SCHOOL1		

Of course, you're not limited to only these files when you create combination pictures. You can take any number of pieces of clip art and group them together. They can come from the same clip art disk or from different disks.

As long as the pieces don't overlap, you don't have to do anything out of the ordinary. If you do put one piece atop another, though, you'll have some editing to do. *Newsroom* clip art is transparent—whatever's already on the screen shows through clip art. Text, lines, boxes, other clip art—it doesn't matter what it is—everything shines through.

Figure 4-16. The Invisible Men

The two men in Figure 4-16 overlap at the shoulder of the one on the left; the jumble of lines is distracting. It just doesn't look good.

You need to clean up the mess with the Magnifying Glass icon. Select it and move the rectangle to the left man's shoulder. You'll have to turn off pixels in several steps, moving the rectangle when you finish with each 28 × 16–pixel grid.

It may be hard to tell which pixels should remain and which should be changed when you see something like this.

Figure 4-17. What a Mess

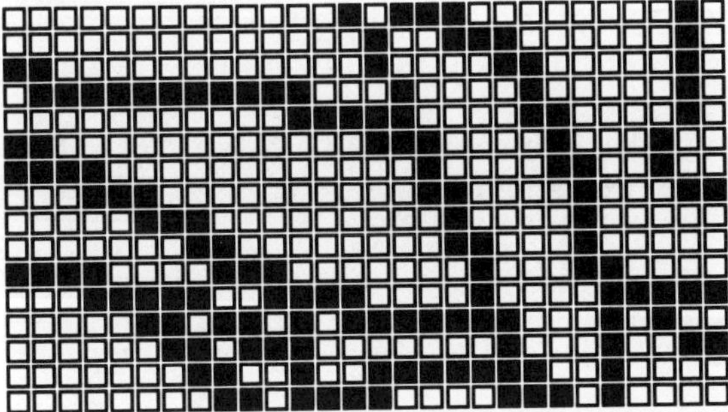

Actually, everything to the left of the gently curving line which begins at the top, about a third of the way across the grid (from the right), needs to be erased. That curving line is the left man's shoulder.

When all the loose pixels have been turned white, the two men should look like Figure 4-18. The man on the right is clearly behind the man on the left. Extraneous details have been eliminated and the combination picture is complete. (The shoulder lines of both men and part of the left man's coat were extended to meet the fence.)

Figure 4-18. Two Men Behind Fence

Keeping Your Masterpiece

Once you've selected, grabbed, positioned, changed, and maybe even combined your clip art, crop it and save it to disk. Especially good creations should be saved not only to your current issue's data disk, but to another data disk as well.

Copying *Newsroom* files is as easy as loading them into the proper work area and saving them out again to a new data disk. You can even use the same name if you want.

Call this special clip art disk something appropriate, like *Good Clip Art*. Make sure you name the files so that you can remember what they contain without having to load them into the Photo Lab for viewing.

Unfortunately, the work you've done can be saved only as photo files, not clip art files. There's a difference. Original clip art can be flipped, moved without distortion, and called with the Clip Art icon in either the Photo Lab or Banner work areas. Photo files, as you've seen, are much less flexible.

CLIPCAPTURE. What you want is a way to save your artwork as *clip art*, not just photos. *Newsroom* can't do that. But a program called *CLIPCAPTURE* can.

> *CLIPCAPTURE* is available only for the Apple II series. It costs $24.95 and runs on any II+, IIe, IIc, and IIGS with at least 48K of memory. *CLIPCAPTURE* is sold almost exclusively by mail. Contact *CLIPCAPTURE*, 477 Windridge Dr., Racine, WI 53402.

Among its many features, *CLIPCAPTURE* makes custom clip art disks from your own artwork, or from other sources like hi-res screens and *Print Shop* graphics. Functionally identical to any clip art disk from Springboard, each *CLIPCAPTURE*-created clip art collection can hold up to 250 pieces of art in up to 70 files (called pages by the program). Once this new clip art has been placed on disk, you can grab it with the Clip Art icon (in both the Photo Lab and the Banner), place it anywhere on the screen, flip it, and move it. In all respects, it's clip art.

Here's how *CLIPCAPTURE* works with *Newsroom* photo files.

Create your original artwork by combining existing clip art, editing art, or adding things drawn with the Graphics Tools (even text!).

Figure 4-19 is a photo which uses all three of these techniques. The clip art was all taken from *Clip Art Collection, Volume 1.* The airplane came from AERIAL1, the two clouds from SCENERY3, and the hills from SCENERY2. Two copies of the hills were laid down, and then the overlapping lines were cleaned up. The same process was used with the two different clouds. The airplane was positioned before its windows and wing stripes were filled with black.

Figure 4-19. New Art

But this is still a photo. If you grab or flip the airplane, clouds, or hills with the Hand, the editing will reappear or stay in place. Once it's saved as a photo file, you can't shift anything around—you couldn't, for instance, move the text *Scott's AirCharter* to the right a bit.

This is a perfect candidate for *CLIPCAPTURE*. A bit of planning is necessary, though. Most flexible would be four pieces of clip art—the plane, the clouds, the hills, and the text. Then you could save them each as separate pieces of clip art and recombine them (or even reuse them) in any number of ways.

Split the photo. As you create the various elements of a complex picture, save each as a photo. In the example of Figure 4-19, for instance, you'd end up with four photo files.

Element	**File**
Airplane	PLANE
Clouds	CLOUDS
Hills	HILLS
Text	SCOTT

You must save these pieces as you create them. You could not, for example, load something like Figure 4-19 into the Photo Lab and then crop each element one at a time. Although all seems to be working, when you later load what you think is a piece of the former photo, the entire photo (as it was originally) appears on the screen. It doesn't even help to erase everything but what you want—the whole photo still reappears. Obviously, a fault in *Newsroom*. You can build a photo from pieces, but you cannot later take it apart.

With those four files on disk, you can load *CLIPCAPTURE* and begin making the files into pieces of clip art.

CLIPCAPTURE is easy to use and shouldn't give even the beginning *Newsroom* user many problems. Simply follow the screen menus and make your choices.

CLIPCAPTURE's instructions must be printed from the disk. Read them carefully before using the program, for they outline in detail the program's features and functions.

Here are some things to note about *CLIPCAPTURE*:

- The Esc key exits you from all menus. It also "clips" the photo on the screen when you're in the clip creation mode.
- If you have a one-drive system (Apple IIc, for instance), be prepared for some serious disk swapping when it comes time to transfer clipping pages from the data disk to the clip art disk.
- You can use the same filenames for the clips you capture as you used for the photo files on the data disk. *CLIPCAPTURE* puts the prefix CL. on all clipping filenames.
- You can reduce the entire screen, or thicken (in either or both horizontal and vertical dimensions) the graphic. You can even invert the image before saving it as a piece of clip art.

Turning these four photos into four pieces of clip art takes about five minutes (less on a two-drive system). Each photo was loaded into the program and then clipped and pasted into a clip page. You manually position the pieces of clip art on the clip art page with the arrow keys. You may have to reposition the clip art if the pieces are too close together, but *CLIPCAPTURE* tells you when things are tight.

When you're done, you'll have a file on the *CLIPCAPTURE* clip art disk (I named mine AIRCHART). It is, for all intents and purposes, a standard clip art file on a standard clip art disk.

With *Newsroom* back in the computer, you can enter the Photo Lab (or the Banner) and select the Clip Art icon. Instead of putting one of Springboard's clip art collections in the drive, stick in your newly created disk. Highlight AIRCHART and—instantly—the four pieces of clip art are on the screen.

Grab and position them as you would any clip art. You can move them, flip them, and lay them atop one another. You can make duplicates of any of these pieces of clip art, just as you can with Springboard's.

One possible result of all this is Figure 4-20. Note that the airplane has been flipped; the black-filled windows and stripes followed along. One set of clouds is flipped. The text and hills were repositioned a number of times before everything was just right.

Figure 4-20. Clip Art Magic

The process of turning photos into clip art takes time, but it's time well spent. Once created, a piece of clip art is always instantly available.

CLIPCAPTURE can make *Newsroom* clip art from *Print Shop* or *Print Shop*-compatible graphics. (The *CLIPCAPTURE* disk comes with more than 180 pieces of clip art made from public domain *Print Shop* graphics.) It can also clip parts of a standard Apple hi-res screen as clip art. Hi-res screens can be created by several draw/paint programs on the Apple, as well as by a technique outlined in Chapter 11.

So much for the quick and easy route to *Newsroom* art. The *Clip Art Collection* disks may have thousands of pieces of art, but there's still one problem. No collection can have exactly what you and your newspaper needs for every situation. At some point you'll want to take the artist's brush in your own hands.

More Talent Required

Freehand *Newsroom* photos take more time, more patience, and more talent than clip art. But then your handmade artwork is more original than clip art, too.

The Graphics Tools menu adds drawing power to *Newsroom, and* makes it possible to put words in the Photo Lab work space. Lines, boxes, and circles come easy; other more free-form art comes with more difficulty.

This section isn't a crash course in computer art. Art lessons would take a book in themselves. And *Newsroom*'s tools are less than impressive, anyway.

What you'll find here are some applications of the Graphics Tools, things you can do almost immediately that will enhance your *Newsroom* newspaper.

Before you leap into the Graphics Tools, though, take a look at them.

The Graphics Tools

Line. Draws a single line from point to point. Straight lines are easier to draw when you use the arrow or cursor keys instead of a mouse or joystick.

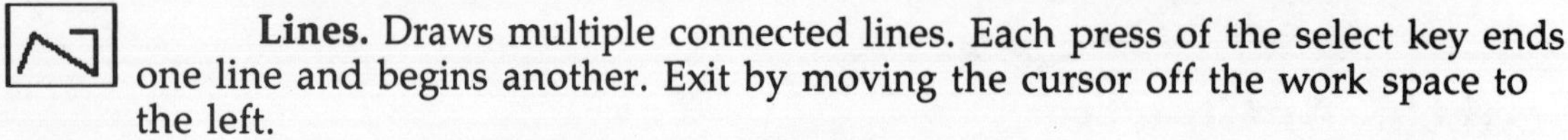

Lines. Draws multiple connected lines. Each press of the select key ends one line and begins another. Exit by moving the cursor off the work space to the left.

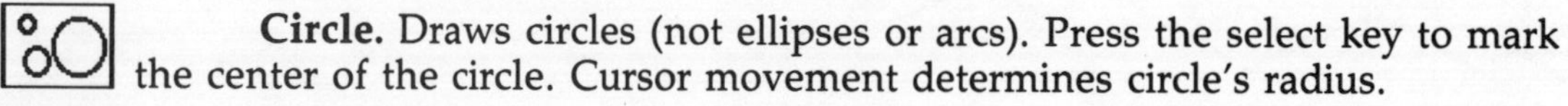

Circle. Draws circles (not ellipses or arcs). Press the select key to mark the center of the circle. Cursor movement determines circle's radius.

Box. Draws rectangles and squares.

Draw. Draws freehand, much like a pen would. Pressing the select key draws; releasing it "lifts up" the pen. This tool is very difficult to control, even in the best of circumstances (with joystick or mouse).

Eraser. Erases whatever it's moved across. Press the select key down to erase; release it to move the eraser. The eraser is often hard to manage since it disappears as it works.

The six tools all require a pen size as well. Pen sizes are set the same way, by moving the triangle-shaped cursor to the appropriate box and pressing the select key.

Pens 1–5. Various sizes and shapes of pens, running from the smallest to the largest left to right. Pen 5 is the size of choice for large eraser tasks.

Pens 6–10. Specialty pen shapes. Pens 6–9 draw thicker lines in some directions than they do in others. Pen 10 (the one that looks like a case of measles) is probably used least of any, though its effect can be interesting.

Graphics Tools Troubles

Though they're drawing tools, the Graphics Tools aren't up to par with those you'll find in graphics-specific programs. Some things the Graphics Tools do very well, while other tasks are beyond their abilities. If you're a *Newsroom* pro, you may have already discovered some of their limitations.

The edge of the world. The left side of the Photo Lab work space is dangerous. When using any of the Graphics Tools near this edge, place your cursor carefully. As soon as you move left from the leftmost pixel, you return to the icon selection area. Your last action, whether drawing a line or erasing something, is aborted. You'll have to return to the work space (Ctrl-L on the Apple and IBM versions takes you back to the middle of the screen) to complete your drawing. The last tool chosen is still in effect, however.

Circles only. The Circle tool makes only circles, not ovals or ellipses (extremely squished circles). This is one of the major deficiencies of the Graphics Tools. There are three ways to make curved lines in the Photo Lab, none of which are really satisfactory.

- Draw a circle and then erase part of it. A curved line remains. This is hard to get right.
- Draw it by hand with the Draw tool (or even more difficult, draw it pixel by pixel in the Magnifying Glass mode).
- Use another graphics program to draw the line and then convert the hi-res screen to *Newsroom*-photo form (Apple version only).

For many *Newsroom* users, all three of these options are too time-consuming. Suggestion: Don't create designs or pictures which require curved lines.

Straight lines. You can be sure a line is straight when it has no kinks as you "rubberband" it. Lines at 45-degree angles are also obvious, as the kinks are suddenly smoothed out.

Erase. Most of your erasing will be done with the large, square pen. To avoid erasing the wrong things, run the eraser from side to side in a level sweeping motion if you're using a joystick or mouse with *Newsroom*. To view the eraser (it's invisible while it operates), release the select key for a moment.

Duplicates. Since there are no guidelines or rulers on the screen, making several shapes the same size is hard. Here's what you do:

- Draw the first shape, counting the number of keypresses (large increment, small, or a combination) it takes to draw the line, circle, or box.
- Jot the number(s) down.
- Create the other shapes with that same number of keypresses.

Even boxes. To draw several boxes in a row, make the first and then move the cursor back to its top side. Move the cursor to the location of the next box with the arrow or cursor keys, counting the keypresses. Begin the second box. Use the counting method to make all the boxes the same size.

Bull's-eye. Concentric circles (like in a bull's-eye), are simple. Choose the smallest pen and the Draw tool. Put a dot on the screen where the center of your circles will be. Begin all the circles at that dot—they can be of different diameters, but they'll all share the same center.

Try These First

When you're adding graphics to your photos with the Tools, it's best to start with the simpler tools, like Line and Box. As you become more experienced, you can venture out with the harder-to-control tools, like Lines and Draw.

Boxes, frames, lines, and rules are the easiest to make in the Photo Lab. They're also the most commonly used graphic elements in newspapers.

When they're used as part of a larger piece of art, boxes and lines can be placed anywhere. More care is necessary when you plan to add the graphics to a panel later, especially when the panel includes text entered at the Copy Desk.

Let's take a look at creating rules in the Photo Lab; these rules will then be loaded into a Copy Desk panel.

Copy Desk rules. Draw the lines in the Photo Lab. Horizontal rules are most common, although you may find uses for vertical rules in special situations. Remember that the Photo Lab and the Copy Desk work spaces are the same width—a line all the way across the screen in the Photo Lab will also be one panel wide in the Copy Desk.

Save the rules as photo files. If you later want the text to come near the line, crop it close. If you want generous space between the text and the line, crop it with more white space.

Figure 4-21. Rule Cropping

Rule and Crop *Result*

Dropping Shadows. Boxes or frames that include a shadow really stand out. They're quite simple to make in the Photo Lab and can be constructed a number of ways.

- Use either of the diagonal pens (pen 8 or 9) to draw two of the sides for a three-dimensional look. Finish off the box with a standard pen shape.

Figure 4-22. 3-D Boxes

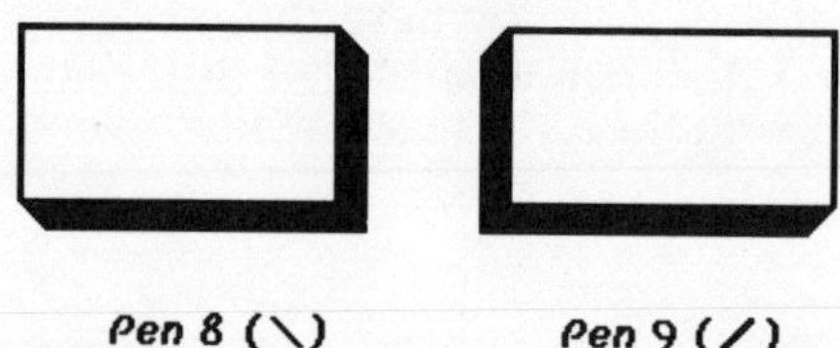

- An entirely different look can be created with the large, square pen. Use it to draw two sides of a box. Switch to a thinner pen and complete the box. Figure 4-23 shows several ways you can use this two-pen combination.

Figure 4-23. Floating Boxes

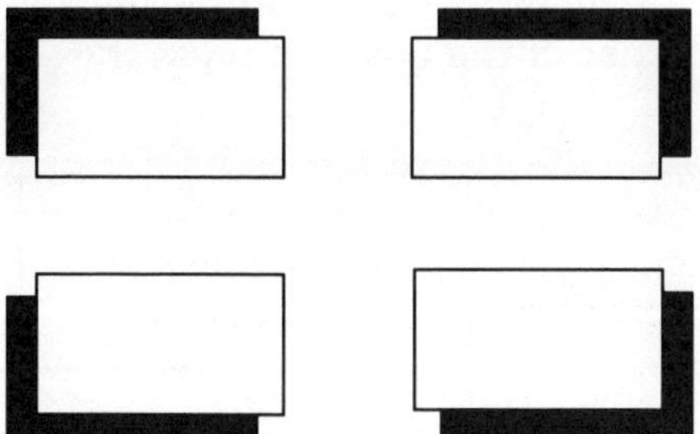

Words in the Photo Lab

Most of the time you use text in the Photo Lab, it's in small chunks—captions for pictures, labels for charts or diagrams, and other things of that sort.

Occasionally, though, you'll want to use the text features of the Photo Lab for longer sections. The Copy Desk is the natural place to type in words for your *Newsroom* newspaper, of course, but there are some things—graphics primarily—that cannot be done in the Copy Desk.

Photo Lab text entry is quite different from the Copy Desk.

- There's no Delete key. You must retype or space across a mistake.
- Only the right and left cursor or arrow keys work. Use them to backspace over text you've already entered.
- The Return or Enter key moves the cursor one line down.
- There's no word-wrap feature.
- To change or retype something once you've "picked up" the cursor, you must position it exactly.
- Text typed across any art erases the art.

One writing job you can do in the Photo Lab is making text-filled boxes. Chapter 2 showed you how to do this in the Copy Desk by importing lines. The result, you'll remember, isn't always satisfactory. You almost always end up with something that looks lopsided or misaligned. It's easier to type in the text from within the Photo Lab—even with the Lab's inferior text abilities—and then transfer the entire box to a panel via a photo file.

- Write the text you intend to box and estimate its length. (Estimate with one of the techniques described in Chapter 2.) Add another 10–15 percent to account for the sides of the box.
- Enter the Photo Lab.

- Select the Crayon icon, and choose Box and the appropriate pen. Most boxes will look best using the two leftmost pens. Try one of the three-dimensional or drop-shadowed boxes for an even more impressive look.
- Draw a box a bit larger vertically than the text block you're going to enter. *The box should extend the entire width of the work area.*
- Choose the Crayon again and select the type size and typeface you want.
- Position the cursor near the top left inside corner of the box and press the select key. Begin typing.

> Type slowly and carefully. In many cases, mistakes early in the section can only be corrected by retyping everything from that point on. It's best if you proofread each line before pressing Return or Enter.

- Press the Return or Enter key to end each line and send the cursor to the next line on the screen. Be careful not to go through the line on the right side. Back up with the left cursor or arrow key to correct mistakes.
- Hyphenate words if you want.

Figure 4-24. Text in a Box

Colossus of Rhodes

One of the Seven Wonders of the World, the Colossus of Rhodes was a bronze statue standing nearly 100 feet high.

Though it was reported to have straddled the entrance to a harbor, that's unlikely. More probable is that it was near the harbor entrance, to greet and impress arriving vessels.

Other accounts of the statue say it held a large lamp to guide ships safely to the port.

- Once the box of text is done, crop it. (Make sure to crop clear across the work space so that later text, if any, in the Copy Desk can't sneak by and end up beside it.)
- Load it into the appropriate panel in the Copy Desk. If necessary, add more text above or below the box (or both).
- Save the panel file to disk.

Sidebars. You first read about *sidebars* in Chapter 2. A sidebar is a mini–news story which has some connection with another, longer story on the page. A sidebar contains facts that you think the reader would like to know, but which really don't have a place in the main story. Figure 4-24 could have been a sidebar for a story about the discovery of the ruined remains of the Colossus of Rhodes, for example. Sidebars normally run alongside the main story and are often boxed or shaded.

You can duplicate this journalistic device in *Newsroom* and the Photo Lab. Shaded boxes are possible, though the results aren't really acceptable. The best you can hope for is something that looks like Figure 4-25.

Figure 4-25. Look for the Dots

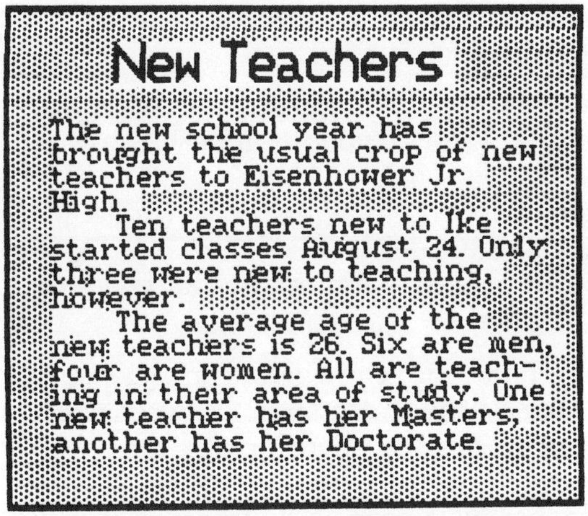

New Teachers

The new school year has brought the usual crop of new teachers to Eisenhower Jr. High.

Ten teachers new to Ike started classes August 24. Only three were new to teaching, however.

The average age of the new teachers is 26. Six are men, four are women. All are teaching in their area of study. One new teacher has her Masters; another has her Doctorate.

Notice the dots scattered here and there throughout the text? They're an unavoidable by-product of the pattern that fills the box. Some patterns create even more distracting problems. The top left pattern, for instance, puts thin lines randomly in the text.

If you're set on trying a shaded sidebar, follow these steps.

≡ Draw a box and fill it with a pattern (Figure 4-25 used the middle pattern, bottom row).
≡ Type the text in a large or small typeface (or a combination of the two).

It's impossible to eliminate the extra dots or lines—all the patterns put them into the text. The least noticeable, however, are the dots which you'll get with the middle pattern in the bottom row. Of course, you can clean up the dots (or lines) in the sidebar with the Magnifying Glass icon. Cleaning up Figure 4-25, for instance, doesn't take more than a few minutes.

More pleasing to the eye are boxed sidebars. They're made the same way as a shaded sidebar, but without a pattern.

Boxed sidebars can be longer than a single panel and still be completely enclosed. All it takes is a bit of planning.

- After selecting the Box tool and the desired pen size, move the cursor so that it's in the upper left corner.
- Now, count the number of small-increment keypresses as you move to the right. A good number is five.
- Press the select key and then cursor down to the bottom of the screen.
- Switch to large-increment movement and cursor to the right. Count the keypresses (11 takes you near the other side, leaving a gap about the same as on the left).
- Press the select key. The box is drawn.
- Go back to the Graphics Tools and choose the Eraser and the large, square pen.
- Erase the box's bottom side.
- Pick the Line tool and the smallest pen.
- Place the cursor at the far left side, near the top. Change to small increments and count the keypresses as you move right (20 is a good number). Draw a very short, vertical line.
- Choose your text and place the box cursor so that its left edge is against the line you just drew. Type in the first part of the sidebar.
- Crop the entire work space and save it to disk. (It's important that you crop the whole photo, from one corner to the other.)

Things may get a bit sticky near the bottom of the work space. Depending on where you first began text, there may be too much space between the last line of text and the bottom of the screen. At times, there's really not much you can do to prevent this.

To create the second half of the sidebar, you need to do things just a bit differently.

- Draw the box with the same pen size, counting the same number of keypresses to start and end the box as you used to create the first box. This makes sure the lines in the two parts meet.
- Instead of erasing the bottom side of the box, erase the top side.
- Draw the vertical text guideline by counting the same number of keypresses in from the left side. Choose the same text as in the first half.
- Position the text cursor at the very top of the work space, with its left edge against the guide.
- Type in the second part of the text.
- Crop the entire work space and save it to disk.

Now you've got two photo files on disk. Take care when you later load them into the Copy Desk—as soon as you load one into the work space, press the select key to set it down. *Don't move the photo.*

Save the panels to disk; then place them in Layout so that they're stacked one atop the other. Make sure that the first panel goes on top.

Here's what a two-panel sidebar might look like in finished form.

Figure 4-26. Long Sidebar

Going to Europe

Before we went on our family vacation to Europe this summer, we had to do a lot of advance planning.

Some of the things that anyone going to Europe needs to have before leaving include:

A passport
All prescription medicines needed
An extra pair of glasses, or contacts
U.S. driver's license (if you plan on renting a car in Europe).
Emergency phone number of person to contact in U.S.
List of all medical problems
List of all medical allergies

Also make sure that all reservations are confirmed and in writing. Take the written confirmations with you when you go. They're proof positive that you made the arrangements.

Watch the foreign exchange rates for several weeks in advance. If it looks like the dollar is dropping against European currency, exchange some dollars right then. Check on how much you can take out of the U.S. in foreign currency, before you do, however.

Have a happy holiday!

Then Try These

Things get harder as you get more ambitious with the Photo Lab and its Graphics Tools. Sidebars were tricky, though the explanation probably took longer to read than it did to do. More advanced Photo Lab techniques take even more planning and care.

As you push the Photo Lab's capabilities to its limits, you'll discover lots of ways you can create more attractive, more informative *Newsroom* graphics.

What's offered here are only two such ways of making even more powerful artwork for your *Newsroom* newspaper. Scores more are waiting to be explored.

Page numbers. Most newspapers run more than one page. That's why pages are numbered. Readers need to know where stories start (perhaps with a small table-of-contents box on the front page) and where pages jump (as in *See Basketball, C4*). Chapter 2 described a page-numbering technique in *Newsroom.* The process works, but it's clumsy and time-consuming. A better method, with the added benefit of boxing the page numbers, is available in the Photo Lab.

Go to the Photo Lab and select the Camera icon, *even though you haven't drawn or typed anything.* Put the cursor in the upper left corner, press the select key, and then cursor down with one keypress (large increment). Move to the right until the cropping box stretches across the work space. Snap this picture and save the file as NUMBLANK. That's step 1.

Step 2 is to return to the Photo Lab screen and type a page number with one of the small typefaces. Start numbering with page 2, since the front page doesn't need a number. If you want to get really fancy, type a hyphen, space, then the number, another space, and another hyphen, so it looks like **- 2 -**.

Put this number in an appropriate corner. Depending on the page number, it should go in the right or left corner. Even page numbers (2, 4, 6, and so on) go in the left corner; odd page numbers (3, 5, 7, for instance) go in the right corner.

Surround this number with a box and then pick the Camera icon again. Go to the top left corner, cursor down one keypress, and stretch the cropping box across the screen. Save this photo as something like NUM2. Repeat the process for each page that you need numbered by returning to the box and typing over the old number with the new.

Figure 4-27. Snapping Space and Numbers

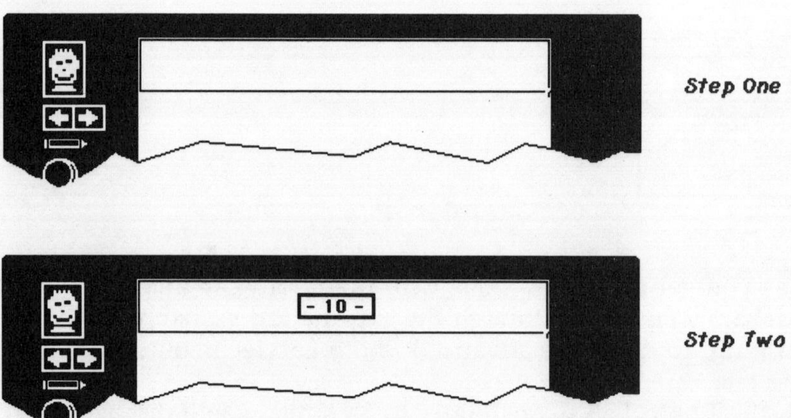

When you're finished (it won't take you long), you'll have a photo file for each page number except page 1. Here's what you do as you enter news stories in the Copy Desk.

Decide which column will have the page number. Match the corner with the column. In other words, even page numbers (left corner) should be placed in the left column. Put odd page numbers in the right-hand column.

Next, decide where you'll put the page number. Top of the page or bottom? Either is fine. Just be consistent once you make up your mind.

If the panel you're starting is in the correct column and place in your planned layout—another reason for planning your pages before you hit Layout—load the appropriate NUM photo file and position it at the top of the panel if this is a top-of-the-column panel or at the bottom of the panel if this panel goes at the bottom of a column.

Type text just as you would normally. If the page number photo is at the top, the text automatically starts below the picture's cropped dimensions. A photo at the bottom of the panel stops the text before it intrudes on the page number.

Figure 4-28. Place Page Numbers

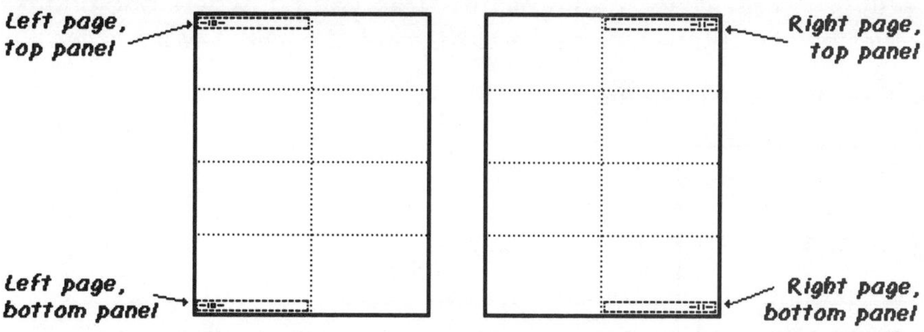

One more thing to do. Place the NUMBLANK photo file in the same location in the panel opposite the page-numbered panel. Thus, if you put the page number at the top of the top panel in the left-hand column (because it was an even-numbered page), then place NUMBLANK at the top of the top panel in the right-hand column.

Figure 4-29. Don't Forget NUMBLANK

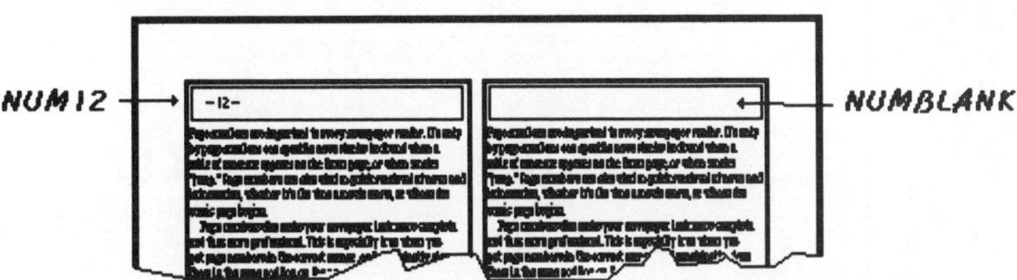

Multiphoto pictures. Just because you can only draw graphics and use clip art in photo-sized pieces doesn't mean you can't come up with larger pictures. It's not hard to build big pictures out of several photo blocks.

It's all a matter of planning the composition. Large graphics made from two or more vertical photos are easier to create than pictures built from two horizontal photos. That's because when you print photos as panels in a page layout, there's no space between panels vertically; there is a gutter between horizontal panels.

Plan your artwork accordingly. If you're using two vertical photos, the only limitation is that clip art can't go across the photo boundary. If you count keypresses, you can do such things as make lines and boxes look like they're drawn across photos. Put the beginning of a line of text at the bottom of the top photo and its end at the top of the bottom photo. With the correct spacing, it looks perfectly natural.

Multiphoto pictures made from vertical photos can even have a box around them. Follow the same procedure you used to draw boxes around two-panel sidebars—the top photo has lines at the top and both sides, while the bottom photo has lines at the bottom and sides.

Figure 4-30 is a vertical two-photo picture. Can you tell where one photo ends and the other begins? (Between the *Baseball* graphic and the word *Fever.*)

Figure 4-30. Vertical Multiphoto Picture

Horizontal photos aren't much more difficult, even though you have to contend with the gutter. Simply put the white space to good use.

You can't create graphics which stretch across the gutter, so boxes and lines are out unless you want to draw the connecting lines by hand after the page comes out of the printer. Depending on how steady your hand is, the results can be dismal or outstanding.

The clip art and text in Figure 4-30 can be rearranged to produce an effective horizontal picture. (The two photos meet between the words *Kings* and *MacMillan.*)

Figure 4-31. Horizontal Baseball

Tigers vs. Kings MacMillan Field, 7:30

Baseball

Fever !!

Catch It !!!

Aligning text and graphics in a horizontal picture takes a bit of work. Text can be aligned by placing the cursor at a work space edge and counting the same number of keypresses up or down in each photo. Guidelines can help align graphics—in Figure 4-31, for example, one was drawn in each photo by putting the cursor at the very bottom and moving up 20 keypresses (small increments). The horizontal line was then used to position the pitcher and batter.

When you load a photo file into the Copy Desk—either for a vertical or horizontal picture—immediately press the select key to set it down. Don't move the photo or the two-photo picture may be skewed.

Later, in Layout, check that you're placing the right panels in the right page-layout boxes.

Straight columns. If you've ever tried to put words or numbers into columns, you've stumbled across one of *Newsroom*'s problems. *Newsroom*'s type isn't *monospaced*—wide letters, like *M*, take up more space than narrow letters, like *J*.

Add to that the absence of any Tab function, and columns look ragged.

When looks are important, you may want to enter your columns in the Photo Lab instead of the Copy Desk. The Photo Lab gives you more precise control over where letters and numbers appear. The disadvantage is that it takes much longer. Trade time for straight columns? It's up to you.

Try this Photo Lab technique for straight-column results.

- Set the start of text by pressing the select key.
- Type in the first column, pressing Return or Enter at the end of each entry.
- When the first column is completed, use the left arrow or cursor key to move back through what you've typed. The cursor will stop when it reaches the first character in the column.
- Press the select key to free the cursor.
- With the right cursor or arrow key (not a joystick or mouse), move the cursor until it's at the spot where the second column should start. This should be slightly to the right of the rightmost character in the first column. Small-increment moves here give you more control.

≡ Type in the second column as you did the first. Return to the beginning of the second column with the left arrow or cursor key.
≡ Repeat the procedure as many times as necessary to enter all the columns. (Unless the entries are very short, you won't get more than three or four columns across the screen.)
≡ When you're through, closely crop the columns and save the photo file to disk.
≡ Load the photo into the appropriate Copy Desk panel and enter more text if necessary.

Figure 4-32. Straight Columns

Sale Items Today

Today's sale items range from paint to our smallest brushes. Keep this list handy today for quick reference as customers ask prices.

Item	Price	Part Number
2" brush	$1.29	2-34-43
3" brush	$1.99	2-34-44
Roller	$3.49	4-00-09
Paint pan	$4.49	4-00-03
Paint, white	$9.99	6-10-10
Paint, brown	$9.99	6-10-14
Paint, gray	$9.99	6-10-17

If you have any questions concerning the sale items, ask Mr. Ause.

You've been trying your talent for some time now in the Photo Lab. With the Graphics Tools, you've drawn everything from shaded sidebars to multiphoto pictures. The last section of this chapter takes you on a tour of some of the most advanced Photo Lab techniques you're likely to ever see. Using more computer software and more computer hardware, you can turn out *Newsroom* graphics that are truly one-of-a-kind.

The Advanced Photo Lab

The Photo Lab's tools aren't the most sophisticated. In fact, they're quite primitive compared to dedicated graphics programs. You'll do well to push their capabilities as far as what you've seen demonstrated in this chapter.

But if you're using an Apple personal computer to publish your newspaper or newsletter, or to a lesser extent a Commodore 64 or 128, you have other graphics means at your disposal.

These advanced Photo Lab techniques range from using other graphics software to scanning art to digitizing video images. They all involve other software and/or hardware. Using these techniques takes time and money. The time is certainly worthwhile, as you'll see in this section. The money—well, that's for you to decide. None of these methods costs more than $200.00, not much more than you've already invested in *Newsroom* if you have all three of the *Clip Art Collection* disks.

The first two techniques—converting art and video digitizing—can be used with both Apple and Commodore personal computers. The last method, scanning, can only be done if you have an Apple II+, IIe, IIc, or IIGS. IBM users of *Newsroom* are, at this writing, out in the graphics cold.

Apple Art Conversion

The simplest (and the least expensive) way to increase your *Newsroom* graphics power is to use the *Convert picture* option in the Apple version of *Newsroom*. All you need is a drawing program that can save its creations to disk as standard Apple hi-res files.

Another method of creating hi-res images on the Apple is discussed in Chapter 11, "News from Work." Look in the section titled "Great Graphics the Easy Way." The technique doesn't require a drawing program.

There are a multitude of Apple drawing programs on the market. The more recent and more powerful ones save out their images as double hi-res files, however. When you're looking at various drawing programs, make sure you check on the way each saves its files. You want one which uses the Apple *hi-res* format. Here's three such programs, actually just a sampling of what's available.

Picture Maker. This simple-to-use drawing program was published in *COMPUTE!'s Apple Applications* magazine as a type-in program, although you can order a disk which contains *Picture Maker* (as well as other programs) for $12.95, plus $2.00 shipping and handling. Specify the Spring/Summer 1987 issue. You can order this disk by calling 1-800-346-6767. *Picture Maker* has tools for creating lines, circles, arcs (something impossible with *Newsroom*), and polygons, and includes a palette of 26 shades and patterns.

MousePaint. Very much like the popular *MacPaint* for the Macintosh, *MousePaint* is a mouse-driven drawing program with pull-down menus and several interesting graphics tools. They range from an airbrush to a variable-sized brush. *MousePaint* was packaged with every new Apple computer for some time, but is not now widely available. You should be able to find one rather easily, however, if you have friends with Apple computers or if you're a member of an Apple users group.

816/Paint. From Baudville, this versatile program is the most powerful of the three. It can save images in hi-res format (among others) and works on all Apple personal computers. It's fast, powerful, and easy to learn. Like

MousePaint, it uses a mouse and pull-down menus. Its tool selection is superior to *MousePaint*'s. The price for *816/Paint* is $75.00. Look for it in your local software store or order it directly from Baudville (1001 Medical Park Dr. SE, Grand Rapids, MI 49506).

Draw your artwork and save it to disk. If your graphics program is working with the ProDOS operating system (*MousePaint* and *819/Paint* do, for instance), you'll have to transfer the file to a DOS 3.3 formatted disk to use it with *Newsroom*. The easiest way to do this is to use the *ProDOS Systems Utilities* disk that came with your computer. First format a disk with DOS 3.3 and then copy the hi-res image files from the ProDOS disk to the DOS 3.3 disk.

As you're drawing your original artwork, keep it a size that will fit within the Photo Lab's work space. That varies with the monitor or television set you're using, but if the art's no larger than about three-fourths of the screen (in both directions), it should fit within the Lab's work space.

With your hi-res image on disk, you're ready.

- Enter the Photo Lab and select the Disk icon. Choose the box labeled *Convert picture*.
- Stick the disk with the hi-res image in the drive and select *OK*.
- Type in the name of the hi-res file you want to convert. If you can't remember the filename, press Control-C to see a list of files. If you press Control-C, any key returns you to the previous screen.
- Read the next screen and select *OK*.
- The rectangle represents the size of the Photo Lab work space. Move the large rectangle with the arrow keys to enclose all or part of the artwork. Switch to small increments with Control-S for fine positioning of the rectangle.
- Press the select key, and the artwork magically appears on the Photo Lab screen.

You can modify the artwork as can any graphic. Draw lines, circles, and boxes; erase sections, zoom in and edit with the Magnifying Glass—you can do all this and more. You can't move the artwork, however, since it's identical to graphics you've drawn, not clip art you've grabbed.

You can also use the *Convert picture* feature in the Banner work area. The only difference is that the selection rectangle is only half as high as the one used in the Photo Lab. On the other hand, the art prints twice as large.

Figure 4-33 is a simple example of artwork converted into *Newsroom* photo format. It was drawn with *MousePaint* in about five minutes. Notice the curves used for the lid of the paint can—*MousePaint* lets you create ellipses, something *Newsroom* finds impossible.

Figure 4-33. Paint by Numbers, Inc.

Of course, you can crop the artwork with the Camera, then save it as a photo file. From that moment, it's a normal photo which you can load into a panel in the Copy Desk or print directly from the Press. As you can see from Figure 4-34, you can load the converted artwork into the Copy Desk and add text to complete the panel.

Figure 4-34. Add Text to Paint and Stir

Our introductory offer can save you 20% off the normal price.
Call us today at 222-0099 for a free estimate.

Complex drawings are a snap when you can use powerful graphics software instead of the clumsy Photo Lab tools. Graphics programs not only offer impressive features, but can save you time. Drawing something like the two pictures in Figure 4-35 would have taken hours in the Photo Lab. Using a dedicated graphics program, though, means you can produce high-quality art in minutes.

Figure 4-35. Apple Art, City Art

Courtesy COMPUTE! Publications, Inc. Copyright 1986 COMPUTE! Publications, Inc.

Other Art Conversions

Own a Commodore computer? Then you don't have a *Convert picture* option. Fortunately, you can still convert hi-res graphics to *Newsroom* photos with one of several graphics conversion programs.

One such package is a companion to the ComputerEyes video digitizing system discussed later in this chapter. It's called *ComputerEyes Newsroom Compatibility Software for Commodore Computers.*

You need the basic ComputerEyes hardware and and software to use this disk. *Newsroom Compatibility Software* saves video images as *Newsroom* photo files (again, see the section, "The Video Generation," for details on using ComputerEyes).

Just as exciting to *Newsroom* users is another feature of the program that lets you convert *any* normal Commodore hi-res image to a *Newsroom* photo. Like the Apple version's *Convert picture* function, this puts considerable graphics power in your hands. You can use graphics-dedicated software to sketch and draw pictures and then convert them into Photo Lab format. Any graphics software that saves its creations as normal hi-res images (9K files with PRG filename suffixes) is a candidate for your *Newsroom* software library.

You can get other conversion software from Commodore user groups and electronic bulletin boards. One program, most recently found in the Commodore 64/128 Round Table on the GEnie electronic database service, is

PS/PM/NR V1.2, a user-written conversion program which translates *Print Shop, Print Master,* and *Newsroom* files to any of the other formats. One advantage of getting programs from user groups or electronic bulletin boards is that the software is either free or very inexpensive.

***Print Shop* to *Newsroom*.** *Print Shop* is the bestselling graphics program. Sold by the hundreds of thousands, you can find the program in homes and schools from coast to coast. With *Print Shop,* you can churn out customized greeting cards, banners, and signs by the dozens.

One of the attractions of *Print Shop* is its huge collection of graphics. Some of the *Print Shop*–compatible graphics are sold by Brøderbund, the publisher of *Print Shop.* Other graphics collections are sold by software companies like Epyx and Unison. Even Springboard has a *Print Shop* graphics disk (called *Graphics Expander*).

Any software that can turn *Print Shop* graphics into something *Newsroom* can use instantly expands your publishing possibilities. You suddenly have access to hundreds more pieces of ready-made art.

For the Apple II, both *CLIPCAPTURE* and the *ComputerEyes/2 Enhancement Software* (see "The Video Generation" for information on the ComputerEyes disk) offer *Print Shop*-to-*Newsroom* graphics conversion features. If you have a Commodore computer, *ComputerEyes Newsroom Compatibility Software for Commodore Computers* and the just-mentioned *PS/PM/NR V1.2* let you translate *Print Shop* graphics to Photo Lab format.

The conversion software describes the process, so that's not necessary here. All you need are some *Print Shop* graphics, the conversion software, and a *Newsroom* data disk.

You can find *Print Shop*–compatible graphics on some electronic bulletin boards and commercial database services like CompuServe and GEnie. These *public domain* graphics usually cost you nothing but the phone and/or database charges. You also need telecommunications software which lets you *download* files over the phone lines.

Most *Print Shop* graphics are quite small (see Figure 4-36). They rarely take up more than a fourth of the Photo Lab's work space screen.

Figure 4-36. Really Small *Print Shop* Viking

When you get tired of the *Clip Art Collection* disks from Springboard, consider transforming *Print Shop* graphics into something for *Newsroom* and your newspaper. You'll discover an entirely new graphics world.

The Video Generation

Video and *Newsroom*. The combination is almost unbeatable.

How would you like to be able to take a "picture" of anything—line art on paper, a car, a landscape, a person, anything—and turn it into something printable by *Newsroom*? If your newspaper could include real photographs, or something very much like real photographs, it would be even more professional, even more like the newspaper that's delivered to your door every morning.

With ComputerEyes, a video acquisition system available for the Apple II and Commodore 64/128 computers, you can do exactly that. ComputerEyes' hardware and software, when combined with any video camera or videotape recorder (VCR), turns reality into *Newsroom* photos.

The Apple and Commodore versions of ComputerEyes include different kinds of hardware and work slightly differently. Their results, however, are almost identical.

And since you're using ComputerEyes with *Newsroom*, you should also buy the appropriate *Newsroom*-specific software from Digital Vision, the makers of ComputerEyes. For the Apple II, that means getting *ComputerEyes/2 Enhancement Software*. If you have a Commodore computer, you should pick up *ComputerEyes Newsroom Compatibility Software for Commodore Computers*. Both disks let you convert ComputerEyes images to *Newsroom* photo file format with the least fuss and bother.

ComputerEyes is available directly from Digital Vision, 14 Oak St., Suite 2, Needham, MA 02192 for $129.95. You may be able to find it at your local computer or software dealer. The *Newsroom*-specific software can also be bought from Digital Vision. *ComputerEyes/2 Enhancement Software* (Apple) costs $24.95, while *ComputerEyes Newsroom Compatibility Software for Commodore Computers* (Commodore) costs $15.00.

Plug and load. No matter which version you use, you need to install the hardware and run the software.

The hardware ranges from a board that plugs into an empty slot (Apple II+, IIe, IIGS) to a small box that plugs into the back of the computer (Commodore and Apple IIc). Follow the directions in your ComputerEyes manual to install and connect everything—computer, monitor, camera/VCR—and to initialize the program. If you're using an Apple, pick DOS 3.3 as the operating system. It just makes things much simpler, since *Newsroom* uses DOS 3.3, too.

When installing the board in the IIGS, make sure you go to the Control Panel and enter the *Slots* section to change the appropriate slot to read *Your card*. (You don't have to do this if you put the board in slot 7.)

Set up and focus the camera. One of the disadvantages of ComputerEyes is that it's not portable. You can't go far from the computer. A solution to this problem is to use a VCR with good *freeze-frame* capabilities. With a portable video camera, such as a camcorder, you can take video of anything anywhere and then put the tape into your VCR. Run the tape until the image you want to digitize is on the screen and then freeze that frame. The image should be clear, not distorted or disrupted by white lines. Connect the VCR to the ComputerEyes hardware and proceed normally to acquire an image.

Captured images. ComputerEyes's software is menu driven and easy to use. With the *ComputerEyes/2 Enhancement Software* or *ComputerEyes Newsroom Compatibility Software for Commodore Computers,* follow the prompts to capture an image. If you're using an Apple, the best image-capture type to use is *Hi-Res Multi-Level.* If you're using a Commodore, however, *Normal Capture* seems to have the best results.

When you've got an image in memory, and thus on the screen, crop the image to a size suitable for *Newsroom*'s Photo Lab. You do this with an outlined rectangle, much like the one Apple owners use to convert pictures in the Photo Lab. Keep this in mind—you can't stuff the entire screen's contents into a photo file. Then save the file to disk.

With the Apple version and the *ComputerEyes/2 Enhancement Software* disk, you can shrink (or expand) the acquired image before you crop it to *Newsroom* photo-file size. For a full-screen image, try rates of 80–90 percent. There's a slight drop in quality when you shrink an image, but sometimes it's the only way to get everything into the photo file.

It takes only minutes from the time you set up the camera to the moment you have *Newsroom* photo files on a data disk. Those ComputerEyes-created files are identical in all respects to normal photo files.

Digitizing still lifes. Since ComputerEyes takes several seconds to acquire an image, you'll be hard pressed to take video of anything moving. That includes small children, animals, and sporting events. (One way around this is to take video and then freeze a frame as explained earlier.) Still lifes are the easiest video compositions. The subject doesn't move and you can control the lighting. Figure 4-37 is a digital still life of a telephone, while Figure 4-38 is of a collection of art supplies, including spray can, pencils, and scissors.

Note: All the following examples were created with the Apple version of ComputerEyes and used the Hi-Res Multi-Level capture mode.

Figure 4-37. Digital Phone

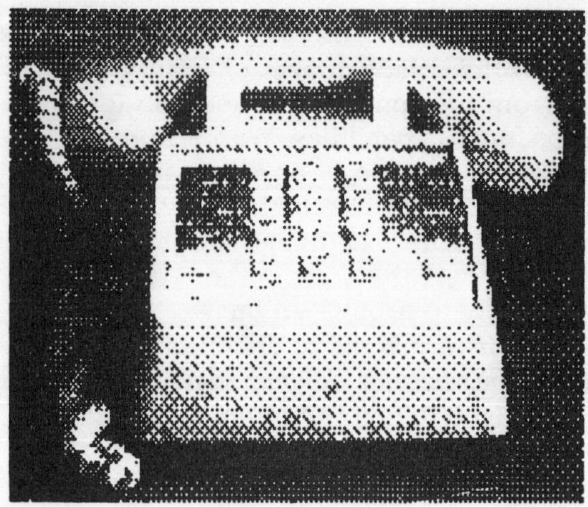

Figure 4-38. Digital Art

Digitizing landscapes. As long as there's not a lot of movement across your camera's view, you can digitize landscapes as easily as still lifes. This view of a parking lot (Figure 4-39), although admittedly fuzzy, was taken through a window on a bright summer day. Even with the best lighting conditions, ComputerEyes results aren't guaranteed. On the other hand, creating something even close to this detail would take hours with the Graphics Tools.

Figure 4-39. Digital Parking Lot

Digitizing people. People are harder to capture on video with ComputerEyes because of the time it takes to acquire an image. It takes at least 6 seconds to acquire an image, and it can take up to 50 seconds if you use one of the more detailed modes on the Commodore 64. That's a long time to remain perfectly still. If the subject moves, the image will come out smeared. Children in particular can't be expected to sit motionless for that long. Figure 4-40 is a self portrait. It's recognizable, at best. Better lighting might have improved its quality.

And using digitized art. As with any photo file, you can load a ComputerEyes-produced file into the Photo Lab, crop just a piece of it, and then save the chunk under a new name. That new file can then be added to a panel in the Copy Desk work area, where text can be added to begin a news story. Figure 4-41 includes a digitized piece of art at the top—it's a shot of a toy truck, not a real one.

Figure 4-40. Digital Self Portrait

Figure 4-41. Digital Trucking

Trucks Hit The Road

The company's new fleet of Volvo/White trucks arrived last Friday, and after a three-day maintenance check, they're all ready to hit the road.

"We're pleased that every one of the trucks came to us ready to go," said Jules Irvings, Maintenance Manager. "We expected to have some problems, but everything's worked out perfectly."

Scanners

If you thought video digitizing was sending *Newsroom* and your newspaper into the electronic future, then get ready for another graphics shock—scanning.

A *scanner* is a device that reads whatever's on a page of paper and translates that image to your computer screen. Once safely stored in your computer's memory, it can be saved to disk and later recalled for viewing or changing. Some scanners read typewritten text so that you don't have to retype a document into the computer. Others work best with pictures.

If you have an Apple IIc, 128K Enhanced Apple IIe, or an Apple IIGS, you can add scanning to your *Newsroom* publishing toolkit with Scannit, an inexpensive optical scanning device. It works with your printer—you roll the art (it has to be on paper that will fit, obviously) into the printer and it scans away.

Scannit is available from JED design, 3300 Central Ave. SE, Canton, OH 44707, for $189.00. You may also find it at your local Apple dealer. You'll need an ImageWriter or ImageWriter II printer, a 5¼-inch disk drive, and an Apple computer. Specify your printer and computer when ordering, as Scannit's hardware differs depending on the printer model.

Another scanner is ThunderScan ($219), from Thunderware, Famous for its Macintosh scanner, the company's Apple II model (Apple IIe, IIc, and IIGS) is much more sophisticated than Scannit. Its ability to scan whole pages in a variety of resolutions is particularly impressive.

Scannit comes with two disks, a plastic box about the size of two cigarette packages, and a small scanning device that replaces the ribbon cartridge (ImageWriter I) or fits alongside the existing cartridge (ImageWriter II). Installation takes a few minutes as you fit the scanning device in the printer, connect the printer to your computer, and connect the small box to the DB-9 connector on the back of your computer (it's on the far left as you look at the *back* of the computer).

After you put the Scannit disk in the drive and turn on your computer, you need to manually focus the scanner. Follow the directions in the Scannit manual. Select *Normal hi-res Scan*—the standard Apple hi-res mode that you can convert within *Newsroom*—put the art in the printer, and press Return. The printhead moves back and forth across the art, reading what it sees and putting that on the screen. You can adjust the contrast and sensitivity to white by turning two knobs on the small box. The Scannit manual offers several hints on adjusting these controls.

When the scanning is complete, you'll be asked to save the file. Put an empty, formatted disk (it has to be formatted with ProDOS; the easiest way to do that is with your *ProDOS Systems Utilities* disk) in the drive, and type a filename in the form */disk volume name/filename.*

Apple IIGS owners take note: Your 3½-inch *ProDOS Systems Utilities* disk does not allow for copying from ProDOS to DOS 3.3. You'll need to buy a copy of the 5¼-inch *ProDOS Systems Utilities* disk from your local Apple dealer. This disk is normally used with the IIc, but it will work with your IIGS (as long as you have a 5¼-inch drive).

You then must copy the scanned image files from the ProDOS data disk to an empty disk formatted in DOS 3.3 so you can use them with *Newsroom.* Again, use your *ProDOS Systems Utilities* disk to do this.

What you've got now is a series of hi-res images stored on a DOS 3.3 disk. Run *Newsroom,* enter the Photo Lab work area, select the Disk icon, and choose *Convert picture.* Grab image after image, saving each to a *Newsroom* data disk as a photo file. You can turn only about 75 percent of the screen into a *Newsroom* photo (the Photo Lab work space is smaller than the screen, remember). Refer to the earlier section, "Apple Art Conversion," for details on the complete picture conversion process.

Scanning simple line art. Simple black and white line art is the simplest to scan. The contrast is easily picked up by Scannit, and the result is generally clear and recognizable. The cartoon figure in Figure 4-42, drawn originally in pen, came through Scannit almost as you see it. The characters were rough, though, and had to be cleaned up. *MousePaint* was used for this, but the Magnifying Glass option in the Photo Lab would have worked about as well.

Figure 4-42. Binky Clone

Scanning complex line art. More complicated line art scans just as well. Figure 4-43 is a reproduction of Thomas (Stonewall) Jackson, the famous Confederate general in the Civil War. Scannit's contrast control was turned up for this picture, which gave the shading across Jackson's face. Notice, however, that his beard is cut off—in the original scan, it was intact. Just one example of how the smaller-sized photo files can be limiting. Keep this in mind as you're selecting your scanning art.

Figure 4-43. Stonewall

Scanning photos. Although photos can be most demanding of your scanning techniques, the results can be equally impressive. This next figure was created by scanning a photo of an Apple IIGS at a magnification rate of 3—Scannit can magnify the image two, three, or four times normal—to make it recognizable. Detail was lost in the lower part of the picture, almost obliterating the IIGS's keyboard.

Figure 4-44. Apple IIGS

Scanning logos. One of the quickest ways to recreate a company logo, club emblem, or school mascot is by scanning. Once in photo-file form, you can clean it up with the Magnifying Glass icon. Figure 4-45 shows the nameplate of the magazine *COMPUTE!'s Apple Applications*. It's not been cleaned up yet (notice the smeared s at the top right). The word *Applications* didn't come through—it got lost in the shaded bar at the bottom. Scanning isn't perfect.

Figure 4-45. COMPUTE!'s Apple

Scanning into the Banner. Except for the size of the art allowed, converting a scanned picture into a banner is identical to converting a picture into a photo. All you have to keep in mind is the size of the Banner work space (half as high as the Photo Lab's). Figure 4-46 shows a completed banner which uses a scanned image on the left. Text, lines, and a box were added to finish the banner.

Figure 4-46. Blaster Master

Picture Perfect

The Photo Lab is a dynamic part of *Newsroom* that can push your newspaper to new graphic heights. With its ability to capture and change clip art, draw line art, and add text, the Photo Lab can produce photos that tell a story as easily as scores of words.

But the true power of the Photo Lab comes from experimentation. Pattern-filled sidebars, multiphoto pictures, and perfectly aligned columns are just some of what this versatile work area can do. Even more impressive are advanced techniques like digitizing and scanning.

With the best graphics *Newsroom* can create, your newspaper will stand out, be noticed, and be read.

The next work area on this tour through *Newsroom* is the Wire Service, arguably the most forgotten part of *Newsroom*. It may be ignored by many, but it's features can make you a more effective newspaper writer, editor, or publisher.

CHAPTER 5

It's a Group Effort

The Wire Service

There's no question that the Wire Service work area is the forgotten part of *Newsroom*. Even the manual gives it just a brief mention.

Perhaps that's because most *Newsroom* owners haven't used the Wire Service—and don't ever want to. Maybe you fit in that group.

Or perhaps you've used the Wire Service once or twice, but it seemed like more bother than it was worth. Setting up the modem, connecting everything, making the phone call, and sending files one at a time—it took time, and when things didn't work, you had no idea why.

This chapter tries to change your mind. It shows why you should use the Wire Service and then shows you how. It also spells out what equipment you need, how to save time and money, and even how to publish a newspaper without turning on your printer.

The Wire Service can make *Newsroom* a more powerful program and can make you a more effective newspaper publisher, editor, or writer.

Pick Up the Phone

The Wire Service lets you call someone on the telephone—call across town or across the country—and share anything either of you have created with *Newsroom*. As you'll find out later, all you need is a *modem*, a device that lets your computer communicate using the phone lines.

The question many *Newsroom* users have, though, is *Why bother?* You may be one of those people. Why should you use the Wire Service? After all, you (and your staff if you have one) have gotten along perfectly well writing, editing, and printing your newspaper. Why do you need someone hundreds of miles away to help you?

First of all, the Wire Service isn't only for transmitting panels, photos, and pages across state lines. It can just as easily send a page across town or across the street. The Wire Service makes more writers able to contribute to your publication, makes some newspapers possible, and opens up new possibilities for printing your newspaper.

Writers in Other Cities, Schools, or Offices

One of the best things about *Newsroom*'s Wire Service is that it expands the number of writers you can have for your paper. Writers don't have to live nearby; they can live anywhere there's a telephone and still contribute to your paper.

Professional newspapers have a similar setup, for many major papers put correspondents in large cities to report on the important news from those places. The *New York Times*, for example, has reporters in Washington, D.C. who report on the news in the capital and then transmit their stories to the *Times'* central office for editing, layout, and finally printing.

Your paper can have far-flung correspondents, too. As long as each writer has a copy of *Newsroom*, he or she can write the story, illustrate it, and place it in a page. Then, by using the Wire Service, he or she can send you the story and photos for more editing or layout work.

More writers in more places means you can expand the kind of news you include in your publication. In some cases, it can make your newspaper or newsletter possible in the first place.

The Wire Service at home. With the Wire Service, you can turn your family newspaper into something for the *entire* family, not just the people who live in the same house you do. Parents, grandparents, brothers and sisters, sons and daughters, uncles and aunts, cousins, and even family friends can become writers and readers of your paper.

Newsroom is the perfect way for everyone in the family to stay in touch. Instead of writing news about your grandparents secondhand, why not have them write it themselves and send it to you with the Wire Service? Why not use that talented brother of yours to help write the news of his family?

The possibilities are exciting. You can turn your small family paper, where you do all the writing and which has just a handful of readers, into something that a dozen people help put together, and scores eagerly read.

The Wire Service at school. The Wire Service makes it possible for a paper's writers to work at home if they have a computer and a copy of *Newsroom*. This may be important if there aren't enough computers at school for your staff or if the newspaper's time on them is limited.

And since the Wire Service lets you transmit files from one kind of computer to another, it doesn't matter that one writer has a Commodore 64 at home, another an IBM PC, and a third an Apple IIe. Stories can be written on any machine and then sent to a computer at school, where the paper is edited, laid out, and printed.

Another possibility the Wire Service opens up is sharing news with other schools, either those in your own city, or one almost anywhere in the country. People have pen pals, cities have sister cities—why can't your school have a "buddy school" in a different city? Your readers won't be interested in all of their news, just as they won't want to print all of yours. But the two schools will have lots in common. Ideas for fund raising; ways to solve problems like vandalism, tardiness, or bad cafeteria food; and feature stories about interesting people and events are just some of the things you could share with other school newspapers.

It shouldn't be hard to find a school to share information with. If you're looking for one out of town, ask some of your school's teachers and administrators where they've taught before.

The Wire Service at work. Sometimes even small businesses have several branch offices—across town or on the other side of the state. It doesn't take a large company to have employees in several places.

If you're publishing the company's newspaper or newsletter, you want access to *all* the company news, not just what you can find in your particular office. *Newsroom* and its Wire Service work area can tie the company together by making it possible for employees at every office or job site to contribute their news and opinions.

In many cases, this is the only way you'll be able to publish all the company news. Many firms can't afford to send a newsletter editor or writer from office to office, reporting on the news. Instead of taking the writer to the news, bring the news to the writer by sending stories from one part of the company to another with the Wire Service. All that's needed is a computer and modem (which are probably already there), and a copy of *Newsroom* at each office.

Of course, not everything about using correspondents is going to work out all the time. Though there are advantages to the Wire Service and what it means—more writers from more places with more news—there are disadvantages, too.

You may never meet some of the people writing for your paper. If they live, go to school, or work in another city, it's going to be hard to get to know them. It's going to be just as hard to know their writing abilities, or their general *Newsroom* skills. You may not have as much confidence in a correspondent's writing as with someone you can talk to every day. And it's harder to show them what you want in a story and how to improve their writing.

Enforcing deadlines is also going to be more difficult. It's a fact that part of the pressure you can put on a tardy writer comes from standing right in front of him or her and asking why the story's late. People find it easier to make excuses over the phone than they do in a face-to-face conversation. (That assumes you can even *reach* them by phone; writers who are late have a habit of not answering phone calls from their editor.)

Overall, the Wire Service's benefits far outweigh its problems. Try the Wire Service on a regular basis for awhile as a test. Your newspaper may be better written, have more news, and be more interesting to your readers when stories from far-away places are included.

Best Print Possible

Another excellent reason to use the Wire Service work area of *Newsroom* is to print your newspaper in the best possible quality.

All printers are not created equal. Some printers create a much better-looking page than others. Figure 5-1 illustrates this by showing the same panel printed by a Commodore MPS 803 printer (left) and an Apple ImageWriter (right).

Figure 5-1. Printers Aren't the Same

The market went bullish yesterday, jumping 24 points in the afternoon after a short fall of 3 points in the morning.

Stock experts attribute the rapid rise to new confidence in the dollar, which rose against both the Japanese Yen and the German mark.

Whether the pattern is going to

Market
Goes
Bullish

The market went bullish yesterday, jumping 24 points in the afternoon after a small fall of 3 points in the morning.

Stock experts attribute the rapid rise to new confidence in the dollar, which rose against both the Japanese Yen and the German Mark.

Whether the pattern is going to

The three versions of *Newsroom* support dozens of printers (see the Appendix for a list of all the printers). You may know someone with a copy of *Newsroom*, a computer, and a printer that's better than yours. The Commodore printers, for instance, generally create poor-quality pages. At the other end of the spectrum, the Apple ImageWriter produces high-quality print.

Print quality is especially important when you're planning on copying your pages on a copier. Light printing or widely spaced dots can make even originals hard to read. When pages are copied, they may become even more illegible. (See Chapter 7 for more details about printing your newspaper.)

Let's say you're using the Commodore 64 version of *Newsroom*, but you don't want to print your paper on your Commodore MPS 803 printer. You'd rather print the paper on an Epson FX100. Unfortunately, you don't have one. Nor does anyone you know who also has a Commodore 64. Without the Wire Service, you'd have to print on the MPS 803.

With the Wire Service, however, you can transfer your pages to an IBM PC connected to an Epson FX100 and then print them on that system.

Laser printing. A laser printer works much like a small copying machine. An image is traced with a low-powered beam of laser light onto a shiny drum inside the printer. Black plastic powder, called *toner*, sticks to the parts of the drum touched by the laser beam, and as the paper moves through the printer, the drum transfers the toner to the paper.

The results are astonishing. Text is clear and crisp. Blacks are truly black, without any of the thin lines you may be used to with a dot-matrix printer. Figure 5-2 shows just how good laser-printed *Newsroom* panels can be.

Figure 5-2. Laser Printing Compared

Golf Lessons Now Available At Olsen

For the first time ever, golf lessons will be given at Olsen Municipal Golf Course. Bob Shelby, acting pro at Olsen, will conduct the lessons every day except Sunday. Hours are by appointment only.

"I think we'll have a really good turnout," Shelby said. "Lots of people

What's the catch? Laser printers are expensive, often costing nearly $3,000. It's unlikely your school has one, even more unlikely you have one at home. Because of their cost, laser printers are found only in offices and businesses. (See Chapter 7 for information about exceptions and ideas about how anyone can find a laser printer to use.)

If your office has a laser printer, or you know someone who works in an office which does, you'll also need an IBM PC, PC XT, PC AT, or PC compatible with at least 512K of memory, and a copy of *Newsroom Pro.*

If you're publishing a business newspaper or newsletter and do the work at the office, you'll probably want to work with *Newsroom Pro,* the more advanced version of *Newsroom* available only for the IBM PC. That way, you can skip the transfer process to print on a laser printer. However, you may be creating a family newspaper, or you or someone in your family may be working on a school newspaper. In that case, you could create the publication with *Newsroom* and then follow the steps below to print the master copy on a laser printer at work. If necessary, make sure you have approval before you use office equipment for home or school paper printing.

You can print your newspaper on a laser printer if you're willing to go through several steps and have access to an IBM PC, PC XT, PC AT, or PC compatible, a copy of the IBM version of *Newsroom*, a copy of *Newsroom Pro*, and one of these laser printers.

Apple LaserWriter
Apple LaserWriter Plus
HP LaserJet Plus

- Send your pages to an IBM PC equipped with *Newsroom* via the Wire Service if you're not using the IBM version already.
- Start *Newsroom Pro* and go to the Copy Desk area.
- Choose the Disk icon and select *Load original Newsroom* page. You can only load entire pages from *Newsroom* into *Newsroom Pro*.
- Follow the directions by choosing the appropriate drive and directory.
- Load the page from *Newsroom*.
- Save the page to a *Newsroom Pro* data disk.
- Go to the Press work area, make sure that the correct laser printer is selected, choose the page, and print.

Print just one or two copies of each page as *masters* and then duplicate those masters on a copying machine.

There are more reasons why the Wire Service makes using *Newsroom* more useful. They range from being able to send or receive stories at the last minute to publishing a paperless newspaper. You'll discover more uses for the Wire Service—and more reasons for using it—as you explore it yourself and work with *Newsroom* day after day.

Talking Computers

The Wire Service work area is different from the three you've already explored in this book. There's no white work space on the screen nor are there icons on the left. Instead, you make some simple selections to tell *Newsroom* what equipment you're using, what pages, panels, banners, or photos you want to send, and what phone number you're calling.

In "How the Wire Service Works," you'll step through a sample session of the Wire Service. Here, though, you'll find information about the one piece of hardware you need to transmit files over phone lines—a *modem*. If you're not interested in *how* things work as files are transmitted, make sure you at least read the section, "Have the Right Modem," which lists the kinds of modems each version of *Newsroom* supports.

Modems Make Computers Talk

Computers talk in a language vastly different from any human speech. That language, no matter what the computer, is made up of thousands of combinations of two numbers—0 and 1. To a computer, 0 means *off* and 1 means *on*.

The pattern of those ons and offs make it possible for computers to use programs like *Newsroom*, print on a printer, and even "talk" over the telephone.

A telephone, however, doesn't understand these patterns of 0s and 1s any more than most people do. The telephone is designed to take voices and other sounds and then transmit them as tones. For a computer to talk on the telephone, the computer's language has to be translated into the tones the telephone can send down the phone line.

Figure 5-3. Computer Talking

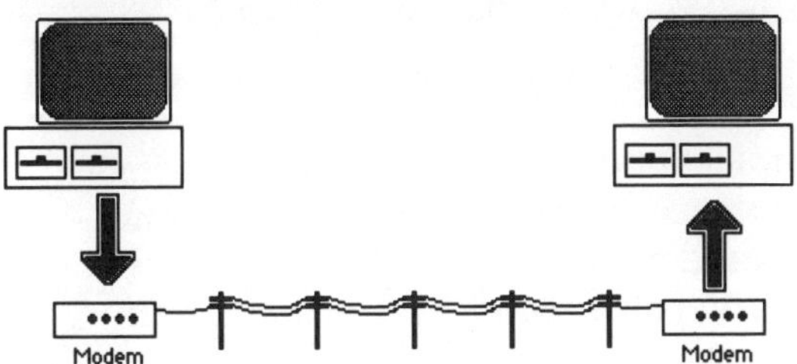

That's what a modem does. When your computer sends a *Newsroom* file, the modem takes the 0s and 1s and translates them into tones the telephone system understands. When your computer receives a file, the modem does the opposite by translating tones from the telephone into 0s and 1s for the computer. The modem works in both directions, *MODulating* and *DEModulating* (hence the name *modem*) tones.

How Files Are Sent

Sending or receiving any kind of computer information—not just *Newsroom* pages, panels, and photos—is done similarly. Whatever program is letting your computer send or receive (usually it's called a *telecommunications* program) breaks a file into a generic "flavor" of 0 and 1 patterns. Collectively, these patterns are known as *ASCII*. The simplest way to think of ASCII is to remember that every computer can understand it. That's why telecommunications is one of the surest ways for two different computers—say an IBM PC and an Apple IIe—to communicate. Files are broken down into an ASCII pattern of 0s and 1s, which is what's sent across the phone lines.

That's also how you can share *Newsroom* files between three kinds of computers. The Wire Service is the telecommunications program which does the translating of *Newsroom* files into ASCII patterns which can be sent across the country.

No other telecommunications program will do, simply because the *Newsroom* files have a peculiar *format*, or way the information is stored on disk. Only the Wire Service is set up to read that format from disk when sending or to write that format to disk when receiving. It's because of this format that the computers at both ends of the connection must be running *Newsroom*.

Have the Right Modem

A number of different modems will work with the three versions of *Newsroom*. Every modem found in the *Change setup* menu of each *Newsroom* version is listed below.

Use this list for two things: To buy the right modem if you don't have one already and to make sure everyone on your Wire Service "network" has an appropriate modem.

Besides making sure that it's on the list, the only other important feature to look for when buying a modem is its *baud* rate. Baud rate is the speed at which the modem transmits or receives information. The Wire Service can send or receive data at either 300 or 1200 baud in the Apple and IBM versions; the Commodore version only allows for 300 baud.

The numbers—300 and 1200—indicate how may *bits* of information—how many 0s or 1s—can be transmitted or received each second. A Commodore 1600 modem, which is a 300-baud modem, can send 300 bits per second. A 1200-baud modem, like an Apple 1200 Personal Modem, transmits four times as fast, at 1200 bits per second.

All things being equal (which they won't be, because higher-speed modems cost more), if you have a choice, you'll want a 1200-baud modem for your Apple or IBM. Not only will you save time, but if you're calling long distance to telecommunicate files, you'll save a lot of money, too.

Modems at both ends of the connection must be running at the same speed. If one computer is using a modem set for 300 baud and the other modem is at 1200 baud, communication can't happen. *Newsroom* makes allowances for this by letting you set the baud rate. Make sure, though, that you know how fast the modem at the other end of the phone line will run before you place your call.

Modems Supported by *Newsroom*

Apple[1]
Apple Modem 300
Apple Modem 1200
AT & T 2224
Bizcomp 1012
Bizcomp 1022
Companion 212A
Datec PAL 212
Executive 212
General Datacom
Hayes Micromodem II
Hayes Micromodem IIe
Hayes Smartmodem 300
Hayes Smartmodem 1200
Hayes Smartmodem 2400

Commodore 64/128
Commodore 1670
Commodore 1660
Commodore 1600

IBM[2]
AT&T 2224
Bizcomp 1012
Bizcomp 1022
Companion 212A
Datec PAL 212
Executive 212
General Datacom
Hayes Smartmodem 300
Hayes Smartmodem 1200
Hayes Smartmodem 2400
Infor-Mate 1200
InforPHONE IPX-1200
Mark X
Mark XII

Apple[1]

Infor-Mate 1200
InforPHONE IPX-1200
Mark X
Mark XII
Maxwell 300V
Maxwell 1200V
Multimodem HC3
Multimodem HC
Multimodem 1200
Multimodem 224
Multimodem IIe
Popcom X100
Pro-Modem 1200
Quadmodem
Qubie
Smart-Cat Plus
Tel-A-Modem
Ven-Tel 1200 Plus
Volksmodem
Wolfcom WD 212X
Hayes Smartmodem compatible
Hayes Micromodem compatible

Commodore 64/128

IBM[2]

Maxwell 300V
Maxwell 1200V
Multimodem HC3
Multimodem HC
Pro-Modem 1200
Quadmodem
Qubie
Radio Shack DC-2212
Smart-Cat Plus
Tel-A-Modem
Ven-Tel 1200 Plus
Volksmodem
Wolfcom WD 212X
Hayes Smartmodem compatible

[1]If you're using the Apple II+, IIe, or IIGS, you'll also need a serial card installed. The cards listed in *Newsroom* are listed below (though other cards will work, especially those that perfectly duplicate the functions of the Super Serial Card—cards like Apricorn's Super Serial Imager, for instance):

Apple Communication Card
Apple Super Serial Card
ALS Dispatcher
AST Multi I/O
California Computer Systems 7710
California Computer Systems 7711
Prometheus VersaCard
SSM AIO serial
SSM ASIO

[2]*Newsroom Pro,* the professional version of *Newsroom* for the IBM, supports the same modems.

You have a modem, *Newsroom,* and files to transfer. What comes next is a lesson in using the Wire Service.

Calling Across America

The Wire Service is one of the three *Newsroom* work areas that don't use icons or a work space on the screen. Boxed choices fill the screen instead, letting you quickly select the feature you want. The procedure is straightforward and brief instructions help you make the choices. As you send or receive files, a display keeps you informed about the progress of the transmission. Everything is kept as simple as possible.

Load *Newsroom*, select the Wire Service work area, and you'll see a screen that looks like Figure 5-4.

Figure 5-4. The First Wire Service Screen

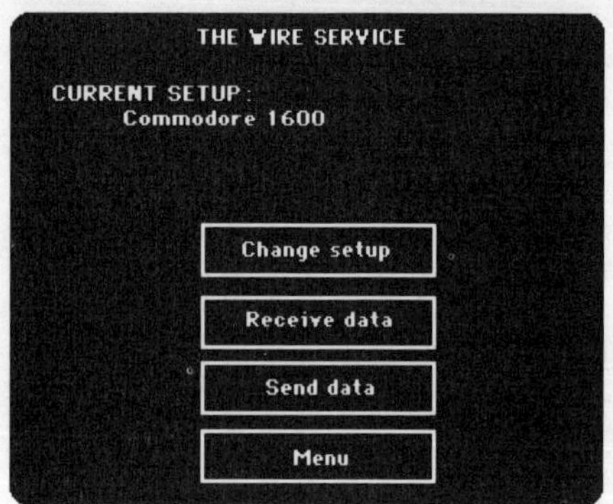

Before going on, make sure the modem, phone line, and your computer are all connected properly. Although your modem's manual will have complete instructions on how to connect it with both your computer and a phone line, here's a quick check list you can run through before any Wire Service session.

If you have an Apple or IBM computer.

- If you have an internal modem (one inside the computer case), check that the card is firmly set in the correct slot. Note the slot number if you have an Apple computer.
- If you have an external modem (one outside the computer case), plug in its power cord and if necessary, turn on the modem.
- Remove the phone cable which runs into the telephone and insert it in the modem's modular phone jack.
- If you have an external modem, take the modem cable and connect the modem with the correct serial port.

If you have a Commodore 64 or 128 computer.

- With the computer turned off, gently push the modem's connector end into the User Port (the one on the far right as you look at the back of the computer).
- Place the phone beside the computer.

You're ready to telecommunicate. Let's watch a typical Wire Service session, where Margaret is sending a panel to Peter. Margaret has an Apple IIe and an Apple Modem 1200; Peter owns a Commodore 64 and a Commodore 1600 modem.

How the Wire Service Works

Margaret and Peter must both prepare their computers and modems for telecommunications, make several selections, and then begin the transmission. They will be choosing different options because one is sending and the other is receiving, and because they're using different computers. You may see slightly different menu lists and make different choices than what's outlined here.

Make the first setup call. Margaret calls Peter and tells him she wants to send him a *Newsroom* panel file. Peter reminds her that the transmission must be at 300 baud, even though she has a 1200-baud modem, since his modem is the slower of the two. Margaret says that she'll call back in five minutes to see if Peter is ready. Total time on the phone, two minutes.

Margaret gets ready. First, she makes sure the correct data disk—the one which contains the panel STORY—is in the right-hand disk drive. Next, she pops the top of the computer case and checks that the Super Serial card in slot 1 is set to use the modem. The white triangle on the small block at the back end of the card is pointing up, toward *MODEM*, so it's ready.

Replacing the computer case, Margaret plugs one end of the modem cable into the modem and the other into the Super Serial card's port. She plugs the modem's power cord into an outlet and turns on the modem. For the moment, she leaves the telephone line plugged into the phone.

Now she turns on the computer, loads *Newsroom*, and selects the Wire Service work area.

- Margaret selects *Change setup* from the first Wire Service screen (see Figure 5-4). She chooses *Apple Modem 1200, Touch, Apple Super Serial Card,* and *Slot 1* in the four selection menus presented.
- She checks that her selections are displayed correctly beneath *CURRENT SETUP:* on the screen now on her monitor.
- Next, Margaret selects *Send data.* The four types of files she can send (along with the always-offered *Cancel* option) are listed. Since she's sending a panel, she presses the down-arrow key twice and then hits the Open Apple key.
- The disk in the second drive is automatically read, and a list of only its panel files is displayed. Margaret moves the highlight bar until it's atop STORY and then presses the Open Apple key.
- *What will the baud rate of the transmission be?* is the message at the top of the screen now on the monitor. Since her Apple IIe will telecommunicate with a Commodore 64, which can only transfer at 300 baud, she presses the Open Apple key while the box around *300* is blinking.
- The next screen is the last before dialing takes place. It asks for the phone number to dial. Margaret types in *15552344343* (not a real number, but you get the idea) but doesn't press Return.

When calling long distance, don't forget to begin the sequence with a *1*. You can only type numbers and commas when entering the phone number. A comma is interpreted as a five-second pause between numbers, something often necessary if you're calling from a phone which makes you dial a single number for an outside line. Many offices and some schools have this kind of system. The most common digit used for reaching an outside line is 9; dialing a local number from such a phone could look like *9,2345678* in the Wire Service.

Peter gets ready. He makes sure there's an empty, formatted data disk handy. Making sure the computer is turned off, he inserts the connector end of the modem into the User Port at the back right (as viewed from the back) of the 64. He sets the switch on the side of the modem to *A* for *Answer*. Peter brings the phone close to the computer and modem, but leaves the line plugged into the phone. He turns on the computer, disk drive, and monitor, loads *Newsroom*, and chooses the Wire Service work area.

- Peter chooses *Change setup* from the first Wire Service screen (see Figure 5-4). He selects *Commodore 1600* in the one selection menu shown. (If Peter were using a Commodore 1660 or 1670 modem, or a Hayes-compatible modem, the Wire Service would ask him to specify *Touch* or *Pulse*.)
- He checks that the selection is displayed correctly beneath *CURRENT SETUP:* on the screen now on his monitor.
- Peter selects *Receive data* from the list.
- He verifies that the transmission will take place at 300 baud by choosing *OK*.
- The next screen has a long message which asks if he wants to replace any existing file with a transferred file if the two have the same name. Since the data disk is empty, he chooses *Replace existing files*. If the data disk had held files he wanted to keep, he would have picked either *Replace some . . .* or *Do not replace. . . .*
- Peter inserts the data disk in the drive and selects *OK*.
- The screen now on the monitor (begins with *Switch modem to answer mode*) is the last before transmission takes place.

Make the second setup call. Everything is ready and the five minutes are up. Margaret calls Peter again, tells him that she's ready, and hears from him that he is, too. She'll start sending in one minute, she tells him, and hangs up. Total time on the line, less than a minute.

Sending and receiving. Margaret pulls the phone line from the phone and plugs it into the modem jack. She presses Return and after a short pause, the modem begins dialing.

At the other end, Peter's phone rings. He unplugs the cord from the handset and plugs it into the modem.

Margaret hears the phone ring; then there's a pause followed by a high whine. Connection has been made.

Peter presses the Commodore key to choose *OK*.

Margaret's screen looks a lot like Figure 5-5.

Figure 5-5. Transmission in Progress

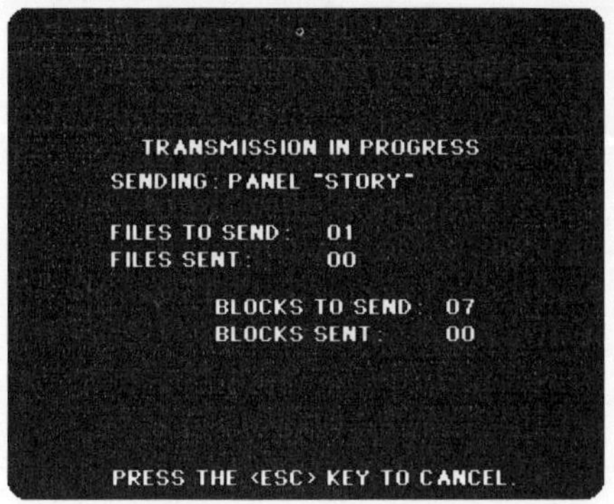

And Peter's screen soon looks much the same, though instead of indicating the progress of sending a file, it shows that the computer's receiving a file.

At the end of the transmission, both computer screens display the message *The transmission has been completed.* Neat and simple.

Since STORY was the only file to transmit, both Margaret and Peter press Return to acknowledge the message. Margaret switches off her modem, and Peter pulls the phone line from his modem and plugs it back into the phone's receiver. The connection is broken.

Peter selects *Menu* from the screen now on his monitor, enters the Copy Desk work area once *Newsroom* returns to the main menu, and loads the panel STORY. Everything looks fine.

Transmission successful.

When Things Go Wrong

Telecommunications can be frustrating. Not because it's difficult in itself, but that when things go wrong, it's often hard to pin down just what's making things go wrong.

The problem is that there are so many parts to sending or receiving files. First of all, you have to assume the person at the other end knows what he or she is doing. That may be the furthest thing from the truth. Second, all the equipment—the computer, modem, and phone line—must be in working order. And third, you have to use the Wire Service correctly.

A failure in any one of those things, or in any number of others, can make it impossible to send or receive. Finding out which link in the chain is broken is sometimes a matter of trial and error. However, there are some general suggestions which may help when you feel like the Wire Service was designed to make you go crazy.

When nothing happens. This is the worst—you think you're ready to send or receive a file, and nothing, absolutely nothing, happens. The computer just sits there, with the *Transmission in Progress* or *Waiting for call . . .* message on the screen.

≡ First of all, *wait*. Not long, but wait for 30–60 seconds, just to make sure that things really aren't working.
≡ Check that everything—modem, card (if there is one), cables, and power cord—are turned on, plugged in, or firmly connected. If you can assume the person at the other end is doing the same, try to send or receive again. If you can't assume that, call and tell him or her to check all the connections. Then try again.
≡ Check the *CURRENT SETUP:* selections. Are they right? If you have an Apple II+, IIe, or IIGS, check that the communications card is in the same slot as is listed on your screen. Try again.
≡ If you have an Apple IIGS, check that the Control Panel agrees with your current setup. Press Option, Control, and the Reset keys at the same time, press 1 to enter the Control Panel, and use the arrow keys to highlight *Slots* on the next screen. Set the appropriate slot so that it reads *Your Card* by highlighting the slot number and pressing the Return key.
≡ If you have a Commodore 64 or 128 and you're using a Commodore 1600 modem, check that it's set on Originate if you're sending, or on Answer if you're receiving. Try again.

When the connection is broken. This is the second-most-frustrating disaster. Right in the middle of sending a photo file, you hear the modem go "click" and you know the connection is broken.

≡ Someone may have accidentally pulled the phone line loose from the modem or pulled the modem cable out of the serial port or dropped something on the computer. You get the idea. Put things back together and try again.
≡ Someone may have picked up an extension on your line or on the line at the other end. This is often enough to either scramble the transmission (especially if whoever picked up the extension talked into the phone) or break the connection altogether. Tell everyone who might pick up an extension that you're going to be sending or receiving files and not to touch the phone until you say it's okay. Try again.
≡ Either end of the connection may have a *call-waiting* service, and an incoming call broke the connection. Call waiting wrecks havoc on telecommunications, for a modem will usually interpret the second call or the signal which indicates you have a second call waiting, as a break in the line and will shut

things off. If you're going to transfer files, remove the call-waiting feature or install a second line.

≡ You're unlucky and you have a bad connection. This happens. One time you can dial a number and everything's fine; the next time, you can't keep the connection open. Calls are routed through different telephone circuits different times. Hang up and try again.

The one thing all these suggestions have in common is *try again.* Don't be discouraged if you can't get the Wire Service to successfully send or receive a file the first time you use it. Keep at it.

If these suggestions don't help, or if your problem seems to be something else, you can call Springboard's Technical Support number (612-944-3912). The more details you can provide, the likelier they can help.

Save Money, Save Time

Time is money. That's never easier to understand than when you're talking long distance (or even locally when you're charged for the length of the call) on the phone. Just imagine a meter ringing up the charge as the time ticks by.

If you send or receive files with the Wire Service, you probably do so long distance. Telecommunications, just like phone conversation, costs money. The less time you're *online* with the phone line open, the less money you'll have to pay. It only makes sense to be as efficient as possible with the time spent transferring files in the Wire Service.

Some of these suggestions are general to all telecommunications, so if you're a modem whiz, these may be old news. Other tips, however, are specific to *Newsroom* and the Wire Service. No matter what your experience, following these guidelines will save you time and then save you money.

How long will this take? This may not save you money so much as tell you how much things are going to cost. At least you won't have shocking surprises when the phone bill comes.

Calculating the time it will take to send a file or files is pretty simple. First, you need to find out the length of the files you're going to send. Do this by placing your data disk in the drive before loading and running *Newsroom.* For each computer, type in the command(s) listed and press Return or Enter.

Computer	Command
Apple	CATALOG[1]
Commodore	LOAD "$",8 LIST
IBM	DIR

[1]DOS 3.3 must be installed. There's no way to break out of *Newsroom* and enter DOS directly. Replace the *Newsroom* disk with one that has DOS 3.3 on it (many commercial programs are on DOS 3.3–formatted disks). Press the Open Apple, Control, and Reset keys at the same time. Break out of the program by pressing Control and Reset together. Now you're in DOS 3.3.

Here's what you'll see on the screen.

Apple

A	**003**	PN.GAME1
A	**004**	PN.GAME2
A	**007**	PH.PLAYER
A	**010**	PH.TROPHY

Commodore

3	"PN.GAME1"	PRG
4	"PN.GAME2"	PRG
7	"PH.PLAYER"	PRG
10	"PH.TROPHY"	PRG

IBM

GAME1	PN	**713**	1-14-88	08:05a
GAME2	PN	**1023**	1-14-88	08:15a
PLAYER	PH	**1652**	1-14-88	08:35a
TROPHY	PH	**2446**	1-14-88	09:00a

The numbers in boldface indicate how large each file is; the Apple and Commodore files are measured in *blocks*, while IBM file lengths are shown in bytes. The unit of measurement doesn't matter—all you need to do is some quick math using one of the formulas below.

Computer	**Formula**	**Results**
Apple	(Number of blocks * 256) / 1800	# minutes at 300 baud
Apple	(Number of blocks * 256) / 7200	# minutes at 1200 baud
Commodore	(Number of blocks * 256) / 1800	# minutes at 300 baud
Commodore	(Number of blocks * 256) / 7200	# minutes at 1200 baud
IBM	Number of bytes / 1800	# minutes at 300 baud
IBM	Number of bytes / 7200	# minutes at 1200 baud

Here's an example: If you have an Apple photo of 12 blocks, and you're sending at 300 baud, the formula works out as (12 * 256 = 3072) / 1800 = 1.7 minutes. In other words, it should take about a minute and three-quarters to send this photo file at 300 baud. At 1200 baud, four times faster, the formula works out as (12 * 256 = 3072) / 7200 = 0.42 minutes.

Always send pages. When you have a lot of files to send, you'll take almost as much time getting ready to send as it actually takes to transmit the files. That's because you must repeat every step each time you send or receive a file. If you're sending, that means you'll have to hang up after each successful transmission, select another file, then redial, and make a connection. *You have to do that each time.*

That can be pretty tiresome—and expensive. Most long-distance services charge more for the first minute than they do for any succeeding minutes. Three minutes in one chunk, then, costs less than three one-minute slices.

To avoid much of this waste of time and money, take advantage of a Wire Service quirk. You may have already noticed that if you send a panel file which included both text and a photo, the Wire Service automatically sent not only the panel file, but also the photo file which the panel needs in order to display and print correctly. The two files are invisibly tied together in *Newsroom*. The Wire Service sent first the panel and then the photo.

Do the same thing, but on a larger scale, by placing all your panel and banner files in pages.

Before you send any files with the Wire Service, go to the Layout work area and compose one or more pages with those files. You don't need to worry about how the panels are laid out—it's not important, since you're only grouping the files together to make for faster transmission.

In Layout, pick the appropriate page type (bannered or bannerless) and size (letter or legal). If you have nine panels, for instance, lay out a bannerless, legal-sized page.

Now, when you send a file, select *Page* when you're asked to choose which kind of file you're transmitting. All the files which were laid out in that page are transmitted, one after another. Photo files linked to panels are still automatically transferred.

The person receiving the files doesn't have to use the page-layout file which was sent—remember that a page file just holds the names of the panels (and possible banner), not the panels themselves. The transmitted panels can be loaded into a different page layout or the photos can be used with entirely new panels.

Create a directory. When you're sending a number of files, it might make it easier on the recipient if you told him or her what files were for which story and how those files are to be organized.

You could do this verbally on the phone, but it would be better if you

Figure 5-6. Sending Directory

Directory of Files

Filename	Page	Description
BALLGAME	1	Recent baseball game with Cubs.
SUSAN	1	Susan Bradford's re-election as mayor
BANNER	1	New banner
NOVA1	1	Story about new supernova; part 1
NOVA2	1	Part 2 (keep in same column)
NOVA3	1	Part 3
NOVA4	1	Part 4 (includes great graphic in lower right of panel)

could send some sort of written record. One way to do this is to create a directory to the files you're sending. List their filenames and whatever explanatory notes are necessary in a panel and place it in the layout before you send the page. A typical directory panel might look like Figure 5-6.

It doesn't matter where in the page layout this directory panel appears; simply use a name like DIRECTRY and the recipient will know to look at it for instructions on filenames and the stories they represent.

Call late or on weekends. When you're calling long distance with the Wire Service, remember that most long-distance telephone services charge less when dialing after 5 p.m. weekdays (it's even cheaper after 11 p.m.) or on weekends and holidays. Save yourself some money by transmitting files during these times.

Electronic Publishing

You can enter the latest age of publishing by skipping the printing process and distributing an electronic-only version of your newspaper.

Such *electronic publishing*—where no paper is involved—has been talked about for years, though it has not really taken hold. It's still cheaper, for instance, to print up 10,000 copies of a newspaper than to send all that information to 10,000 computers. And that's assuming all the readers have a computer.

But if you have a limited circulation for your newspaper or newsletter, want to reach people in distant places, and want to reach them quickly, you may want to give electronic publishing a try.

Here's how it could work.

You write, edit, and lay out your newspaper normally. Make sure that all the pages—and all the panel, banner, and photo files for those pages—are on one disk to keep disk swapping to a minimum and to speed up the transfer process.

Instead of going to the Press work area to print the paper, select the Wire Service. You can send your paper only to those readers who have a copy of *Newsroom*. Remember, however, that it doesn't matter if they're using a different version of *Newsroom*.

Send the entire issue to your readers. When the transmission is completed, each reader will print out the paper on his or her own printer. Instead of waiting days for the news to arrive in the mail, your readers can have your paper within minutes of the moment you finish it. Your paper can be in readers' hands even faster than if you'd used an overnight delivery service.

Electronic publishing is most effective when you have clumps of readers in different locations. Let's say you're publishing a business newsletter, and your company has offices in three other cities. Rather than printing and making copies of the newsletter in one location and then sending those copies through the mail to the other offices, you can distribute your publication electronically.

Send the newsletter to each office—that's a total of three different transmissions—with the Wire Service. Each office then prints the newsletter, makes copies, and distributes the newsletter to the people who work there. The news still reaches every employee in the company, but it does so much faster than if you had mailed the newletter and probably for about the same price as the postage.

Figure 5-7. Electronic Publishing

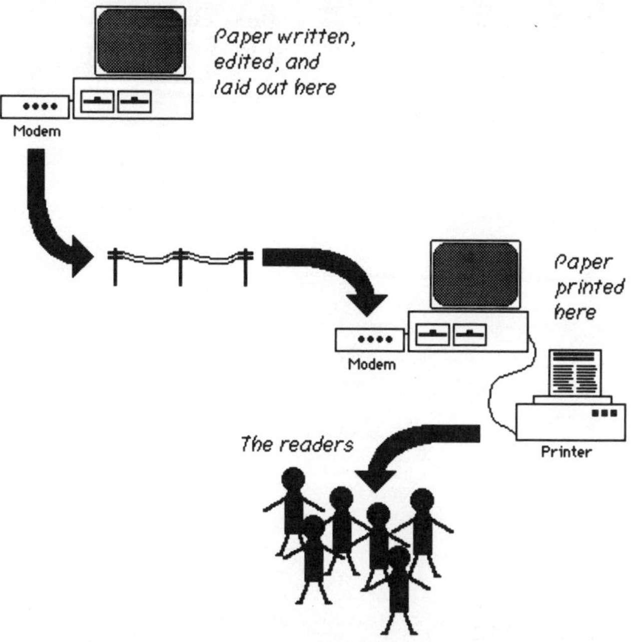

Some of the ways you could use electronic publishing might include:

- Sending a family newspaper to distant relatives.
- Sharing a school newspaper with schools in other cities (or even countries).
- Keeping in touch with friends who've moved away.
- Exchanging computer user-group newsletters with other user groups.
- Writing personalized newspaperlike bulletins to the family back home.
- Providing the handicapped or shut-in with church news.
- Informing every employee in a far-flung company of new policies or practices.

Think about who you want to read your newspaper or newsletter. You'll probably come up with a few people who could best receive your newspaper electronically.

Dial Tones

No other work area in *Newsroom* is more overlooked than the Wire Service. And no other work area has more potential for changing the way your newspaper or newsletter is written and read.

More and more computer users have a modem and are accustomed to telecommunicating. Many of those people have *Newsroom*. That means the future of things like electronic publishing with *Newsroom* can only get brighter.

The Wire Service doesn't have to be intimidating or unused. Give it a try; you'll be amazed at the opportunities it can offer. The next chapter puts you at a mechanical artist's drafting table, with electronic glue, wax, and paper at your fingertips. Layout—the process of putting together a page—is your next stop in this advanced tour of *Newsroom*.

CHAPTER 6
Looks Count

The Layout

The Layout work area is the first step in the *Newsroom* production process. The areas you've already used—the Copy Desk, Banner, Photo Lab, and Wire Service—all helped you create or gather together the parts of your newspaper. But the panels and banners now on your disk are just a collection of files, not a publication. You need the Layout work area to pull those panels and banners together.

It's in Layout that you build your newspaper pages. Stories are organized and put on the page. Full-panel graphics, saved in panel form in the Copy Desk, are set in the right position. Banners are used or not used as you build front or inside pages.

Layout is far more important than its simple steps indicate. It may take you only a few minutes to lay out a page once the files are on your data disk. But the process of deciding what goes where shouldn't start when you enter the Layout work area. It should begin long before, when you're making panels with words and graphics.

Unfortunately, it's hard to imagine what a page will look like in final form. *Newsroom* doesn't let you preview a page. You can do a lot of work, only to discover that the page looks terrible when it comes out of the printer. That's not very efficient, and probably pretty frustrating.

This chapter doesn't show you how to select files in the Layout work area to build a page—that's ridiculously easy. Instead, it shows how you can use good publication design techniques in your own newspaper or newsletter.

The end result should be a newspaper that's easier to read and one that's read by more people. The design of your publication isn't an end in itself—it's just the tool you use to communicate your message, your news. Good design is unnoticed; only bad design gets attention.

Your Part in *Newsroom* Design

Newsroom is a simple-to-use program. It's meant to be used by people with little or no journalistic experience. To use *Newsroom,* you certainly shouldn't have to be a graphic designer, someone whose job it is to create great layouts.

Actually, Layout is pretty easy. All you have to do is choose a page format, pick the files you want on that page, and save the layout. This simple process may tempt you into not thinking about how your pages look.

Don't let that happen. There's plenty you can do to make your paper better looking and clearer in communicating the news. Some of the methods you can use early in the panel-creating process; other design techniques can wait until you hit Layout. Almost everything depends, however, on how well you can imagine what the final page will look like when it's printed.

Use Your Imagination

This is probably the toughest part of design and using the Layout work area. Because there's no way to see what a page will look like until it's printed, you either have to use trial and error in design or be able to create a mental picture of the page as you work.

If you're a *Newsroom* pro, you can probably imagine what a page will look like rather easily. If you're a *Newsroom* novice, though, it's not nearly so simple. Experience with *Newsroom* is the best way to learn how to create such mental images.

Even if you're a master at design and the Layout work area, it may still be difficult to keep everything straight. One way to help yourself plan pages, and thus design better layouts, is to create a sketch (called a *dummy* in newspaper terminology) of each page. Figure 6-1 shows two dummies of a single page.

Figure 6-1. Layout Dummies

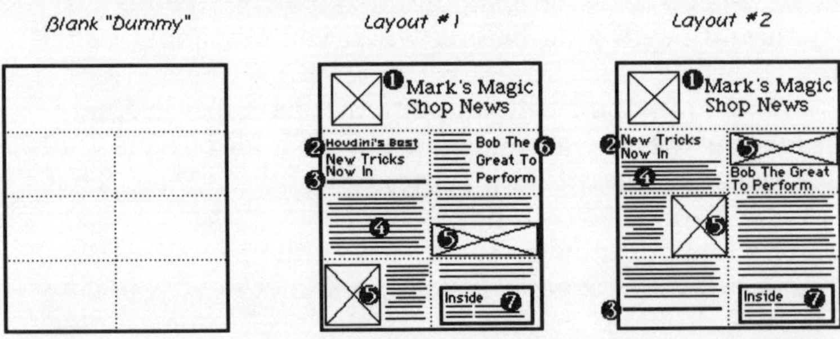

1. The banner includes a graphic (the box with the X through it, the usual way to represent a picture, figure, or photo in a dummy) and the name of the paper.
2. In layout 1, the headline for the story *New Tricks Now In* occupies an entire panel. (A smaller headline, called a *kicker,* is placed above the main headline.) In layout 2, however, the body copy begins immediately after the headline.
3. The heavy black line shows a thick rule. Layout 1 uses the rule to separate the headline from the article, while layout 2 uses it at the bottom of the first column to indicate the end of the article (not a bad idea, since the copy doesn't use up the entire panel).
4. The text of one of the stories occupies part of the left column in each layout.

5. The two photos remain the same size from one layout to the other. Placement is different, though. Notice that the first photo in layout 1 is simply shifted to the other side of the panel to create a new look in layout 2.
6. Layout 1 used the Photo Lab to create the headline for the story *Bob The Great To Perform*. This way, the body copy can be placed to the left of the headline photo. (As you saw in Chapter 2, placing large- and small-sized typefaces in the same line only leads to bad-looking panels.)
7. Both layouts put the box which lists the stories inside the newspaper in the same place on the page.

In Figure 6-1, a blank dummy is followed by two possible layouts of the front page of a newspaper called *Mark's Magic Shop News*. Each layout includes two stories, two photos, and one graphic (a box at the bottom right). But each layout positions those elements quite differently.

To create your blank dummy, you can do one of two things, depending on the size dummy you want to work with.

- If you want a small dummy, sketch an outline of a sheet of paper. (Before they were reduced to place in this book, the dummies in Figure 6-1 were 2 × 2½ inches, approximately the right dimensions.) Divide the small page in two vertical columns, and if you're using layout for paper that's 8½ × 11 inches, divide the page horizontally into four equal areas.
- You can make a full-sized dummy with *Newsroom*. Create a banner which has a thin-lined box as large as the work space. With the Photo Lab, draw a box as large as the work space, save it as a photo, and then place it in a panel. Go to Layout; place the banner once and the panel six (or eight) times. Print it out. You should have something that looks like Figure 6-2.

Figure 6-2. Full-Sized Dummy

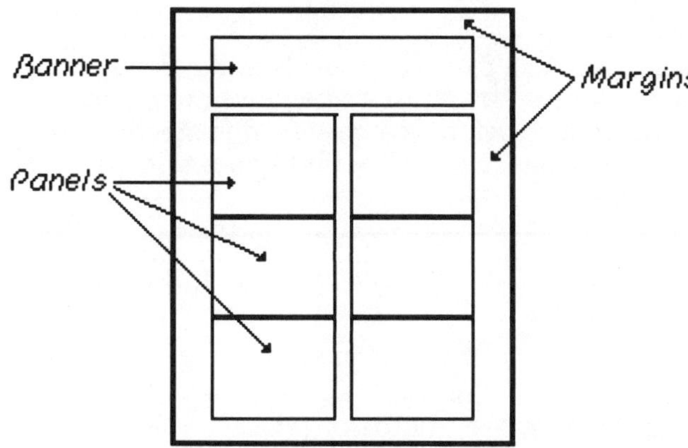

You can quickly sketch in the major headlines, show the approximate size of any graphics, and fill in the panel areas with lines to represent text (see Chapter 2 for information on how to estimate story length before typing in the Copy Desk).

The best time to make your layout plans is *before* you create panels for your stories and photos. Write the headlines and copy for your stories, draw any custom graphics, and choose the clip art you'll use. List each element with its approximate length (in panels). For instance, a list for layout 2 in Figure 6-1 might look like this.

Piece	**Length**
Banner	Banner length
Headline: "New Tricks"	½ panel
Text: "New Tricks"	1½ panels
Photo: "New Tricks"	½ panel
Headline: "Bob"	½ panel
Text: "Bob"	1½ panels
Photo: "Bob"	½ panel
Inside box	½ panel

By adding everything up, you can tell that only 5½ of the possible 6 panels will be filled. Layout 2 simply left white space at the bottom of the left column, but layout 1 used that extra room in a panel-sized headline for a story. If you hadn't listed the page elements this way, you wouldn't have noticed there was room to do that until you went to the trouble of going to both Layout and Press.

Of course, if you want, you can sketch a dummy when the panels and banner are completed and on disk. Measurements are much more exact, obviously, but you won't be able to make as many dramatic changes as easily. It will be more of a simple shifting of panels than anything else.

If most of your stories are only one panel long—as is common in many *Newsroom*-produced papers—it will be easier to wait until you have the panels done and on disk before you create a dummy. Since each story is a self-contained panel, all you'll want to do is put the stories in a pleasing arrangement.

With page dummies in hand, you're ready to go to Layout and start putting together your paper. Or are you?

By now, you should have a good idea of how to picture a page, either in your mind or in a dummy. But you may not have the foggiest idea of what will look good in that layout. Is it better to use more photos or fewer? What's the best way to make the text easier to read? Which special elements can work for your newspaper?

The rest of this chapter introduces you to several principles of good publication design and offers a large number of techniques, tips, and tricks to make your newspaper *look* good and *read* well. That, after all, is the whole point of good design and layout.

Be Consistent

Readers come to expect certain things from your newspaper. Whether they realize it or not, they get used to the look of your publication. Almost without knowing it, they recognize a headline by its placement and typeface. When you regularly use space to show the end of one story, they look for that. Or they subconsciously notice that text set in sans serif is always used for photo captions, never body copy.

All these things, and more, make up your newspaper's design consistency. A consistent design means readers can get the news more easily and more quickly. It also usually makes them more comfortable with the newspaper.

The other side of that, however, is that readers can become quickly confused when the consistency is broken. If they expect to see headlines in sans serif, for instance, and suddenly come across one that's set in serif, they'll pause. Perhaps for just a moment, but they'll wonder what the change means. Does it mean a more important story? An advertisement? Or just a mistake (most readers *love* to find mistakes in a publication, yours included)?

Newsroom's Consistency

Newsroom makes several design decisions for you. You may think that's a restriction, but it's one of the best things about the program. In many instances, *Newsroom* forces you to be consistent.

The design elements which *Newsroom* takes care of for you include

- Page size—just two are available: 8½ × 11 and 8½ × 14.
- Page format—each page size has two, and they differ only in that one has a banner and the other doesn't.
- Margins—preset at approximately 1¼-inches on each side.
- Banners—can be placed only at the top of a page.
- Columns—each page uses two columns of equal width.
- Photo size—can't be larger than 1/8 or 1/10 page, and can't cross columns.
- Gutter—the narrow space between columns can't be crossed by either text or graphics.

Figure 6-3. Graphic Restrictions

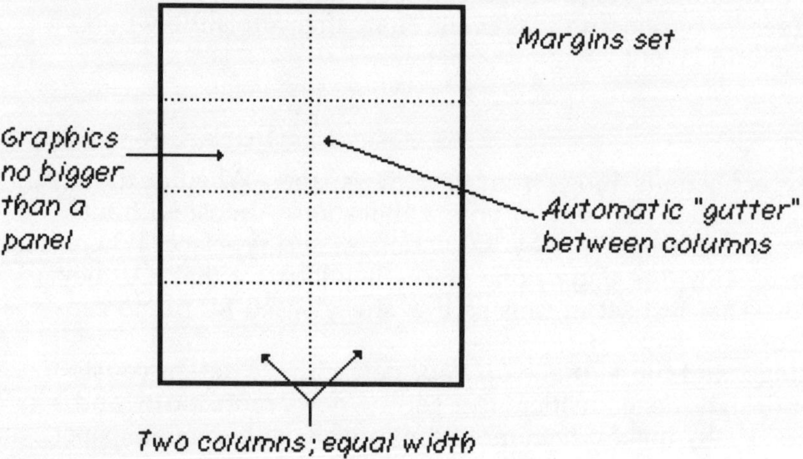

Your Consistency

Don't worry—*Newsroom* doesn't take every design decision out of your hands. There are plenty for you to make.

Once you make a design decision, however—like which typeface to use for body copy—stick to it. You may think that because *Newsroom* has five typefaces, you must use them all on each page. All that does is confuse your readers and make them work harder to get the news.

If your paper or newsletter has more than one page, be consistent not only within a page, but also within the publication as a whole. Of the two, however, it's more important that pages be consistent.

Most rules are made to be broken, and design rules are no exception. If you want your paper's sports page to look different from your front page, you can break with tradition. Have a good reason for any design that's different from your normal one, though.

Here are the things you've got control over.

Headlines. Use the same typeface and size for all headlines. Just as importantly, position your headlines in the same place in each panel. If you usually set your headlines *flush left* (they start at the left edge of the panel), always set them that way. If you center them, always center them. If they sometimes appear with a rule separating them from the body copy, always do that.

Body copy. Use the same typeface and size for all your newspaper's body copy. A good idea in *Newsroom* is to use one typeface (serif or sans serif) for the headlines and to use the remaining face for the body copy. Save the other small typeface for special purposes, where you want your readers to notice the difference.

Figure 6-4. Consistent Headlines

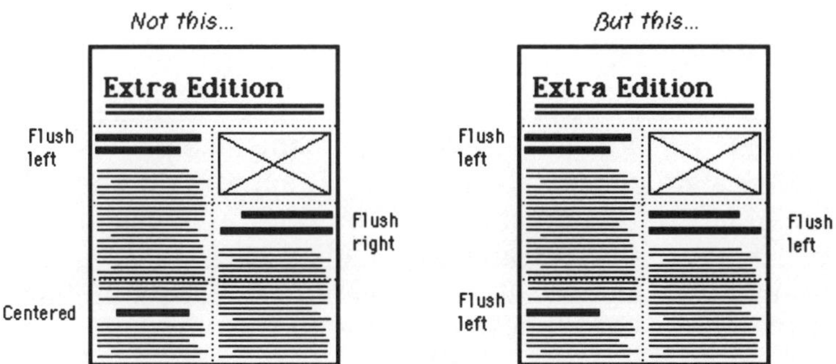

Captions. Set *captions,* the words which accompany a photo or graphic, in the same typeface throughout your newspaper or newsletter. Make them stand out from the rest of the small-size type by using a different face from the normal body copy. As Figure 6-5 shows, you can place captions below the photo or to either side. They can be centered or flush left. Position captions consistently in your publication.

Figure 6-5. Caption Positions

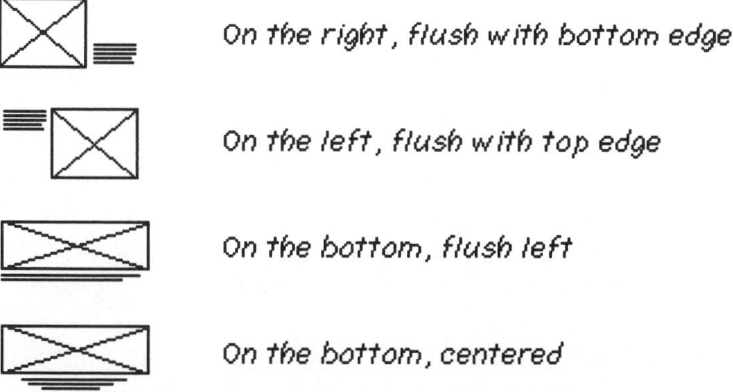

Rules, boxes, and frames. Rules, boxes, and frames should be the same thickness throughout your newspaper. If you use the thinnest pen to draw a rule which separates one story from another, for example, use that line thickness every time for that purpose. If it's not possible to use the same thickness, don't use more than two pen widths on any one page. None of this applies to banners.

Be consistent—but don't lock yourself rigidly into a pattern that's never broken. These design guidelines are just that. When you really want to attract the reader's eye, for instance, there's no better way than to use a completely different design. Break from your normal design only rarely, however. The effect will be lost if it's used all the time.

Be Off-Balance

Many publications try to create *balanced* pages, where elements like photos, headlines, stories, and graphics are positioned so that what appears on one half of the page balances with what's on the other half. If you drew a vertical line through a balanced page, you'd see that the amount of space taken up by photos, the size and thickness of headlines, and the mass of body copy on one side was almost equal to the photos, headlines, and copy on the other.

Figure 6-6. Balanced Page

You can balance a page's top and bottom halves the same way.

Balanced pages don't have to be perfect. If a large headline is in the upper left corner, for example, a headline of approximately the same *weight* (size and thickness of the type) could be anywhere on the right half, not just in the lower right corner. This is called *informal balance.*

Newsroom forces you to create pages which are already somewhat balanced. Pages have the same number of panels in each column, graphics can't be larger than a panel, and headlines can't stretch across columns.

Tilt to One Side

Beyond what's forced on your layout by the program, however, you should try to create *unbalanced* pages. Here's why.

When a page is balanced—and the more perfectly it's balanced, the more this happens—a reader is confused. What's important on this page? If there are four headlines on the pages, two in each column, and every headline has about the same weight, how are your readers to tell that one story is far more important than another? If two of those stories use photos, but those photos are of equal size, how do your readers tell which story is more newsworthy and interesting?

Balanced pages are also usually boring to look at, especially when one balanced page follows another, and another, and another. When everything looks the same, nothing looks interesting.

By avoiding a strictly balanced page, you can create reader interest and avoid confusion. Unequal balance, either left/right or top/bottom, can help to focus a reader's attention at what *you* think is important. The reader's eyes automatically move toward the largest graphic, the blackest and thickest headline, and the most prominent design. Use this to your advantage by planning your pages right.

Most Important Story

One way to make use of an off-balance page is to direct your reader's attention to the story you think is the most important on that page.

Though layouts differ, most newspapers place the biggest story in the upper right of the front page. That may sound odd, since we read from left to right, but there's a good reason for it. The banner stretches across the paper, and our eyes follow—all the way to the right edge of the page. Even if readers don't actually "read" the banner, they still look at it.

Once the eyes reach the edge of the page, their natural movement is

Figure 6-7. Upper Right

Threader's Times

down the right-hand column. That's why you should put the most important story on your front page (which may be your only page) in the upper right.

You can make this imbalance even more dramatic by using photos only with the most important story. Consider placing the photo above the headline; if it's the only photo on the page, your readers will naturally look at it first. Put the headline for that story below the photo. Notice the short caption at the upper right corner of the photo in Figure 6-8.

Figure 6-8. One Photo

Once you've placed that first story, you can decide where to put the rest. With *Newsroom*, you may not have more than another story or two to put on the front page. No matter how many stories you're running, try to imagine how your readers look at the page. Once they read the top story, what will keep them on the page? Will their eyes simply skip off the page or is there something you can use to keep their attention long enough so that they read every story?

If you were laying out a page like the one shown in Figure 6-8, you might try boxing the short story near the bottom or running a rule above it.

Page 2 and on. On bannerless pages, it's best to place the most important story at the top left. That's where readers look first. After that, arrange your stories in the pattern most likely followed by a reader's eyes. That means you have to guide the reader from the end of the most important story to the beginning of the second-most-important story. You can do that by placing graphics and photos to lead the reader from one story to the next, or by simply starting the second story immediately after the first. Figure 6-9 shows how photos can help channel the reader's attention. The numbers indicate the relative importance of the stories.

Figure 6-9. Lead Your Readers

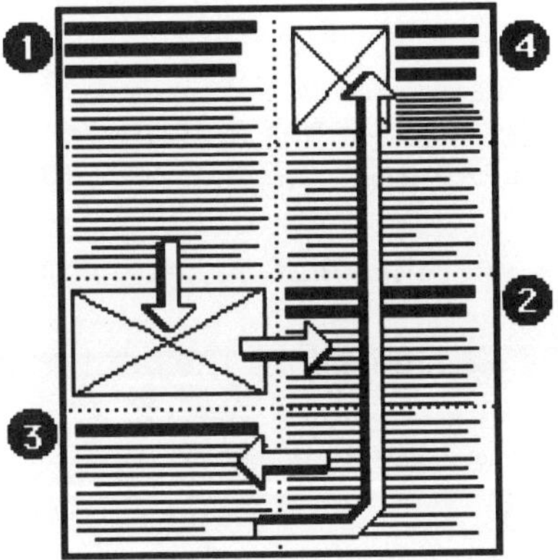

Try to create pages that are not truly balanced. Sometimes it's hard when you have a lot of stories and want to use a lot of graphics, or when stories and photos are close in size and importance.

Remember that your job in Layout is to make an appealing, easy-to-read and easy-to-follow newspaper. You'll get more comfortable in designing pages as you work with *Newsroom*, especially if you can get reader comments about how your design works.

Be Spacious

One of the most common beginner's mistakes in Layout is to design pages that are cluttered with headlines, photos, and text. It's easy to do—part of the problem is that you can only see one panel on the screen at a time. You can't have a perfect idea of how a page will look until it's printed.

And then there's the temptation of *Newsroom*—you want to *really* give your readers the news. So you pack every possible piece of clip art, every headline typeface, and as much text as possible in one page. But when you cram a page with graphics large and small, change typefaces with every story, and try to squeeze the maximum number of words into each panel, all you do is make the page harder to read.

Readers get confused. With so many things to look at, it's impossible to decide which is the most important or worth reading. And when stories are packed together, it's even hard to tell where one story ends and another begins.

White space, the design term used for blank parts of the page, helps funnel the reader's attention to the right story or photo. White space acts as a backdrop to whatever you're trying to make noticeable.

But white space is necessary for other reasons. It makes a page more attractive. It gives the reader's eyes a rest, if only for a moment, from the work of reading text. And it makes a page easier to read.

A number of white-space suggestions follow; use some or all to make your pages better looking and more readable.

White Space in Text

Newsroom's small-sized text is hard to read in large chunks. It has nothing to do with the way the letters are formed or how many you can put on a line. On the screen, in fact, a panel looks perfectly readable.

But print a page of text and it changes into something that makes reading hard work.

The lines of text are too close together. There's little *leading*, the white space normally found between each line of text. It's amazing how readers depend on leading to make printed words easier to read. Here's an example.

This is set with no leading. There is no extra space between the bottom of one line of text and the top of the next line. Notice how it's hard to read?

This is set with the normal leading for this book. Extra space has been inserted between each line. It's not much, just a fraction of an inch, but notice how much easier this is to read.

This is set with even more leading. The text is still easy to read, and the open space gives the text a light, airy feeling. However, this takes up more space and might give the impression that the lines are separate and not part of a unified paragraph.

Unfortunately, there's no way for you to specify the spacing, or leading, between lines of text in *Newsroom*. That's set.

You can, however, "open up" your text with a simple technique.

Figure 6-10. Text Closed and Text Open

The annual Art Fair was held in the media center during the week of January 18 through 22. All 85 entries were displayed in one of three galleries Mr. Willard set up in the South Wing of the center.
The Grand Prize winner in the Painting gallery was Marsh Tucker, a seventh grader. His painting, named "Worms," was done with watercolors.
Grand Prize winner in the Sculpture gallery was Reka Vande-Grost. An eighth grader, her "Man on Horse" was made from clay.
The Grand Prize winner in the Sketching gallery was a ninth grader, Tosh Anders. The pencil-on-paper sketch, named "Marilyn," was also voted Best of Show by the judges.
"We had a really good turnout,"

The annual Art Fair was held in the media center during the week of January 18 through 22. All 85 entries were displayed in one of three galleries Mr. Willard set up in the South Wing of the center.

The Grand Prize winner in the Painting gallery was Marsh Tucker, a seventh grader. His painting, named "Worms," was done with watercolors.

Grand Prize winner in the Sculpture gallery was Reka Vande-Grost. An eighth grader, her "Man on Horse" was made from clay.

The Grand Prize winner in the Sketching gallery was a ninth grader, Tosh Anders. The pencil-on-paper sketch, named "Marilyn," was

Instead of pressing Return or Enter only once to end a paragraph, press the key twice to insert a blank line between paragraphs. It's not the same as leading between individual lines, but at least long columns of text are broken up into separate paragraphs. Reading those long columns is easier.

With stories that are only a couple of short paragraphs long, it's not a good idea to insert such space. Use this technique only if the story runs at least one panel long.

White Space in Headlines

When you look at many *Newsroom* pages, you may have a hard time finding the headlines. That's because the story's body copy begins immediately after the headline.

White space around headlines sets them off and makes them far more noticeable. Take a look at the two examples in Figure 6-11.

Figure 6-11. Headline White Space

Packed Headlines *White Space Used*

Flying Squirrels

The layout on the left crams headlines and text together, making it harder to spot the headlines. The layout on the right, however, uses white space both above and below the headlines to make them stand out.

Whenever you use white space—between paragraphs, in headlines, or for other purposes—you can't put as much text on a page. You can either create a longer newspaper or write shorter news stories. Though you get to make the choice, shorter stories may be your best bet. If your audience is typical for *Newsroom*-produced papers, many of your readers won't want to read a story that runs more than two or three panels.

You can add white space around headlines in one of two ways. Try both as you experiment, but remember to keep your pages consistent. Find which technique works best for you and then stick with it through a page and throughout your paper.

Press Return. The simplest way to add white space is to use the Return or Enter key more than usual. To insert space above the headline, enter the Copy Desk work space and press the Return or Enter key as many times as you want before typing the headlines. For space below the head, do the same after you type in the headline but before you type in the body copy.

For a bit less white space, try this.

- Type in the headline using one of the large type sizes. Don't press Return or Enter.
- Go to the Crayon icon and select one of the small type sizes.
- Move the cursor until it turns into a hand. Now press Return or Enter once or twice. The cursor is small-sized, and so small-sized lines are inserted.

Full-panel headlines. Even more white space can be used around headlines if they're by themselves in a panel. Using an entire panel for a headline cuts down on the text you can run on a page, but the effect may be worth it.

If the story doesn't start at the top of a column, you may want to center the headline vertically, as Figure 6-12 shows. That may look strange, however, if the head is at the top of the page and the other column has text beside the space.

When you're using a full panel just for a headline, you can do some interesting things. One possibility is to use a *kicker*, a kind of subhead that introduces the main headline. Usually a kicker is shorter than the headline, often is underlined, and many times is not a complete sentence. Kickers are always placed above the headline. The headline in Figure 6-12 includes a kicker.

Figure 6-12. Full-Panel Headlines

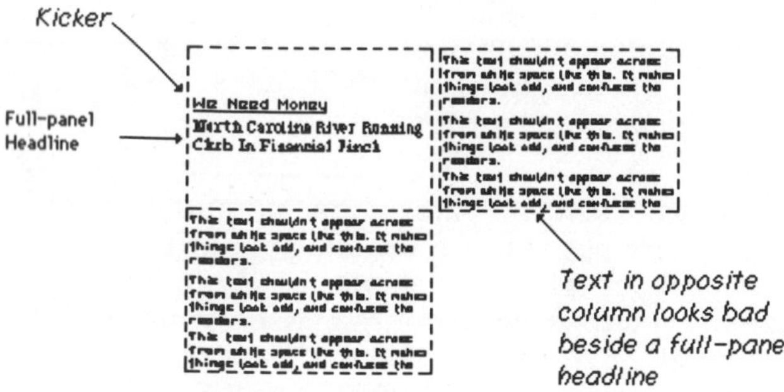

White Space in Pages

Cluttered, crowded pages are too often the normal layout for *Newsroom* newspapers. Opening up your pages so that the type has room to "breathe" isn't difficult, as you've already seen. In many cases it's as simple as using the Return key. Here are a few more tips and techniques you can try.

Every panel doesn't need a photo. It may be tempting, especially when you have hundreds of pieces of clip art to choose from, but it's not necessary to put a photo in every panel. Not only does that make the page incredibly confusing to most readers, but because of the way *Newsroom* wraps text around photos, it can result in some strange-looking layouts.

Use photos and graphics to highlight important stories or to help communicate the news—don't use photos just because they're easy to add to a panel. When you're creating a page's panels, make sure each photo is really helping tell a story. Throw out any photo that isn't contributing to the news somehow.

Figure 6-13 shows two sample page layouts. Which is the more attractive and easier to read?

Figure 6-13. Not Every Picture Tells a Story

Half-filled panels are fine. Another way to effectively use white space to improve your pages is to leave part of a panel empty. When you're writing and illustrating stories, there will be many times when you won't need to completely fill each and every panel. That's okay—just leave the rest of the panel blank. Don't worry about writing more, looking for a photo, or adding a filler.

This unintentional white space can create an attractive and informal look to your paper.

The best place to put these panels is at the bottom of the page. When you put half-filled panels in the middle of a page, it can make the page look unfinished.

Figure 6-14, the front page of the family newspaper *Busy Times*, shows how you can use this leftover panel room.

Figure 6-14. Half Panels

White space left from partial panels

Compare this page to the one on the right in Figure 6-13. A number of headlines and stories were moved up, tightening the layout so that there would be more room at the bottom of the page. Notice that the headline for the story at bottom left, *Muffy Has Kits*, was moved up so that it appeared in the bottom of the middle panel. If you know what kind of layout you're using, and the approximate length of your stories (you will if you follow the suggestions in this chapter and in Chapter 2), you can plan for this *before* you begin typing in heads and stories in panels. Nothing prevents you from starting more than one story in a panel.

White space is an easy-to-use design tool that can make any newspaper—whether it's seen by your family or everyone in your company—better looking and better read. It's not just the news that counts, but also how the news looks.

Be Imaginative

One of the keys to creating a good-looking newspaper is your imagination.

No other *Newsroom*-produced newspaper or newsletter will look exactly like yours. You'll put *your* ideas into its design, lay it out according to what *you* think your readers want to see, and change it when *you* think it's not working.

Be creative and imaginative in how you lay out your paper. Better yet, use that creativity and imagination long before, when you're building panels and selecting photos.

Creativity and imagination usually mean a lot of hard work. Few publications are designed and laid out perfectly the very first time. You'll probably have to use trial and error to arrive at your final newspaper design.

Sketch out your ideas on page dummies. Try things out by taking existing panels, modifying them to fit the layout and design you're after, and printing sample pages. Fine-tune those pages as many times as it takes until you have a paper that looks its best in every story and every page.

Then, once you think it's finished, look at it again. Ask your readers (if you can) what they liked (or didn't like) about how things were organized in the paper and arranged on the page. If the suggestions make sense, use them to create a new design. Print out a page or two and see if you like what you see. If things aren't working, you can always go back to your paper's old look.

The rest of this chapter presents some design ideas you may want to try. Not all of them will be appropriate to your newspaper. Use these ideas as a starting point for your own experimentation. You've got nothing to lose, and a better-looking paper to gain.

Two-Column Stories

Newsroom's panels are only a column wide when you lay them out on a page. That's why most *Newsroom* users lay out stories in single columns, as shown in Figure 6-15.

Figure 6-15. Single File

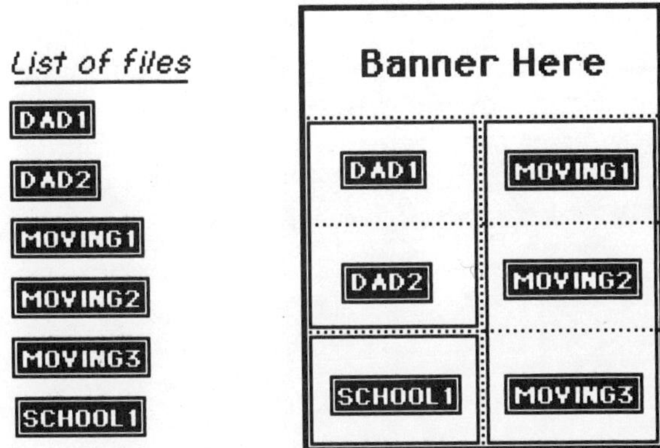

Nothing prevents you from laying out stories differently, however. If you want, you can create layouts like the one in Figure 6-16.

Figure 6-16. Double Column

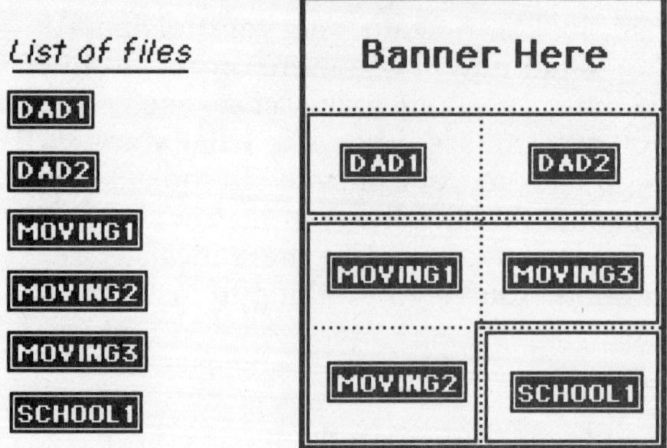

This puts the two-panel story of DAD1 and DAD2 at the top of the page in a horizontal layout. The three MOVING files are grouped into the second story, which starts in the middle left panel, runs down a panel, and then finishes in the middle right panel. The single-panel story SCHOOL is placed in the lower right.

You may have to guide your readers through these stories, though, with graphics which makes the arrangement clear. Several different kinds of graphics can be used, from rules and boxes to inset caps and identical photos. Figure 6-17 shows one way to eliminate any reader confusion.

Figure 6-17. Graphics Help

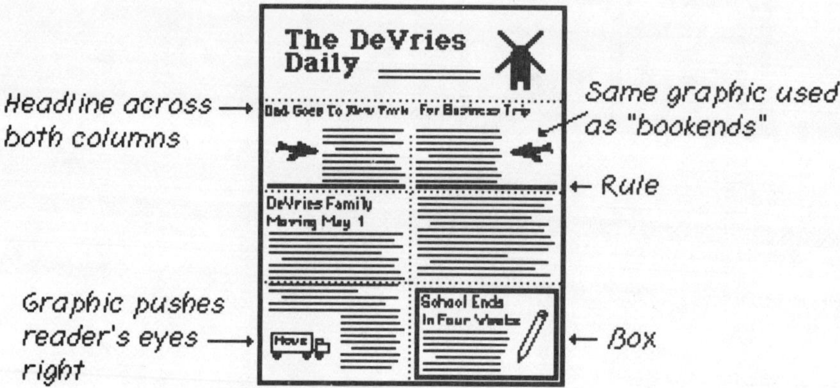

The two-column headline (it's not really two columns, but looks that way; more on it in a moment) tells the reader that the story runs *across* the page, not down. The two identical photos (they've been flipped) bracket the story and act as bookendlike devices to hold the story between them. The photos indicate to the reader that the two panels have a connection. Finally, the heavy rule at the bottom of each of the panels keeps the reader's eye from moving down into the next story.

The second story uses a photo in the bottom left panel as a way to "push" the reader's eyes into the middle of the page, preparing him or her for the move up and to the right when the third panel is reached. The box at the bottom right also channels the reader's eyes up and to the right.

This may seem complicated, but all it takes is some common sense and the ability to imagine where your reader's attention will be focused.

Faking two-column headlines and graphics. *Newsroom* doesn't let you write or draw across columns, of course, but you can create much the same result with some thought and planning.

Headlines, for instance, can easily run across columns. Here's how.

- Write your headline, counting characters as you go (average of 28 across a panel in one of the large type sizes). A break between words should be as close as possible to the right edge of the panel.
- In the Copy Desk, type in the first half of the headline and then as much text as you want. Save the panel.
- With a blank work space, type in the second half of the headline. Make sure it's on the same vertical line as the first half. In other words, if you spaced down one line before typing the first half, do the same when entering the second.
- Type in the rest of the text. Save the panel(s).

With a two-panel story, such a headline could look much like the one in Figure 6-18.

Figure 6-18. Headline and Rule Split

Drawing a graphic across two columns (a thick rule, for instance) is just as simple. Select a pen width and tool, and draw the graphic in the first panel. Assuming this is to be in the left-hand column, make sure the drawing extends to the right edge of the panel. If it's a box, don't close it on that side.

Save the first panel to disk and when the work space reappears, select the Eraser icon. This removes all the text, but keeps any photos or graphics.

You can quickly touch up the graphic so that it's the opposite of what will show in the left-hand column. If you drew a line in the first panel, for example, just make sure the line in the second panel runs all the way to the left edge. The left edge of boxes or frames can be erased with the Eraser and right edges inserted.

No line can cross the gutter, the space between the two columns. If you're drawing a rule like the one in Figure 6-18, it may not matter. A box, however, will look odd if it's broken in two. The only thing you can do is connect the two panels' graphic by hand with a fine-lined, black felt-tipped pen after you've printed your master and before you've duplicated it.

Varying Column Widths

Newsroom sets column widths and side margins for you. The widths vary, but depend on the printer you're using. An Apple ImageWriter, for instance, prints narrow characters in *Newsroom;* columns are 2⅞-inches wide. But an Epson FX-80 prints broader characters and stretches out photos and graphics; its columns are 3¾-inches wide.

Figure 6-19. Printers and Columns Compared

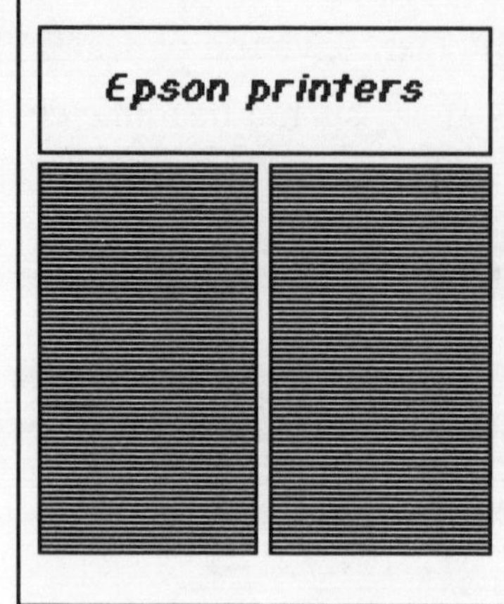

The simplest way to change the width of your columns is to change printers. In fact, it's theoretically possible to print one column with one printer—say the ImageWriter—and then print the other column with another printer, an Epson MX-80 for example. That would give you one wide column and one narrow column.

If you really want to try this out, create two page-layout files for each page. In the first page-layout file, place the banner and the files for the left-hand column. Leave the right-hand column panels blank. Build the second page-layout file by filling the right-hand column with the appropriate panel files. The banner and left-hand column panel areas remain empty. Print on the first printer after noting the starting position of the printer head on the paper. Put the paper in the second printer; make sure the printer head and paper are lined up as before. You may have to print several times to get the top lines of the top panels aligned.

Such a technique is probably more trouble than it's worth. Lining up the paper for the second printing isn't always easy. More bothersome is that the columns look so different. Each kind of printer creates its own style of characters. Your newspaper would have no consistency at all if you mixed printers.

There is a way to alter column width, however, without switching printers. You can't widen columns with this technique, nor can you actually change the margins. But you can create some interesting page designs.

≡ Enter the Photo Lab and select the Camera icon.

≡ Using the crosshairs, crop part of the *empty* work space (remember, the Photo Lab and Copy Desk work spaces are identical in size). The area you're cropping should reach from the top of the work space to the bottom. Its width will set the new column width. The wider the area you select in the Photo Lab, the narrower your columns will be. Save the blank photo to disk.

≡ Go to the Copy Desk, select the Disk icon, and load the blank photo file. If necessary, move the photo—panels which will be in the left-hand column should have the photo on the left side; right-hand panels should use the photo on the right.

≡ Choose your typeface and size and begin entering headlines or text. The blank photo will act as a new margin for the text.

≡ When you're finished with one panel, save it to disk, Return to the work space, and choose the Eraser icon. Only the text will be erased; the blank photo remains. Type in the headlines and text for another panel which will appear in the narrow column.

Figure 6-20. Narrow Columns

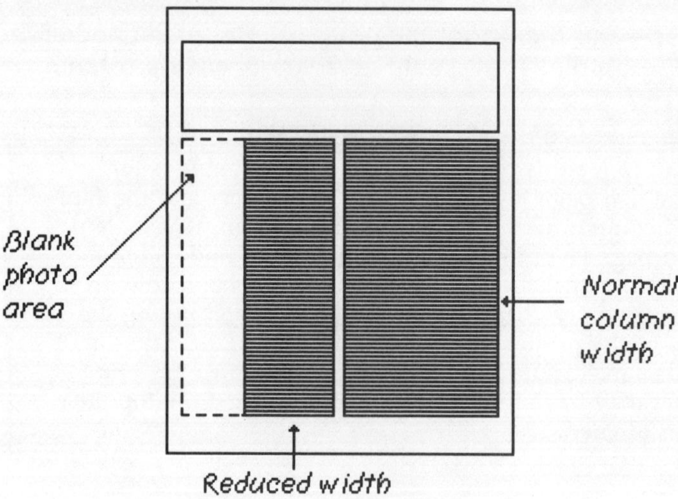

≡ Any clip art you add to narrow panels must be chosen and cropped carefully if it's to fit. If you use clip art and/or graphics, it will be easier to select the Garbage Can icon and start with a fresh work space when you begin another panel. Load the blank photo into the new panel and position it as you did before.

White space, text, or graphics. You can use this new page design—where either one or both columns are narrower than normal—for a variety of interesting effects.

Figure 6-21. Unbalanced Columns

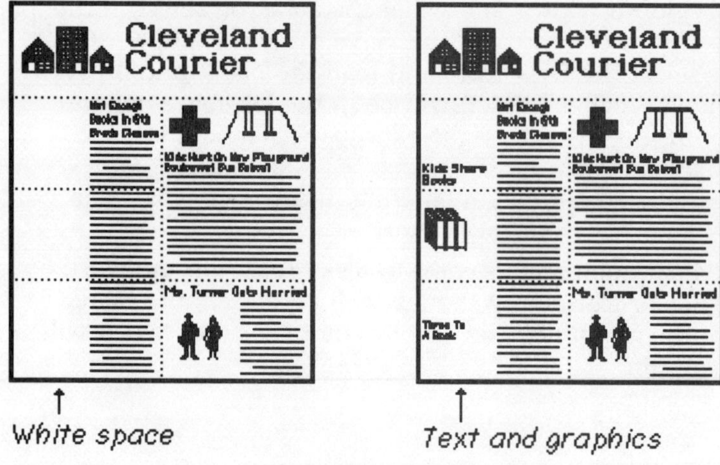

Just leave the space empty. Unbalanced column widths can make for an attractive and unusual page design. Since the reader's eyes will normally be attracted to the large area of white space before anything else on the page (especially if it's on the left side of the page as in Figure 6-21) you'll want to place your most important story or stories in the narrow column.

Use the space for text or graphics. This takes some planning, but can result in a unique page layout. Instead of using a blank photo to create a narrow column, you can use one which includes text or graphics.

Most of the time you'll want to use the text in this area for headlines, subheads, captions, or readouts. Because the width of the photo, it's best if you stick with the small type sizes, even if you're using the text for headlines.

≡ Decide on the width of the photo you'll insert to reduce a column's width.
≡ Make a *master* file by drawing a thin-ruled box of that width in the Photo Lab. The box should extend from the top to the bottom of the work space. Make sure all four sides are visible. Crop it just outside the lines and save it to disk with a name like MASCOL.
≡ When the Photo Lab screen reappears, crop the area just *inside* the box, but not the lines of the box itself. Save this to disk, too, perhaps with a name like COL1.
≡ In the Copy Desk, load the blank photo file (COL1) and place it in the work space. Type your text and save the panel file. Make a mental note of where you'll put the text or graphics.
≡ Return to the Photo Lab and load the MASCOL. Enter the text or graphics in the desired locations. The box is a guide; don't place text or graphics outside of the box.
≡ Again, crop the area just within the boundaries of the box. Save it to disk,

Figure 6-22. Pigs in the Space

Tonight's the Night

Tonight's the night for the annual "Pig Out" pig-picking, all-you-can eat dinner.

As always, proceeds from the dinner will go to the Bob R. Shelby Memorial Fund. It's hoped that enough money will be raised to send two deserving children to summer camp for three weeks.

"We still need cooks,"

using the same name as the blank photo file. Call it COL1, for example. When *Newsroom* asks whether you want to replace the existing file with the same name, select the *OK* box.

- Load the panel you saved earlier, and the new text or graphics you entered in the Photo Lab magically appears. You don't need to save this panel again; panels keep track of associated photo filenames, not what's in those photos.

When it's all done, the panel should look something like Figure 6-22.

Readouts

A *readout* is a short quotation or phrase that calls attention to a story. You'll find a use for readouts in stories or on pages when there's no available or appropriate art, but where you still want some kind of graphic device to break up the mass of text.

Creating a readout is simple. Look for an interesting phrase that summarizes the story. If there are quotations in the story, all the better; find one that will spark the reader's interest. Whatever you select, make sure it's an attention grabber. Bland, say-nothing readouts will only turn readers away from the story.

Readouts act much like graphics. In fact, many readouts are bordered by rules, boxes, or set on gray or black squares.

Once you've chosen your readout, you're ready to create it and place it in a panel.

Just like a photo. *Newsroom* readouts are basically text entered in the Photo Lab. Though you could create readouts in the Copy Desk by inserting spaces and typing in text, in the Photo Lab you can create the rules or boxes which set off the readout from the rest of the copy.

- Go to the Photo Lab and select the large size of the body copy typeface from the Graphics Tools menu. Type in the readout, not forgetting quotation marks if they're needed.
- Draw rules above and below the readout, or draw a box around it. Get as fancy as you want; try a drop-shadowed box for a particularly interesting effect.
- If you're using rules to mark the readout, draw the upper line with a thicker pen than the lower line. This draws attention to the readout when it's first encountered, but makes it easy for the reader to continue with the text once the readout is scanned.
- Crop the readout horizontally across the entire width of the work space, even if the readout takes up only a portion of the screen—you won't want text in the Copy Desk to somehow find its way to the sides of your readout. Crop it close vertically, though. Save it to disk.
- Load it into the Copy Desk and position it. Readouts don't have to be centered in a panel. Type in the body copy. Usually, a blank line will be automatically left above and below the readout.

Here's your first readout.

Figure 6-23. Readout Deluxe

in the water and swam for the two
children.
"I got to them just as the little
boy was going under," Barrons told
police later. "I reached down and
pulled him out of the water with one

"I reached down and pulled him out of the water..."

hand, and grabbed onto the rope
with the other. He was sputtering,
but he was breathing."
The police credit Barrons with

It's probably best if you use readouts only on pages without banners. The main purpose of such a graphic device is to attract attention and break up the grayness of large quantities of type. Inside pages, where eight or ten panels of text are staring at the reader, are more likely to need a readout.

Figure 6-24 offers a typical inside page with readouts. Notice how just two such devices give the page some variety.

Figure 6-24. Readouts on the Page

Design elements like two-column stories, unbalanced columns, and read-outs are just some of what you can produce with *Newsroom*'s Layout work area. Many more are possible. All you have to do is use your creativity and imagination as you put together your newspaper. What you'll discover will amaze you.

Electronic Glue

Layout is terribly simple to use. Too simple, really, for it can fool you into thinking that it takes no thought or care to lay out a publication.

As you've seen by now, that's not the case. Layout—the process, not the work area of *Newsroom*—is as much a matter of hard work as creativity. You have to plan ahead, know what you're doing, and be able to carry out a consistent design. With the information in this chapter, you're well on your way to becoming the best possible *Newsroom* layout artist.

Use the suggestions, tips, and techniques offered here, but don't stop with that. Develop your own design, your own methods. They'll work for no one better than they'll work for you.

The next chapter puts ink on your hands and the smell of hot presses in the air—or comes close. The Press, where you finally print your paper, is the last stop on the tour.

CHAPTER 7

Start the Presses

The Press

The Press is the last step in the long process of creating your newspaper with *Newsroom*. Only when it comes out of the printer, when it's no longer just a collection of files on a disk, does your newspaper become real. Only then is your paper something people can hold in their hands and read.

In the easy-to-use spirit of *Newsroom*, the Press work area is as simple as Layout. Like Layout, it's a three-step process: You identify your printer (and perhaps the printer interface card), line up the paper, and choose the files you want to print. Do it once or twice and you've got it mastered.

The whole thing's so simple, in fact, that there's little to say about it. Little to say, that is, if all you're doing is printing each copy, handing one to a reader, and hoping they like what they see. But if you want to use some attention-getting printing effects, or duplicate tens or hundreds of copies, or even produce multicolored newspapers, then this chapter has information and techniques you can use right now.

Building Your Press

You've written news stories, snapped clip art photos, built banners, and put them all together in attractive page layouts. Your newspaper is ready to go to press.

Newsroom's Press work area doesn't ask you to ink type or turn a press. It's a simple matter of making a few decisions and pressing a few keys on your computer. After that, the program takes over and does everything for you.

That's not to say you won't have problems with *Newsroom*'s Press. One in particular comes up time and again among *Newsroom* users. It's most common among beginning users, though most *Newsroom* publishers have trouble with it now and again. The problem is getting everything ready to print and print correctly.

Before you print, you have to have a printer properly connected to your computer—with the right cable and perhaps an interface card—and you have to tell *Newsroom* what printer it is. Then, if things don't work (as is sometimes the case with printers), you've got to figure out what went wrong and how to fix it.

This section briefly shows you how to build your press by connecting your printer and using the *Change setup* feature of the Press work area. You'll also find hints and tips about solving some *Newsroom* printer problems. If you and your computer are new friends, you'll especially want to read this. If you're a *Newsroom* pro, there's information here that you'll find useful, like the Press checklists.

Connections

Let's assume you have your printer and computer set up on the same desk. Before the computer can "talk" to the printer, there has to be a connection of some sort between the two machines. That connection is a *cable* with one end plugged into the back of the computer and the other end plugged into the printer.

When you bought your printer, a cable may have come packed with it. That's most likely if you own a Commodore 64 or 128, and bought a Commodore or Commodore-compatible printer. Many other printers don't include a cable. The reason for this is because most printers can be used by several different makes of computers—say IBMs, Apples, and Ataris—and each computer generally requires a different cable. It wouldn't be feasible to include cables for all possible connections.

If your printer is without a cable when you take it out of the box, you'll need to buy or build a cable.

> Unless you (or someone you know) is technically minded and handy with a soldering gun, you'll be much better off buying a cable than trying to build one. If you want to try making a cable yourself, look for the pin-configuration diagrams in your computer and printer manuals.

The most convenient place to buy a cable is at the same computer store that sold you the printer. They're more likely to have cables in stock or to know how to make one for you. You can also usually buy quality cables from a mail-order company (look in almost any computer magazine that's dedicated to the kind of computer you use), but it means a longer wait, and if things don't work the first time, even more delays as the cable goes back and forth in the mail.

When you walk into the computer store or call up a mail-order company, here's the information they'll need to sell you the right cable.

- The kind of computer you're using. Be exact. For instance, your Apple computer isn't just an Apple; perhaps it's an Apple IIe. Or maybe your IBM computer isn't really from IBM but is an IBM compatible made by PC Limited.
- The kind of interface card (if your computer needs one to connect to your

printer). Again, be specific as to the kind of card and its manufacturer. It's not a bad idea to take the card's manual or instructions with you in case the store has to special order or hand-build your cable.

≡ The kind of printer you're using. Once again, be as exact as possible. An Epson MX-80, for instance, may not be quite the same as an Epson FX-100. The printer documentation is the first place to look for this information.

With cable in hand, plug one end into the printer's *port*, the receptacle usually in the back which matches one end of the cable. Plug the other end of the cable into the computer's printer port. If you're not sure which port on your computer is for the printer, refer to the computer's manual. Figure 7-1 shows the back of a Commodore 64 computer and gives you an idea of the kind of diagrams you'll find in your manual. Note that on the 64, two ports can be used to connect the computer to a printer. Commodore and Commodore-compatible printers can connect directly to the computer through the *serial port*. Other kinds of printers connect to the computer through a printer interface which in turn is plugged into the *user port*.

Figure 7-1. Around Back

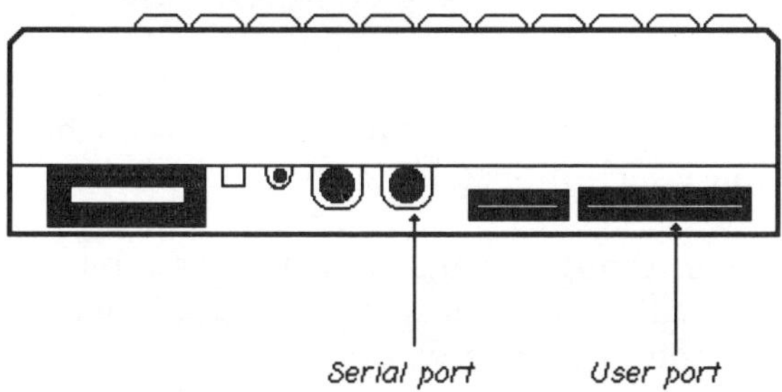

Some computers—like the Apple II+ and IIe, and the IBM PC—don't come equipped with printer ports. You have to buy a separate plug-in board and install it inside your computer before you can connect to a printer.

Installing a board isn't hard. Turn the computer off and open the top of the computer (easy with an Apple; difficult with an IBM). Locate the right slot (one of the narrow connectors inside the computer) and plug the board into place. It's best if you gently rock the board into position with a front-to-back motion.

With the computer and printer connected, make sure that the printer's power cord is plugged into an outlet and the power is turned on. The final step is to make sure the printer is *online* or *selected*. A button and indicator light on the printer should be labeled with one of those two terms.

Figure 7-2. Connection Checklist

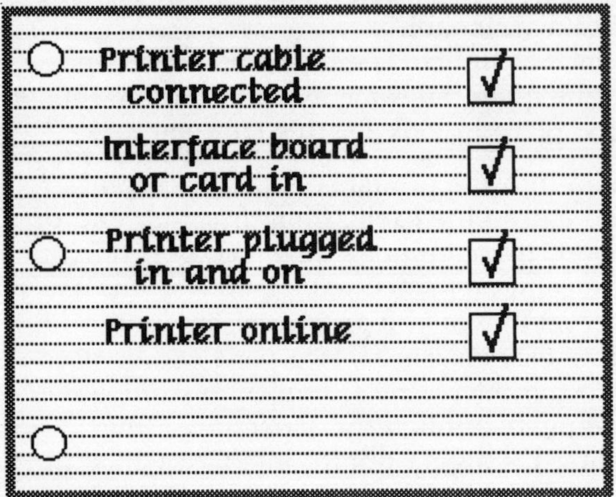

Paper

Printing requires paper. Before you can create your masterpiece, make sure there's paper in the printer.

If you're using *fan-fold* paper, the kind where the individual sheets are connected, insert the paper and roll it into the printer so that the *printhead* (the part of the printer right behind the ribbon which moves back and forth) is just below one of the perforations.

If you're using single sheets of paper, though, you'll need to take a bit more care. It's important that you position each sheet the same, especially its horizontal location, before it is rolled into the printer. If you don't, side margins won't be uniform. For a standard top margin, roll the paper far enough into the printer so that the *bail* (the thin metal rod with the small rubber rollers) can hold the top edge of the paper against the platen.

Use inexpensive paper if you're printing each copy in the printer. Look for fan-fold paper that has what's called *micro-perfs*. When you tear the sheets apart and remove the holed strips on the sides, the edges are very sharp and clean.

But if you're printing just one master copy for later reproduction, consider buying more expensive paper. (You can find more variations in paper if you buy sheets, not fan-fold paper.) Paper with a shiny or slick finish, for instance, will make for a clearer final product. Although there's a danger of the ink smearing as the paper is drawn through the printer, the type and graphics should be sharper when you copy or print from this master. The coarser the paper, the more the ink "bleeds," or spreads out. Using a paper with a finish prevents this.

Figure 7-3. Paper Checklist

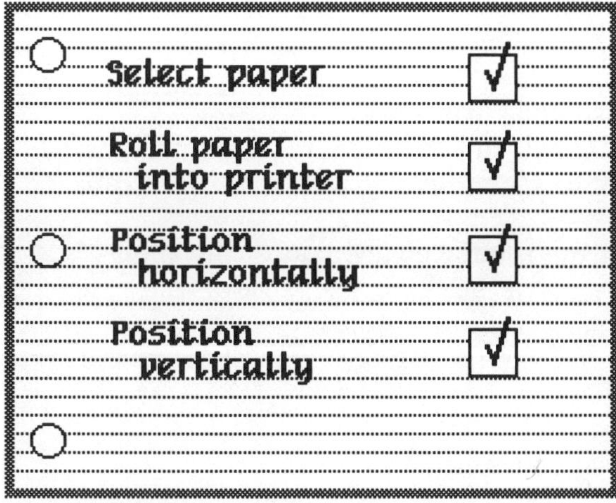

Choose Setup Now

Getting *Newsroom* ready to print is just as important as setting up the printer and computer. *Change setup* is where you customize *Newsroom*'s printing abilities. Using it properly is crucial to the printing process.

When you enter the Press work area, you'll see a list of selection options which looks like Figure 7-4.

Figure 7-4. The Press Screen

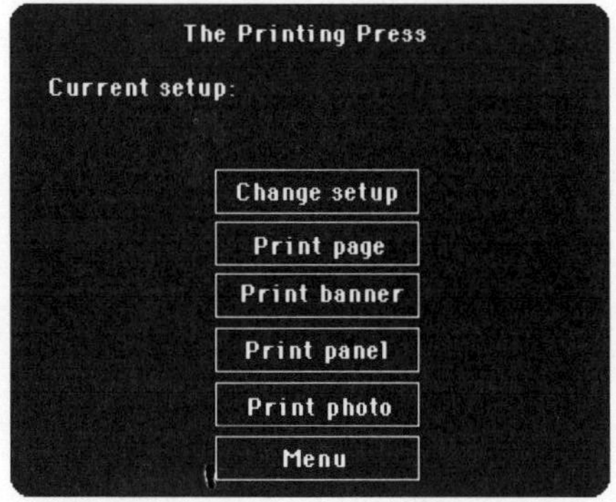

If this is the first time you've used the Press, the items shown under the heading *Current setup:* may not be correct. Select *Change setup* now and make your choices in the following categories for your computer.

Apple II+, IIe, IIGS

Select printer	Choose your printer
Line feed	Pick *Default* (few printers require linefeeds)
Slot	Check to see which slot your interface card is in[1]
Interface card	Select the interface card you've installed[2]

[1]If you're using a IIGS and using the built-in printer port, make sure you've selected *Printer Port* for Slot 1 within the *Slots* area of the Control Panel.

[2]If you're using a IIGS and have the GS-specific update of *Newsroom*, pick *Apple IIgs Printer Port* from this list to print through the built-in printer port.

Apple IIc

Select printer	Choose your printer
Line feed	Pick *Default* (few printers require linefeeds)

Commodore 64 and 128

Select printer	Choose your printer
Select interface card[3]	Select the interface card you've installed
Line feed[3]	Pick *Default* (few printers require linefeeds)

[3]This choice does not appear when you select the Commodore MPS 801, Commodore MPS 803, or Okimate 10 printers.

IBM

Select printer	Choose your printer
Select printer line feed control	Pick *Default* (few printers require linefeeds)

Many potential printing problems can be traced to your *Change setup* selections. If you pick the wrong printer by mistake, for instance, it's possible that nothing will happen when you try to print.

More common, however, is that you can't find your exact printer or interface card on the list. Though *Newsroom* supports a wide range of printers and cards in all three versions, it doesn't account for every combination. The Appendix lists all the printers currently supported by the program.

If your printer or interface card is *not* on the *Change setup* list, you'll want to choose the one that's most similar, in the hopes that it will work. Sometimes that's not hard, other times you may be stymied. Consider these things as you're trying to decide which printer and/or card to select.

- Look in the manual that came with your printer or card (or even on the box it came in). Does it say this printer or card is compatible with one that *is* on the list? If so, pick that printer or card when in *Change setup*.
- Try selecting a printer on the list that's made by the same company. Printer manufacturers often change model numbers without making substantial

Figure 7-5. Change Setup Checklist

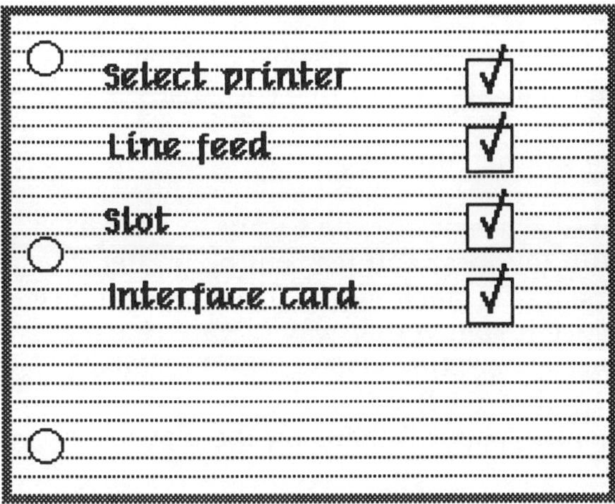

changes in the actual machine. If you have an ImageWriter II, for instance, choose *Apple Imagewriter (normal).* A Commodore MPS 1200 printer works just fine when you select *Commodore MPS 803.*

When All Else Fails . . .

You've done everything by the book, but still the printer just sits there when you tell it to go to work. That's one of the most frustrating moments in computing: You're sure it should work but it doesn't.

Figure 7-6. When Things Go Wrong

✓	Is the printer plugged in and turned on?
✓	Is the printer cable firmly inserted in the computer and printer?
✓	Is the printer online or selected?
✓	Is the printer top on and in place?
✓	Paper has a free path as it feeds into the printer
✓	Paper isn't wrapping around the platen as it comes out of printer
✓	Ribbon is on the right side of the printhead
✓	Ribbon is not worn
✓	In Apple--printer interface is in slot 1 or 2
✓	In Apple--multifunction card is set for printer, not modem
✓	In Apple IIGS--Control Panel matches Change setup selections
✓	Change setup has correct selections

No book can tell you how to make your printer and computer talk to one another. There are too many things that can go wrong, too many combinations of equipment, too many variables.

At best, all *Using Newsroom* can offer is a list of possible problem areas. When things aren't working, or working right, glance at this checklist.

The Master Copy

Unless its circulation is really small—under ten—you won't want to print each individual copy of your newspaper. With the wear and tear on the printer, the ribbon used, and especially the time spent, it's much more efficient to produce a master of each page and then reproduce it some other way.

Think of these masters as *Newsroom*'s *printing plates*. A professional newspaper creates metal or plastic plates that are fixed on the presses; the plates are inked and place an impression on paper. What's on the plates is exactly reproduced.

The same holds true when you're copying a master page printed by *Newsroom*. That's why a master must be perfect. No faint lines of text, smeared photos, or double-vision headlines. If it takes several tries in the Press work area to create a satisfactory master, then take the time to print a page several times.

Later in this chapter, you'll see several copying methods described. But before you actually step up to the copying machine or into a printer's office, there are a number of things you can do with the master so that your newspaper stands out in a crowd.

To use some of these techniques, you need to make plans before you create the master. Others are easiest after the master is printed.

Keep In Stock

For a terrific-looking school or business newspaper, consider printing your newspaper on *stock*, or preprinted paper.

Something that remains the same from issue to issue—most commonly the banner—is printed on a large quantity of paper (you get to choose the kind and color of the paper, of course). This stock of paper is what the newspaper is later printed on.

There are a number of advantages to using preprinted stock, including

- Much better printing quality for the part of the issue printed on the stock, especially when you photocopy the rest of the issue.
- A chance to produce a two-color newspaper. The preprinted stock can be done in color and the rest of the paper in black.
- Hand-drawn art, a formal logo, or even a photograph can be printed on the stock. You're not restricted to printing *Newsroom* clip art on such stock since the printer can use more sophisticated printing techniques.

≡ Possible two-page spreads when the stock is larger-sized paper, say the popular tabloid size of 11 × 17 inches.

> If you're printing a newspaper for the home or family, it doesn't make a lot of sense to print stock. You can use some of the same techniques if you have access to a copier which can print in more than just black. See the section in this chapter called "Colors" for more information on copying in color.

Although such stock can be printed in several ways, the most common is on an offset press at a print shop. Here's how you can arrange for your preprinted stock.

First, decide what you want to print on the stock. Creating preprinted stock is only economical when you print on a large quantity of paper. You'll use the stock for several issues at least. That means whatever you print on the stock must remain unchanged from issue to issue.

The biggest part of your newspaper that doesn't change is the banner. Other parts which don't change very often are the return mailing address (if you're printing it on the last page and then folding the paper in thirds for mailing) or the staff box (which lists the people who produce the paper). Stick with the banner, however, for best results.

Design the banner and lay it out in a page. Save the page-layout file to disk and print the page, aligning the paper in your printer normally. If you're going to include noncomputer art or a photograph, leave room in the banner for these elements.

This is what you take to the printer. Get quotes from several print shops and quick-print stores for the best price; you'll have a more accurate idea of the total cost if you know what kind and size of paper you want the banner printed on.

When you walk into the print shop, be prepared to describe exactly what you want done. That means you have to tell the printer which color you want the banner printed in, where the banner should appear on the stock (in the same relative spot that it would appear on a page from your printer), and how any photographs must be cropped. If you're including art or graphics other than what's in the banner, make sure you have the originals for the printer to use.

If you're putting the banner on large stock so that you can later print a four-page newspaper on one sheet of paper, make sure the printer understands how the stock will later be used. Proof the job before the entire stock is printed or you may waste money and paper.

Figure 7-7 shows what two different sizes of stock would look like when printed.

Figure 7-7. Stock Paper

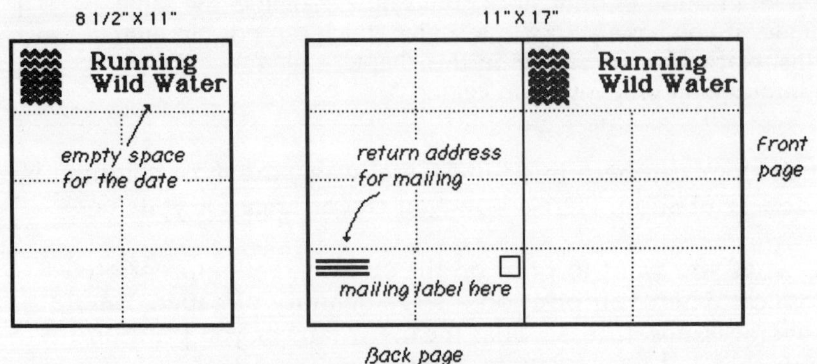

The only thing printed on the 8½ × 11–inch stock is the banner. Note the art on the left—it's not computer-created, but was pasted into place by the printer. Empty space was also left at the bottom of the banner so that a date could be inserted for each issue.

The 11 × 17–inch stock is a bit more complicated. Notice how the banner is printed on the right half of the sheet of paper. That places it correctly when you fold the paper down the middle. And since the newsletter will be mailed to subscribers, the return address was also printed on the stock. Printing the return address shouldn't add much, if anything, to the final cost. You can print the return address in a banner (type is twice as large in a banner as in a panel) the normal way and then tell the printer to paste it down where you indicate.

It's actually cheaper to use larger paper, for much of the cost in printing is the time it takes the printer to set up the job. Many printers charge a fee each time they make a photographic printing plate—shooting two pages separately costs twice as much as putting them together and making just one plate.

If you're using the same printer to print your newspaper issue, the paper can be kept in the print shop. All you need to bring in are the pages you want printed and then tell the printer which pages go where and specify the number of copies.

If you're photocopying your newspaper, make sure the paper you've chosen will work with the copy machine you'll use. Take your preprinted stock to the copy center and tell them how you want the pages organized (see below). Or, if you're using a self-operated copying machine, load the paper in the correct paper tray or cartridge.

Don't forget that you'll need extra paper—the same kind of paper used for the printed stock, but blank—for the inside pages of your newspaper. Buy this blank paper from the printer.

Open Spaces

Another technique you can use to create a unique publication is to vary the top and bottom margins of your pages.

Newsroom always keeps the same margin widths on the left and right (they differ with individual printers, however). You can easily change top and bottom margins, however.

For a wider top margin, just roll the paper further into the printer before printing. Wider bottom margins result when you position the top of the paper slightly below the printer's printhead (the normal top margin of *Newsroom* should make the printer begin printing *on* the paper; you may have to run a few samples to get things right).

You can't get more on a page this way—*Newsroom* only allows so much on a page. The effect, however, can be stunning, especially when you know where to place panels and banners, and how many to use.

Depending on how wide you want the top margin to be, you may use a banner and only four panels, instead of the normal six. Figure 7-8, for instance, shows two results of such a page layout. Since there are no bottom panels to worry about, you can center the printing (as in the middle of Figure 7-8) or simply drop everything down so that there's a lot of white space at the top (as on the right).

Figure 7-8. Big Margins

Column Rules

Many newspapers and newsletters have something impossible to reproduce with *Newsroom*—column rules. These rules, or thin lines, separate columns and give the publication a more formal (and sometimes professional) appearance.

Because of the way that *Newsroom* puts pages together, and because of its automatic spacing between columns, there's no way to insert column rules with the program.

Once the page comes out of the printer, though, anything's possible. With a steady hand, a ruler, and a fine-tipped pen, you can draw column rules on the master before you head for the print or copy shop.

- Use a black pen, preferably one with a very fine felt tip. You can always draw a thicker rule, but it's impossible to make a fat one skinny.
- Measure and mark where the column rule should appear so that each page is consistent.
- Use white out (correction fluid) to cover mistakes. (You can buy a white tape for the same purpose in many art or graphic supply stores.)

Figure 7-9. Column Rules

If you have a little more money to spend, you can buy ready-made rules. These are actually thin strips of adhesive plastic which you unroll. You can buy press-on rules in various thicknesses and styles. You may, for example, want to use a double rule—hard to get right each time when you have to draw the lines by hand. Look for these rolls of rules at any graphic-arts-supply store.

Copies by the Hundreds

Even if your circulation isn't in the hundreds, or you don't have the money for expensive offset printing or fancy photocopying, you don't have to turn your printer into a press. Although most *Newsroom* users make copies on a photocopying machine, there are plenty of other ways to duplicate your newspaper.

Each method requires that you make a master in your own printer. The form that master takes and then what you do with the master differs with each technique.

No matter what the process, you're transforming your printer from a printing press into a plate maker. That's an excellent idea, since your printer isn't suited to serve as a press—it takes too long to print an issue and, considering the wear on the printer, it's expensive.

Choose the reproduction method that best fits your newspaper, its audience, and your pocketbook. A newspaper printed by a print shop wouldn't be appropriate for a home, for example, while a company newsletter run off on a ditto machine gives the impression of smallness and unprofessionalism.

Ditto That

The least expensive way to reproduce your newspaper is with a ditto master, sometimes called a *spirit* master. Most commonly found in schools, they're typically used for making copies of worksheets, tests, and handouts.

The process is simple. Take a ditto master and write, draw, or type on the white side. Any imprint is duplicated (but reversed) on the back by the carbonlike sheet underneath. This master is then placed on the ditto machine's drum, a fluid is poured into a reservoir, and paper is placed at one end of the machine.

Ditto machines come in both hand-operated and electric models. With either, paper is drawn into the machine as the drum revolves. Only those parts of the master which show in the blue carbon print on the paper.

Dittos are convenient because you can actually write, even draw on them. They're limited, however, in the number of copies they can reproduce. Since it's the blue carbon that's transferred to the paper as each copy is made, the more copies you make, the fainter the printing. After approximately 100 copies, the quality goes down.

If your school uses ditto equipment, it may also have a heat-transfer machine which creates a ditto master directly from a printed sheet. Typically, you feed your printed sheet (in your case it would be what came out of your printer from *Newsroom*) and a special ditto master into the machine. Try out this method and compare the results with a ditto master created on your computer printer.

Ditto and *Newsroom*. To run off your newspaper with the ditto process, just follow these steps.

- Create your newspaper normally in *Newsroom*.
- When you're ready to go to Press, remove the paper from your printer and insert a ditto master, white side facing the front of the printer. Set the printer to *friction feed* instead of *tractor feed*.
- Align the ditto master as you would a single sheet of paper.
- Start printing. When done, remove the master from the printer.
- Repeat the above steps for each page of your newspaper.
- Attach a master to the ditto machine's drum. Check the fluid level and fill if necessary. Stack paper in the paper tray.
- Set the machine's counter (if it has one) for the correct number of copies (the machine will stop automatically). Turn on the ditto machine and run off the page. If you're using a hand-operated machine, count the number of times you crank the handle to print the right number of copies.
- Repeat the last two steps for each master.

There are several factors to consider when trying to decide whether you should use ditto reproduction or another method of duplicating your *Newsroom* newspaper.

Category	**Explanation**
Home	Is suitable for home papers *and* provides easy access to equipment?
School	Is suitable for school papers *and* provides easy access to equipment?
Work	Is suitable for newsletters *and* provides easy access to equipment?
Inexpensive	Costs less than 4¢ per page?
Easy to do	Can *Newsroom* users do it themselves?
Fast	Takes less than two hours to print a paper?
Good quality	Has sharp, clear printing?
Long print runs	Is suitable for more than 100 copies per page?
Add other art	Can insert non-*Newsroom* art or graphics before printing?

The short checklist in Figure 7-10 wraps up the strengths and weaknesses of ditto reproduction. The other printing methods described in following sections include similar checklists.

Take a Mimeo

The second-most-inexpensive method of printing your newspaper is with a mimeograph machine. Many schools and churches use mimeograph machines (though they're being replaced by small photocopiers).

A mimeo stencil is created differently than a ditto master. Instead of

Figure 7-10. Ditto Yes or No?

Ditto Process	Yes	No
Home		X
School	X	
Work		X
Inexpensive	X	
Easy to do	X	
Fast	X	
Good quality		X
Long print runs		X
Add other art		X

drawing on it, you cut through the stencil. Normally, this is done with a typewriter. Instead of the typewriter keys striking the ribbon and transferring ink to paper, the keys strike the stencil and cut through the first layer. That part of the stencil is then placed on the mimeograph machine's drum, ink is poured into a small tank or bottle, and paper is drawn through the machine as the drum turns. Ink is spread across the stencil on the drum, and the ink only comes through the places where the stencil's been cut.

Mimeograph stencils last much longer than a ditto master, and so can print more copies before they wear out (they eventually do). Printing is also usually sharper than a ditto, and most often in black, not blue like a ditto.

Mimeo and *Newsroom*. To print your newspaper on a mimeograph, just follow these steps.

- Create your newspaper normally with *Newsroom*.
- When you're ready to go to Press, remove the paper from your printer and insert a mimeo stencil, blue side facing you. Set the printer to *friction feed* instead of *tractor feed*.
- Remove the printer's ribbon. (You want the printer's pin to strike the stencil directly. If you leave the ribbon in, the printer may not cut through the stencil.)
- Align the stencil.
- Start printing. When done, remove the stencil from the printer.
- Repeat the above steps for each page of your newspaper.
- Attach a stencil to the mimeograph machine's drum. Check the ink and fill if necessary. Stack paper in the paper tray.
- Set the machine's counter (if it has one) for the correct number of copies (the machine will stop automatically). Turn on the machine and run off the

page. If you're using a hand-operated machine, count the number of times you crank the handle to print the right number of copies.

≡ Repeat the last two steps for each stencil.

Fast printers may not cut through a mimeograph stencil properly. A good example is the Apple ImageWriter II printer. The ImageWriter II prints so quickly that the pins don't cut all the way through the stencil. Print is either faint or absent on the final mimeographed page. Other than using another printer (the ImageWriter I, perhaps), there's not much you can do about this. Try cutting a stencil—if it doesn't work, choose another printing method.

Figure 7-11. Mimeo Yes or No?

Mimeograph

	Yes	No
Home		X
School	X	
Work		X
Inexpensive	X	
Easy to do	X	
Fast	X	
Good quality	X	
Long print runs	X	
Add other art		X

Copy Cat

The most common duplication method—by far—is photocopying. It's easy to do, available almost anywhere, and provides excellent results.

The pages that come out of your printer are your masters. All you have to do is take them down to a copy shop or find a self-serve photocopy machine.

If you go to a copy shop, your options are more interesting. Tell the staff how many copies you want and then ask how much extra it will cost to use a better-quality paper, colored paper, or both. Unlike dittos and mimeos, you can print on both sides of a sheet of paper when you use a photocopying machine.

You can also add non-*Newsroom* art or graphics before you photocopy . As long as you've left space in the layout, you can paste or tape almost anything to the master after it's out of the printer, but before you copy it. Although the results are not always the best, you can even insert a photograph in the page. Line art or high-contrast graphics work best, however.

Many copiers let you adjust the intensity of the copy. If your printer ribbon was a bit light, for instance, you can make up for it by adjusting the copier to a darker setting.

The biggest disadvantage of photocopying is the cost. Unless you live in a major city with discount copying centers, expect to pay at least 5¢ or 6¢ a copy. That can add up—a four-page newspaper with a circulation of 75 would run $15.00 at 5¢ a copy, $18.00 at 6¢ a copy.

If you run off more than 100 copies of a page, the price usually drops, sometimes as much as 50 percent. Keep that in mind when you're deciding on a print method.

Call several copy centers in your vicinity to get an accurate idea of price. Make sure the price you're being quoted is on the same thing; it's a good idea to ask for a price based on copying standard letter-sized or legal-sized pages (the two sizes *Newsroom* can produce) using normal copying paper.

For an extra fee, copy centers will usually collate and staple your newspaper. Look into this—it saves you a lot of time in putting the paper together.

Photocopying and *Newsroom*. To print your paper or newsletter by photocopying, follow these steps.

- Create your newspaper normally.
- In the Press work area, print each page on the paper of your choice. Try a better grade of paper, one with a finish, for clearer printing.
- Proof the pages for faint printing, double printing, or streaks through large black areas. Print another page if necessary.
- Take the pages to a copy center.
- Specify the number of pages, the kind of paper, and whether you want it collated and stapled.
- Tell the copy-center staff if you want the pages printed on both sides of the paper. If you do, indicate which pages go where.
- If you're waiting while the copies are made, ask to see the first copy of each page. If it's too light or too dark, tell the people at the copy center. They'll adjust their machine.

Figure 7-12. Photocopy Yes or No?

Photocopying

	Yes	No
Home	X	
School	X	
Work	X	
Inexpensive		X
Easy to do	X	
Fast	X	
Good quality	X	
Long print runs	X	
Add other art	X	

Print It Quick

The fourth printing process you can consider is offset printing at a quick-print shop. It's more expensive and takes longer, but the results may be worth the money and the time.

As with photocopying, the pages that come out of your printer are your masters. These masters can be altered before printing, though, by adding non-*Newsroom* art and graphics, or by drawing in such things as column rules.

Once at the print shop, the master page is photographed and an inexpensive plate made from that image. The printer places the plate on an offset press, which uses a mixture of oil, water, and ink to produce the pages. The result is usually much clearer and sharper than you'd find on a typical photocopy.

Print shops generally offer more kinds of paper than a copy center. They can also (for a price) print your newspaper in more than one color. The easiest and cheapest way to do this is to print a banner in one color and print the rest of the newspaper in another color. A more difficult and more expensive way is to let the printer create *masks* for the various parts of a page that you want in each color. The printer makes multiple plates and uses each plate to print a different color on the paper. Check with your local print shop for detailed information on what you need to provide if you want your paper printed in more than one color of ink.

Print shops are your best choice, and are most economic, when you need several hundred copies of each page. Printing less than 100 copies at a print shop, for instance, usually costs more per page than photocopying. At 500 copies, however, a print shop is usually a clear price winner. Get price quotes from several quick print shops in your area—an average price is about 3¢–4¢

per copy for 500 copies on 8½ × 11–inch paper.

One of the big disadvantages of using a print shop is the time involved. It's not uncommon for a print shop to need several days to do your job. (Not because it takes that long, but because they have other work scheduled before yours.) You'll get the job done fastest if you take it to a quick-print shop—one that guarantees they'll deliver the printed pages in a specified time. When you're calling shops for prices, also ask how long it will take them to do the work.

Because many print shops charge per plate and not on the size of the plate, it may be more economical to have the printer place two of your newspaper pages on the camera at the same time to make one plate. That plate is then used to print on both sides of 11 × 17–inch paper, which is folded to make a finished paper. A eight-page paper, for instance, can be made with four plates and printed on two sheets of paper. Figure 7-13 shows how the paper's pages would be laid out, printed, and folded by the printer.

Figure 7-13. Eight Pages, Four Plates, Two Sheets

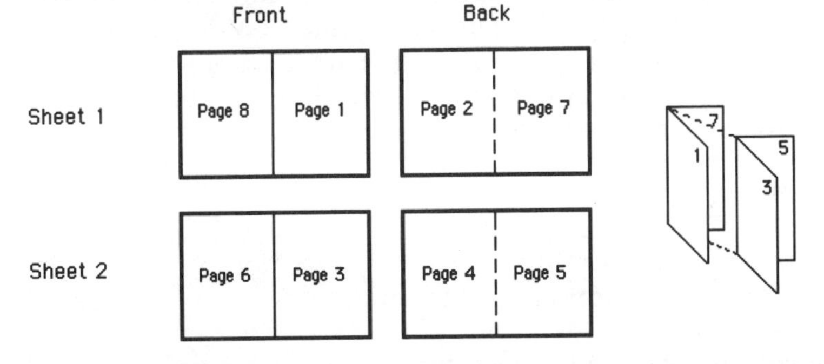

Quick printing and *Newsroom*. To print your newspaper at a quick-print shop, just follow these steps.

- Create your newspaper with *Newsroom*.
- Print each page on the paper of your choice in the Press work area. A better grade of paper will create clearer, sharper type.
- Proof the pages for faint printing, double printing, or streaks through large black areas. Print another page if necessary.
- Take the pages to a quick-print shop.
- Specify the number of copies of each page, the kind of paper, and whether you want it folded and/or stapled.
- Tell the print-shop staff if you want the pages printed on both sides of the paper. If you do, indicate which pages go where. They'll be able to advise you on this.

Figure 7-14. Quick Print Yes or No?

Quick Printing	Yes	No
Home		X
School	X	
Work	X	
Inexpensive		X
Easy to do		X
Fast		X
Good quality	X	
Long print runs	X	
Add other art	X	

No matter what your choice of printing methods, make sure the final product is appropriate for your audience. Teachers and students are used to seeing ditto-produced pages, for instance, and wouldn't think twice about seeing a ditto-made newspaper. On the other hand, a businessperson expects to see higher-quality printed material, and would do a double take if the company newsletter was a slightly smeared ditto.

Advanced Printing

As you've discovered, printing your newspaper doesn't have to be as simple as turning on the printer. You can make printing as complicated and expensive as you want to.

As you publish with *Newsroom*, you'll come across new techniques that make your paper more interesting to look at, easier to produce, or more effective in communicating the news. This section discusses two of these techniques.

Laser printers are one of the hottest-selling computer devices on the market. Giving super-sharp type and smooth graphics, laser printers are a big part of the desktop publishing revolution. You'll see how to use *Newsroom* with a laser printer.

Color can have a tremendous impact on how people react to newspapers. More and more papers are following the lead of such publications as *USA Today* and using color photographs and graphics to catch the reader's eyes and make the news more interesting. You can add color to your *Newsroom*-produced newspaper or newsletter—and here you'll see how to do that.

Laser Beams That Print

The best possible computer printing today is done by laser printers. Based on the same principle as a small copying machine, a laser printer can produce text and graphics that are sharper than any dot-matrix printer.

There are two hurdles in the path of *Newsroom* laser printing, though. The first is money—laser printers aren't cheap. Although prices are coming down, it's still unusual to find one under $2,000. That means it's unlikely you have one in your home or at your school. The second hurdle is even higher—*Newsroom* won't print to a laser printer.

There's a way around the second problem. Chapter 5 outlined the process of transferring your *Newsroom* files to *Newsroom Pro*, the more advanced version for the IBM PC family of computers. Using the Wire Service work area, you send your *Newsroom* pages to an IBM PC (if they were created on an Apple or Commodore) and then translate the pages into *Newsroom Pro* format. *Newsroom Pro can* print with a laser printer.

What about the first problem, then? If you don't work in a laser printer–equipped office—and most people don't—finding one of these machines can be even harder than transferring files to *Newsroom Pro*.

Computer stores. Call several computer stores in your area and ask if they have a laser printer connected to an IBM PC, PC XT, or PC AT. You'll have better luck if you only call dealers who carry IBM personal computers and who also handle Hewlett-Packard equipment (makers of the LaserJet, the most popular laser printer). Tell them you want to rent time on a laser printer. If that's possible, ask what they charge, and how. Is it based on the page you print or on the time you spend on the machine?

More and more computer stores are renting time on a computer–laser printer system. In many cases, stores are doing so because people like you have called and asked about such a service.

Rates vary from city to city, and even from store to store. Some stores will charge by the hour—perhaps $10.00 or more. Others charge by the printed page—maybe $1.00 or $2.00 per page. Still others charge in combination—a fee per hour and an additional surcharge per page.

When you decide on a computer store, make an appointment. That way you know you'll be guaranteed time on the computer. Walk into the store with your copy of *Newsroom Pro* (you should have already transferred your pages to an IBM PC and then converted them to *Newsroom Pro* format) and your data disks. You should have proofed your pages at home, school, or work to make sure everything was perfect. The less time you use and the fewer pages you print at the store, the less it's going to cost you.

Load *Newsroom Pro*, select Press, and begin printing. (You can even make the correct *Change setup:* selections if you know the type of computer and laser printer beforehand.)

All you need is one copy of each page. If you've planned ahead, it won't take more than a few minutes per page. These are your masters, which you can later photocopy or take to a print shop.

Copy centers. Copy shops are another source of laser time. As desktop publishing attracts more users, more businesses try to serve those customers. Many desktop publishers can't afford their own laser printer, and so need to rent laser-printer time. Copy centers and some small print shops, first in California and now in many large cities, saw and filled that need. Kinko copy centers and AlphaGraphics copy shops are just two of the chains that have installed computers and laser printers.

Because desktop publishing first became possible on the Apple Macintosh, many such centers have set up Macs and LaserWriters. But as more and more IBM owners turn to desktop publishing, more of these copy centers will include IBM PC computers. Look for IBM PCs and PC-driven laser printers to pop up in many more of these laser rental stores as time goes by.

Such places charge much like computer stores—by the hour, by the page, or both.

All of this may sound like a lot of work. It is, but once you see your *Newsroom* newspaper printed on a laser printer, you'll realize it was worth the time, effort, and money.

Not everyone's newspaper is suited for laser printing. The time and money involved are substantial. You have to have access to an IBM PC with at least 512K of memory, a copy of *Newsroom Pro*, and a modem if you're currently using an Apple or Commodore to produce your paper.

Many of the advantages of laser printing can be duplicated by taking page masters to a print shop and having the newspaper printed on an offset press. The best candidates for laser printing are business newsletters, publications that use graphics heavily, or pages which include large areas of black shading (most dot-matrix printers do poorest with that).

Colors

In case you hadn't noticed, newspapers have exploded with color in the last few years. Color photographs in every issue, color graphics on almost any page. Led by papers like *USA Today*, newspapers have become more magazinelike in their use of color and have sold better because of it.

Newsroom-made newspapers can use color, too, if you're willing to spend some extra time and money in printing and production.

Here's what you'll need to set up your color printing press.

- *Newsroom*-created masters
- A can of Spray Mount (found in art and graphics supply stores)
- White paper

≡ Scissors or X-acto™ knife
≡ Personal copier or access to one. The most popular are the Canon Personal Copier series
≡ Toner cartridges in the colors you want to print in

Easy enough list to accumulate until you hit the personal copier and toner cartridges. Keep in mind, though, that you don't need to buy a copier yourself. Because of their low price, these small photocopying machines can be found in many offices and schools, and you may be able to use one for your work or school newspaper.

If you can't get access to one, and you're serious about color printing, buy a copier yourself. Considering what it can do, it's not an extravagant purchase. You can buy a copier from a reputable mail order company (like 47th Street Photo in New York City) for under $600. Toner cartridges run less than $70 each.

And with a copier always at hand, you won't have to worry about taking your newspaper somewhere for printing; you'll always have the means to run off as many copies as you want.

Switch colors. The key to your color printing, and the great thing about personal copiers, is that you can easily change the color of the copier's *toner*. Toner is the plastic powdery substance that's fixed to the paper in the copying process.

Normally, copiers use black toner to copy in black type on white paper. Machines like Canon's Personal Copiers have their toner built into a cartridge about 12 inches long by 6 inches wide. That's different than most larger copiers, where the toner is poured from a bottle into a tank. In other words, changing toner colors in a small, personal copier is as simple as opening the machine, taking out one cartridge, and snapping another into place. The whole thing takes about five minutes.

Two masters (or more). First, you need to decide how many colors your paper will use. Unless you're willing to go to a *lot* of work, stick to two colors. In fact, it's a good idea to print only the front page, and perhaps the back page, in color until you're comfortable with the process.

Create your paper in *Newsroom*. If you're going to have a two-color newspaper, print two copies of each page that will use color.

Take those two masters and decide what you want printed in each color. Since one color will probably be black—used for the text at least—start with the second color.

The way you use the second color is up to you. You may want to highlight only the banner, or the banner and all headlines, or all headlines and all graphics. Or something else entirely. Pick major elements on the page; it's almost impossible to color individual words or sentences within the body copy (though with some experience, you should be able to use second color on selected paragraphs).

Figure 7-15 shows two page mock-ups, with the different color elements shown. You may want to sketch something like this to help you decide where to use color.

Figure 7-15. Color Decisions

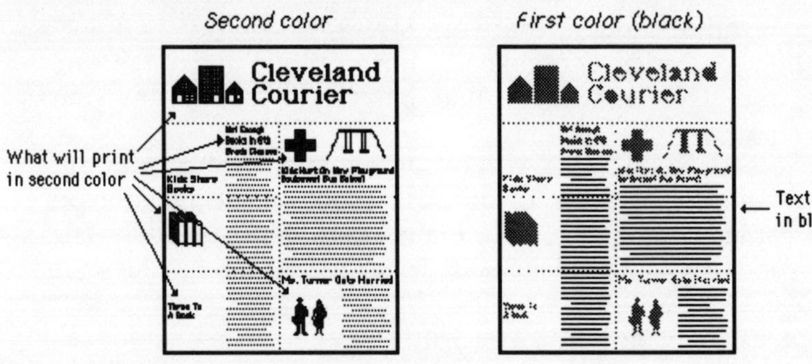

Once you've decided what to print in each color, you'll create what's called a *matte*. This matte will be a piece of white paper cut to expose only those elements on the page which will print in the selected color.

Using your scissors or art knife, cut a piece of paper so that it covers all the parts of the page which *won't* print. Fix this matte to the master with the Spray Mount, a spray adhesive which lets you pick up the matte and reposition it if necessary.

When you're finished, you should have two masters which look like those you see in Figure 7-16.

Figure 7-16. Mattes for Color

Second color

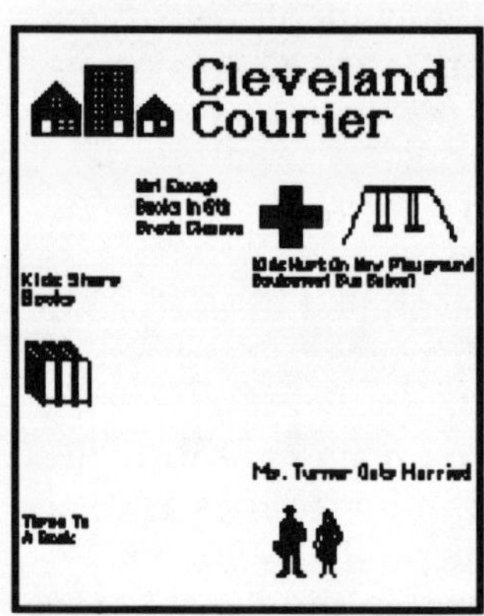

First color (black)

Registering. You're ready to begin printing. Take one of the masters and position it on the copier. Make sure you note exactly where the paper lays—most copiers have marked guides along the edges of the copy glass.

This is called *registering*. For the final copy to print correctly, with all the elements in the right places, all the masters must be positioned in the same spot. If they're not, you'll end up with a page where elements in one color are out of place and overlap what's printed in the other color. Figure 7-17 is a good example.

Figure 7-17. Out of Register

Copy this first master. Make more copies than you'll need—an additional 20 should do—to account for paper jams and other mistakes later on. Take these copies and put the paper back in the paper tray. Make sure the printed side is positioned so that the second pass through the machine copies to that same side.

Change the toner cartridge and place the second matted master on the copy glass. Again, make sure the second master is placed in the exact same spot as the first.

Run a copy through the machine; then check the color registration. If things are off, readjust the second master and run another copy. When you're satisfied, create the remainder of your copies.

That's it. You've just made your first two-color page!

Quick steps. Use this quick list as a reminder of the steps you need to follow as you color copy.

- Print as many masters as there will be colors.
- Decide which page elements will appear in which colors.
- Cut and glue mattes to the masters so that only the material in the selected color shows.
- Copy the first master after carefully noting its placement on the copy glass.

- Put printed paper back in the paper tray.
- Change toner cartridge.
- Place the second master in the same position on the glass.
- Run one copy and check registration. Adjust the master if necessary.
- Copy the second master.
- Repeat last five steps as many times as there are additional colors.

Desktop Printing

You make printing with *Newsroom* as simple or as complicated as you want. At the lowest level, you can use your printer to create every copy of every issue. At the most advanced level, you can use laser printers for sharp type and a color process for a snappy look. The best thing is that you get to decide how to print your paper.

You've explored all six of *Newsroom*'s work areas, from the beginnings of a banner to the final printed product. You're a *Newsroom* pro and have dozens of techniques, tips, and tricks now at your command.

This is the last chapter of the first section, "Make News." What comes next is a fascinating look at how other *Newsroom* users—real people—create newspapers and newsletters for their family, school, organization, or office. This second section of *Using Newsroom at Home, School, and Work* is called "Real News," and is a great source of ideas on how to find news stories, lay out pages, and print hundreds of copies.

PART 2

Real News

CHAPTER 8

News from Home

Newsroom is ideal software for the home. It's easy to learn, an important trait when your leisure time is involved. It's easy to use, which means everyone in the family can participate. And *Newsroom* puts your home computer to work doing something valuable and productive. That alone is worth its price, if only to answer the question so many computer users ask—*what can my computer do*?

Newsroom can do a lot in and for the home. It entertains as children and parents have fun putting together family newspapers, bulletins, greetings, and announcements. It educates as you and your children learn how to write stories, select appropriate illustrations, and combine them into a readable publication. And it communicates as you reach out to your readers, whether that means dozens of friends or just grandma and grandpa.

The program is fun to learn and fun to use. The results are even more exciting, for within every *Newsroom* user is a writer or editor or publisher waiting to be noticed. All it takes is some practice and some encouragement.

Wally's World

That encouragement may just be what Wally Benson offers. He uses *Newsroom* for a variety of tasks, both at home and at work. And some of what he does with *Newsroom* is not only interesting, but unique.

Benson is a captain in the San Diego Fire Department, and as such uses *Newsroom* to publish a newsletter about and for the paramedics which San Diego employs. Though not typical in its subject matter, the *Hartpoon* is a typical *Newsroom* newsletter. It has news, gossip, humor, and satire, all illustrated with customized clip art.

At home, though, he uses *Newsroom* and its clip art disks for something entirely different.

A Funny Publisher

Wally Benson publishes his *Newsroom* home creations with a Compaq computer and prints them with an Epson LX-80 printer. The Compaq, an IBM PC compatible with 640K of RAM, two floppy disk drives, and both a color and monochrome monitor, runs the IBM version of *Newsroom*.

That's the upstairs computer system. Downstairs is the Chameleon computer, another IBM clone (512K, internal monochrome monitor, external color monitor, and two 5¼-inch drives), hooked up to a different printer. Benson usually creates his *Newsroom* productions downstairs on the clone and then takes the disks upstairs to the Compaq and the Epson for final printing.

Benson was introduced to *Newsroom* by a friend who, like Wally, took his IBM-compatible portable computer to work. The friend, a paramedic, was publishing a paramedic's newsletter. A small section of that newsletter was called "The Captain's Corner."

"I started making little articles for that," said Benson. "I started enjoying it. Then I started making funny birthday cards and stuff like that for relatives." Over the last 18 months, his efforts have gathered momentum, and now Benson makes entertaining announcements and greetings for friends and relatives at the slightest excuse.

Grins and Giggles

Benson produces personalized one-page newspapers that he gives as gifts, or gives just on a whim. Each paper's subject matter is completely different from the last because each revolves around a different person.

These newspapers are sometimes cute, sometimes humorous, sometimes even a tiny bit biting. But they always reflect Wally Benson's genuine affection for the people whoh are their topic.

His brother-in-law and sister-in-law took a vacation last year, for instance, and Benson created a single-page publication to memorialize the trip. "I just sat and listened to them, what they did, where their problems were," he said. Benson's brother-in-law related a story about getting a speeding ticket, his first ever, so that was an easy story in the newspaper. To add to the short story, Benson grabbed a piece of clip art showing a car and then modified it so that it looked like it was traveling far above the speed limit.

More car troubles seemed to plague his sister-in-law, for hers kept breaking down. Out comes another car from the clip art disk, and in a few moments there's an astonished woman beside it with dollar signs flying away.

"It just kind of snowballs," Benson claimed with a laugh.

He may laugh, but do the recipients of these newspapers laugh? What do they think of it all? They're the readers, the audience, and if they don't like what they read, then it's just an exercise in laughing at others.

"They really enjoy it," he said. And he had proof to back that up. "Almost everybody that I've run these off [for] have framed them and put them up in a room someplace. Because they're so individual and so geared toward them, much like a photograph of themselves. It's a part of their life that I've written for them and chronicled for them."

There's more. On the receiving end of several such creations, his brother-in-law takes coloring pencils to all the Benson newspapers he gets. "He can't wait for the next one," Wally said with some pride.

Pretty Typical

The mechanics of Benson's work with *Newsroom* are typical of many home users. Once he knows what he's going to write about—whether it's a relative's trip or an Easter greeting to his wife—he grabs clip art from one of the three *Clip Art Collection* disks he owns. Sometimes he modifies the clip art to make it more appropriate. What kind of modifications does he make? "Maybe splitting the picture and lengthening it a little bit. Doing drawings of smoke, and things like that," Benson said. The Graphics Tools, according to Benson, are "extremely easy to use, and a lot of fun."

With the art chosen and changed, Benson makes notes about what text he'll enter. For Benson, the art comes first—in fact, picking out the clip art "gives me ideas for the copy portion," he said.

He makes notes and creates a dummy of the page so that he knows where the page elements will go once he reaches the Layout work area.

First, though, Benson creates the banner. Then, as he loads each illustration, he creates and edits the accompanying text. Benson repeats the process until the page is filled or all the clip art has captionlike copy beside or beneath it.

Layout is casual, with art and text scattered across the page. What consistency exists is in the form of one typeface for the body copy and an occasional use of graphics to define stories.

With the newspaper illustrated, written, and laid out, Wally takes the disk upstairs to his Compaq and Epson LX-80 for printing. That's his proof page, which he uses to correct any errors. The final version of the newspaper is printed to complete the project. Though one would expect he runs off just one copy and simply hands it to its subject, he doesn't quit at the Epson. "I run it off on the printer; then I go down to the copy place and usually get a little heavier stock and colored paper," Benson said. He usually picks pastels, he added, light yellows and pinks in many cases. The heavier, colored paper adds to the total effect.

A Benson paper generally takes about an hour to complete, though it's gone as fast as only 20–30 minutes. But Wally admits he can get carried away. "Sometimes when I get wrapped up in it, and making changes and printing, and everything, it's taken four hours." His wife makes suggestions, or he finds a misspelled word, and it's back to *Newsroom*. "I've gotten so wrapped up that I couldn't shut it down." Now that's an excited *Newsroom* publisher.

All in all, Benson's approach to *Newsroom* is relaxed, and in tune with the kinds of publications he's doing at home. To thousands of people like Wally Benson, *Newsroom* is more than a newspaper-creating program—it's an entertaining program that's a lot of fun to use.

It's important to remember that. If you have fun like Wally, you'll come back to *Newsroom* again and again. You'll certainly get your money's worth then.

Tips from Wally's World . . .

The best thing about *Newsroom* is "all of the pictures that you can move around and make little cartoon-type things [from]," Benson says.

There's a lot of disk swapping involved with *Newsroom* if you keep all the picture files on one disk, all the panels on another, all the page-layout files on yet another disk. That may be a neater form of organization, but it means a "tremendous amount [of disk swapping]," according to Benson.

. . . and Making a Better *Newsroom*

Wally Benson, like many *Newsroom* users, isn't willing to let a good thing alone. He wants Springboard Software to change *Newsroom* for the better. Benson's first suggestion is unique. "What would I suggest to them [Springboard]? Make it for the Amiga," he said. "Actually, that's what I would tell them. Simplify it and make it for the Amiga, so that it could run off one disk." The Commodore Amiga, Benson's newest computer (that means he has at least three machines in one house), is mouse and menu driven, using a graphics way of communicating with the user. It's much like the Apple Macintosh in those respects (or like the Apple IIGS, which is like the Macintosh).

As of this writing (late summer, 1987), Springboard has not announced any additional versions of *Newsroom*. So far, the three systems it currently works on—Apple II, Commodore 64, and IBM PC—seem to be it. Part of this reluctance may stem from Springboard's announced (but not yet released) desktop publishing package for the Apple II line called *Springboard Publisher*. An impressive program in its demonstration form, *Springboard Publisher* may have taken up a majority of the company's resources, giving it little time for translations of software like *Newsroom* to newer and more powerful computers like the Amiga, Atari ST, or the Apple IIGS.

His second suggestion is that the program should load directly into the computer's memory. Most IBM PC *Newsroom* users have plenty of RAM in their machines. Putting all of the *Newsroom* program into memory would eliminate disk swapping entirely, says Benson.

Newsroom is Fun, and Funny

Wally Benson's one-of-a-kind newspapers demonstrate the range of *Newsroom*. Not only can the program produce professional newspapers and newsletters suitable for any school or business, but it can keep its users entertained and its readers in stitches.

That's hardly common among desktop publishing software. *Newsroom* is unique, as Wally Benson demonstrates, in not only its product but also in its process. What other desktop publishing program can claim that thousands of its users think it's *fun* to put together publications?

Benson's creations are just one example of what you can do with *Newsroom* at home. It's certainly possible to write, edit, and print more normal newspapers for the family. News about family events, news from relatives, and news from friends can combine to make a lively paper.

But because of Wally Benson's newspapers, you now know that *Newsroom* doesn't have to stick to such tradition. You can have as much fun as you can imagine.

Wally's the perfect example.

What follows are two of Wally's creations, printed in their original form. Facing each page are remarks pointing out some of the particulars, and highlighting the most interesting techniques Wally used.

1 st
ANNIVERSARY
NORMA & TERRY

1986

1

2

Happy First Anniversary to Norma and Terry, Wed on the 17th of August they made it through their first year together of happily wedded bliss.

It's more fun to do things together.

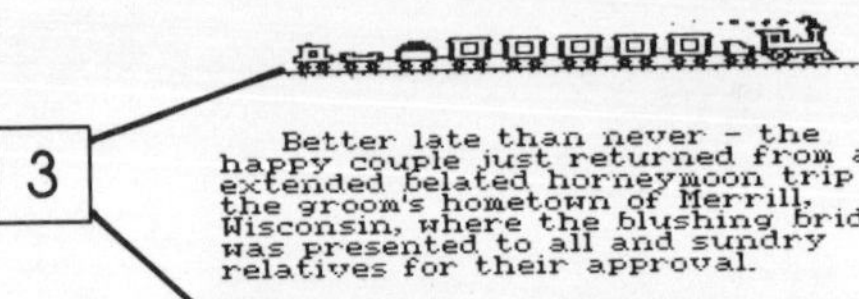

3

Better late than never - the happy couple just returned from an extended belated horneymoon trip to the groom's hometown of Merrill, Wisconsin, where the blushing bride was presented to all and sundry relatives for their approval.

The question of the week ---
Who's sick Norma or the car?
If you call her at work and she's not there-- you can bet the car is in repair.

$ $ $ $

5

Is it true that a soft, purring object sometimes insinuates itself between the loving couple to demand its share of attention.

How fast does a Lincoln travel down the open road ?

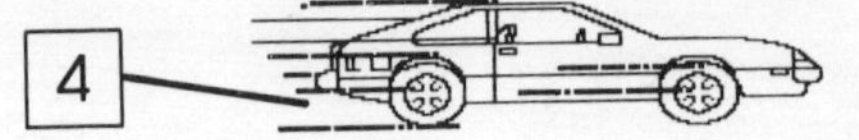

4

6

Terry and Norma took many pictures of historical sites while on their vacation, along with recording the background sounds.

1 Even though it uses two typefaces, this is an effective banner. The clip art (taken from the HOLIDAY2 file on the *Clip Art Collection, Volume 1* disk) is placed at the far right, and creates an unbalanced banner. The text on the left, especially the top two lines of *1st ANNIVERSARY* shout out the name of the announcement. *NORMA & TERRY,* since it's set in a different typeface, is obviously not part of the name or title of the issue. Because they're the subject of the newspaper, it makes sense to violate the usual rule of only one large typeface per banner. Notice how the top side of the box is thin—that was probably an accident. That happens sometimes when you draw boxes as large as the banner work space. A solution is to draw a box just inside the dimensions of the work space, ensuring equally thick sides.

2 Both this photo and the one at the top of the right-hand column were created with clip art from the *Newsroom* Clip Art disk. The cannons are simply flipped versions of the same piece of art. The woman is a flipped copy of the figure found in the upper left of WOMEN3. Both characters were selected for the way they seem to be lighting the cannon fuse. Unfortunately, the two photos really only make sense when you read the line below the rightmost photo *(It's more fun to do things together.)*

3 These two flipped copies of the train from VEHICLE1 of the *Newsroom* Clip Art disk graphically separate the text from the rest of the page. A good choice in clip art, since the copy describes a trip.

4 This modified piece of clip art started out as the car in the middle of AUTO2 from the *Clip Art Collection, Volume 1* disk. Broken lines were added once the clip art was grabbed and placed in the Photo Lab to show the car's high speed. Compare the dimensions of the car in the *Clip Art Collection* manual and its printed form. Notice how much the Epson printer stretches out clip art. In the manual, the car looks thicker and shorter.

5 The dollar signs at the left of this block of text are copies of one piece of clip art taken from the file MONEY2 on the *Clip Art Collection, Volume 2* disk. The Epson-style printing doesn't leave much of an outside margin. The gutter between the two columns is almost as wide as the margins, in fact.

6 The two photos in the bottom right corner of the newspaper were created with a collection of clip art from several clip art disks. Multipicture photos can tell entirely new and different stories simply by juxtaposing clip art that you wouldn' think of putting together (such as the outhouse and photographer at the bottom).

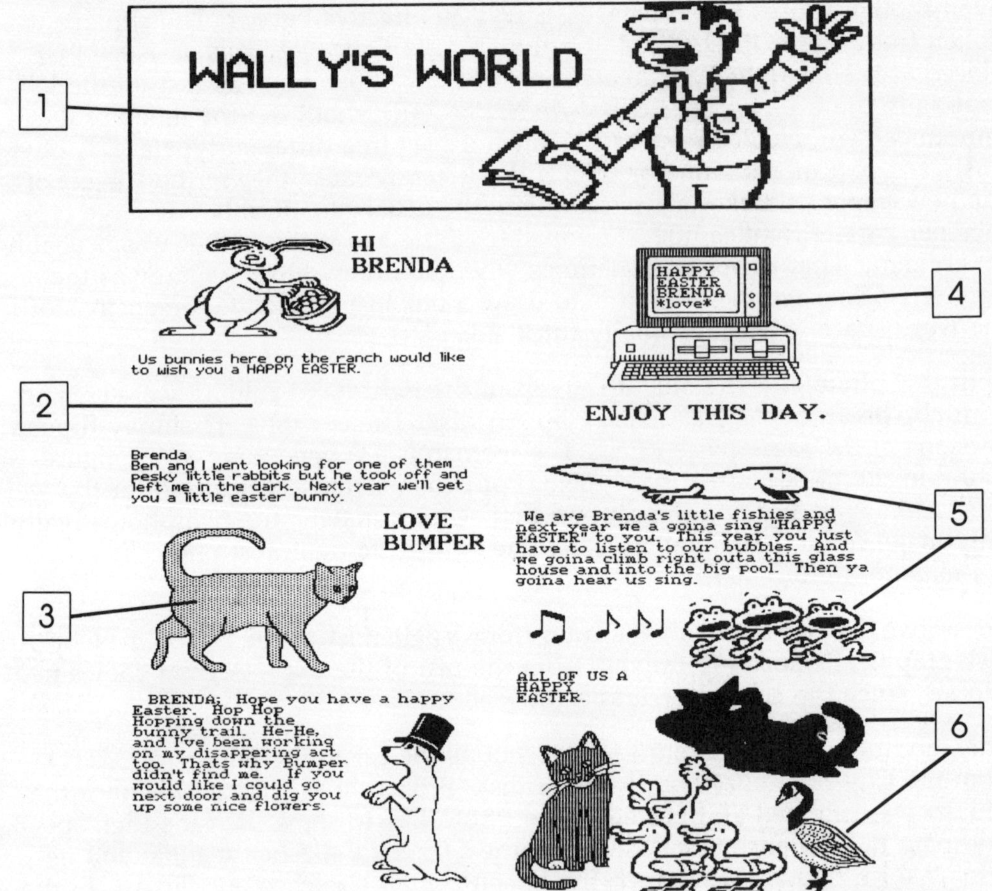
WALLY'S WORLD
1
HI
BRENDA
Us bunnies here on the ranch would like to wish you a HAPPY EASTER.
2
Brenda
Ben and I went looking for one of them pesky little rabbits but he took off and left me in the dark. Next year we'll get you a little easter bunny.
LOVE
BUMPER
3
BRENDA: Hope you have a happy Easter. Hop Hop Hopping down the bunny trail. He-He, and I've been working on my disappering act too. Thats why Bumper didn't find me. If you would like I could go next door and dig you up some nice flowers.
HAPPY
EASTER
BRENDA
love
4
ENJOY THIS DAY.
5
We are Brenda's little fishies and next year we a goina sing "HAPPY EASTER" to you. This year you just have to listen to our bubbles. And we goina climb right outa this glass house and into the big pool. Then ya goina hear us sing.
ALL OF US A
HAPPY
EASTER.
6

1 Another effective banner, this uses a catchy title *(Wally's World)* and a just-as-appropriate piece of clip art. Few people would notice that the original graphic was much larger than the Banner work space. Almost half of it was cut off. Just goes to show how well some large clip art works in a banner.

2 White space is put to good use throughout this newspaper. Part of the informal look to Benson's creations comes from the extensive white space between the short items or stories. More white space results from using so much art without wrapping text around the photos.

3 There may be more than two dozen cats on the *Newsroom* Clip Art disk, but this realistic cat was grabbed from the file BEASTS1 on the *Clip Art Collection, Volume 1* disk. It was filled with one of the patterns from the Graphics Tools menu after it was flipped to face into the page.

4 The artwork, pulled from COMPUTER1 on the *Clip Art Collection, Volume 1* disk, is large enough that you can add text to the screen. Careful positioning of the cursor and using one of the small type sizes ensures that several words fit.

5 Tadpoles and frogs, both appropriate to the story, bracket the copy to set it apart from other elements. Unfortunately, the artwork at the bottom right confuses the issue, and makes it seem as if the singing frogs are only a small part of a larger piece of art. The notes were taken from the MUSIC2 file on the *Clip Art Collection, Volume 1* disk.

6 This appears to be a filler, with four animals placed at random in a panel-sized photo. The two cats have been painted with a pattern, unsuccessfully in the case of the reclining cat. Benson may have intended the cat to be a silhouette, but its outline is hard to distinguish.

CHAPTER 9

News from School

Newsroom is superb school software. It's easy to use—even children can create their own newspapers. It appeals to a wide range of users, for teachers love writing, editing, and publishing as much as their students do. It teaches children and adults all about producing a newspaper and what goes into a paper.

Newspapers are a part of almost every junior high and high school. They not only serve as a training ground for future journalists, they also provide school-specific news to students and teachers. But traditional ways of producing a school newspaper often mean expensive equipment and costly printing fees. *Newsroom* makes it easy for any school to write, edit, lay out, and print a professional-looking newspaper for only pennies a copy. *Newsroom* and an Apple, a Commodore, or an IBM computer (hundreds of thousands of computers are already in American classrooms and can quickly be put to good use) team up to put the power of the Press in the hands of students.

And those students can be younger than ever thought possible. Because of *Newsroom*'s famed ease-of-use, even elementary-school children can use the program to type stories, select and position graphics, lay out pages, and run the printer.

Your school's newspaper can be created by a staff of 1 or a staff of 20. Student journalists can do it all, with a minimum amount of help, or any teacher can do it solo. Best of all, the process is entertaining and educational for everyone, a great combination.

With *Newsroom* you can create a school paper that tells all the news while it teaches children all about the news. What teacher or student can pass that up?

Grover's Gazette

Oak Grove School in Decatur, Illinois is an elementary school with an enrollment of about 350 children. It's a typical school, with children in grades K–6 learning about bears, books, and bluegrass; extracurricular activities ranging from swimming to basketball to reading contests; and dedicated teachers who go the extra mile.

One of those teachers is Dolly Bollero, the advisor/sponsor of Oak Grove's monthly newspaper, *Grover's Gazette*. She and her fifth-grade class produce a publication that reaches everyone in the school and makes its way to other schools and the district's administrative offices. It features news important to its readers—what *has* happened, what *is* happening, and what *will* happen at Oak Grove. It keeps students informed of upcoming events, keeps teachers informed of what their colleagues are doing, and keeps parents informed of the latest school activity. And the paper highlights students' writing in a way no report, paper, or scribbling can.

Grover's Gazette is an informative and entertaining school newspaper. Dolly Bollero makes it sound easy.

Teacher or Publisher?

"I was always big on journalism when I was in school," Bollero said. Her passion for news and newspapers is infectious (she typed the school's newspaper and printed it on a ditto machine long before *Newsroom* came along). Every month she and her 27 fifth graders write, edit, lay out, print, and distribute a 6- to 16-page paper. The children do almost all the work. They type in the stories, choose the graphics, fine-tune the banner, lay out the stories to build pages, and oversee the printing. And they do it with great enthusiasm. "The children *do* enjoy it. They really vie to stay in at recess and noon [to use *Newsroom*]," she said.

Part of that eagerness comes from using *Newsroom*. It may be a difficult program to learn, Bollero said, but speaking of her ten-year-olds, added, "once they learn it, they do well." What other program could be used by children with the results you see at the end of this chapter?

Bollero and Oak Grove have been using *Newsroom* virtually since its introduction. At a computer conference in Chicago in February of 1985, Bollero saw *Newsroom* demonstrated by a software retailer who had stayed up all night to learn the program. "I just latched on to it right then. I really liked it," she said.

Ever since then, she and her staff have been using *Newsroom*, an Apple IIe computer, two disk drives, and ImageWriter I and ImageWriter II printers to roll out a monthly newspaper that reads as well as it looks.

But most importantly, it's a student newspaper created *by* students, not *for* them. "I like it to be their own thing," Bollero admitted. Exactly right.

Grover Goes to Press

The staff of *Grover's Gazette* uses an efficient and time-tested process to put together each issue.

"They usually write about school activities," Bollero said when asked what her staff looked for in a good news story. An obvious answer perhaps, but one that should remind every *Newsroom* user, in school or not, to write about news people want to read.

"My whole class doesn't know how to use *Newsroom*," Bollero admitted, "but everyone in the school writes. One thing I've tried to impress upon the other teachers is that I want everyone to contribute." That means teachers and students alike are encouraged to write news. Their stories are dropped in

Bollero's school mailbox, she collects them, and they end up in a *Newsroom*-marked box in her classroom. Her staff (the children in her class, for everyone is a member of the staff in one capacity or another), picks up the stories and handles them from that point on.

Other times, when there's something special going on in school, Bollero will have her entire class tackle the story as a writing assignment and then pick the best one to include in the paper. Otherwise she simply asks for volunteers to take on a specific story assignment. Judging by the length of *Grover's Gazette*, she doesn't lack for eager reporters.

Only once in a while Bollero will make a suggestion. "If I think of something, I'll go ahead and tell them to try it," she said.

With ideas in hand, or assignments to cover, the student reporters write first drafts with paper and pencil. Stories from outside the staff come in on paper, handwritten or sometimes typed by teachers or the principal. Only then does the staff hit the Copy Desk work area of *Newsroom*. The fifth graders type in the stories. What's even more amazing is that they're not hunting and pecking at the computer keyboard. At Oak Grove, children learn keyboard skills with such programs as *MicroType: World of Pause*. Once they've reached typing speeds of 20 or so words a minute, they switch to word processors like *Bank Street Writer* and *Magic Slate*.

Stories written, the reporter or rewrite person (for some stories are simply typed in by someone on staff), looks for a good piece of art. "The best feature [of *Newsroom*] is being able to call up the graphics," Bollero said. "They like to call up the graphic and then rework it. They may make a smile into a frown, change hair from blonde to black, make it longer or shorter, or change a boy into a girl with a different hairdo. They've even created things from scratch."

As each article is completed, its panels are printed out. Stories are then proofread (Bollero does much of this, the one major task she saves for herself), and errors are corrected. Final versions roll out of the printer and notes are made on the paper. Such things as the disk used, the name of the file, name of the photo file (if any), and whether the story has any extra space at its top or bottom are marked. Layout is next—the most unusual part of *Grover's Gazette* process.

"I only have two girls who know how to lay out the pages. They're the ones I took aside and showed in depth how to lay out a page," said Bollero. The two girls—editors Casey Custer and Sarah Winter during the 1986–87 school year—take all the printed stories and spread them out on the floor and then lay them out to create an attractive page. They look for a number of things, particularly spacing between stories. A story which runs to the very end of its last panel, for instance, isn't placed above a story which begins at the very top of its first panel. The editors have almost total discretion on story placement and thus the appearance of the newspaper.

Bollero duplicates *Grover's Gazette* with mimeograph equipment, which presents special problems. "The ImageWriter II doesn't print out a good mimeograph stencil," she claims. The printer, almost twice as fast as the original ImageWriter, prints too quickly to cut through the stencil. Fortunately, Oak Grove has one ImageWriter I still available, and that's what the newspaper uses to create an acceptable stencil.

The Production Chain

The production and distribution parts of the newspaper process in Dolly Bollero's class deserve some special attention, if only because of the organization it shows.

The school secretaries run the mimeograph machines, printing about 400 copies of each page and then stacking up each page in a separate pile. It takes about an hour to print the typical issue.

Back at Bollero's classroom, the staff turns into a production machine many newspapers would envy. Each student has a specific job; the process depends on each child doing his or her job and even includes a measure of quality control.

Pages are put on desks and the desks arranged in a line. Four people are designated as *staplers*. One child is the *mechanic*, who keeps the staplers loaded and clears any staple jams. Two are *quality-control experts*—they keep an eye on the staplers and make sure that each issue has its pages aligned and stapled high in the upper left corner. Two *counters* stack the completed issues in units of ten, crossing the stacks as the piles grow. Another student is the *runner*, responsible for running the correct number of copies to each classroom in Oak Grove.

The rest of the class is on what's called the *chain*. They circle around, pulling off one copy of each page as they walk by the line of desks, handing a complete issue to one of the staplers. Being a part of the chain is the most boring and least appreciated job. To compensate, Bollero rewards her students for good behavior and citizenship by letting them choose their position. Those with outstanding deportment, of course, choose the better jobs, like stapler or runner.

Everyone at Oak Grove receives a copy of the newspaper, from the principal and teachers to the oldest six grader and the youngest kindergartner.

More Into and Out of *Newsroom*

Newsroom isn't the only software used to create *Grover's Gazette*. Besides the three disks in Springboard's *Clip Art Collection* series, Bollero uses such programs as *Print Shop, Magic Slate,* and even *AppleWorks* to generate specific parts of the newspaper.

At other times, *Newsroom* is used to make nonnewspaper products. No matter what the task—helping *Newsroom* put out a better paper or using *Newsroom* for things besides the newspaper—Bollero uses her imagination.

Calendars. *Print Shop* is used to create the monthly calendar that closes each issue of Oak Grove's paper. The calendar, with boxes large enough for several lines of text, is already formatted. Each day's activity is entered, and the final calendar is printed.

You can create a similar monthly calendar with *Newsroom*'s Photo Lab (see Chapter 12 for details). The final product won't look as good as something turned out by a calendar-creating program, however. Other software, like Epyx's *Create a Calendar*, can also be used. To insert material created by a program other than *Newsroom*, you either have to give it an entire page or manually paste the calendar into a partially empty *Newsroom* page. This works best if you photocopy your newspaper or have it printed at a shop.

Honor rolls. Bollero includes the school honor rolls in *Grover's Gazette*. Oak Grove has two honor rolls, and both are kept in an *AppleWorks* database file. The students' names are printed out from *AppleWorks*, and *Print Shop* is used to enhance the design.

Short stories. Occasionally, *Grover's Gazette* runs a short story written by a student at Oak Grove. *Newsroom*'s small type and clumsy text entry makes it hard to use the program for long works, and Bollero often enters these stories into the simple word processor *Magic Slate*; she then prints them from that program and manually inserts them in the issue. Accompanying art is printed from *Newsroom* clip art (sometimes by printing a banner file so that the art is enlarged) and then cut and pasted by hand before the page is duplicated.

Limericks. After her students read a number of them, she asked each child to write a limerick. They used *Newsroom* to type and illustrate each limerick (one limerick per panel), created a cover with *Print Shop,* and published a small booklet.

Creative-writing class. Bollero's advanced reading class listens to a radio program on creative writing produced at Sangamon State University in Springfield, Illinois. After her students complete their creative-writing assignments, she often uses *Newsroom* to publish a short newsletter with their work.

Bollero uses more than one duplication method to put together the different *Newsroom*-based publications. Although most of *Grover's Gazette* is mimeographed, parts of it may be photocopied from time to time. She has also used a hot thermal machine and special stencils to create mimeograph stencil masters from printed material, like the calendars created with Print Shop.

Tips and Tricks at School

Keep panels and associated photos on the same disk, Bollero advises. This cuts down on disk swapping when printing. Because of the length of *Grover's Gazette,* it often takes three data disks to hold the panel and photo files for a single issue. Banner and page-layout files are kept on yet another disk; then only two disks are necessary to print any given page. When a page-layout file is selected for printing, *Newsroom* will ask for the data disk which contains the banner file (if there is one) or the top left-hand panel. If all of a page's panels (and accompanying photos) are on one disk, only one swap of disks is necessary.

Make sure the children understand the consequences of the *Initialize data disk* command found on the Disk icon lists within the Copy Desk, Banner, and Photo Lab work areas. Even though there is a second screen warning you what will happen, it's possible to lose an entire data disk in moments.

Use serif type for the newspaper's body copy, Bollero suggests. It's a bit larger than sans serif, and so more readable.

Use large type sizes for young children, she says, noting that *Grover's Gazette* uses the type size normally reserved for headlines to print pieces aimed at kindergartners and first graders.

Avoid Epson printers if possible. Their printing is much wider than an ImageWriter and so makes graphics and text unattractive.

Create the paper with students from one class. "I find it easier to work within my own confines, because then if there's some time, 20 minutes or so, they can work on it [*Newsroom* and the paper]," Bollero said.

School House News

Grover's Gazette is not only an example of what *Newsroom* can do for school newspapers, but it's also a testament to the program's simplicity. Dolly Bollero takes her role as *advisor* seriously—her student staff does almost everything on its own, from writing and typing stories to laying out the issue and getting it to its readers.

The paper is packed with news its readers want to hear. That news is well written and fun to read. Art is used to illustrate stories and to make the paper less threatening to the younger readers.

Bollero isn't afraid to use other software where it can help her and her staff turn out a better, more informative, newspaper. From the *Print Shop* calendar to the *AppleWorks* honor rolls, *Grover's Gazette* uses appropriate Apple software to do things *Newsroom* was never meant to do.

It's a publication with personality. Few newspaper publishers could ask for more.

The rest of this chapter shows you four pages from recent issues of *Grover's Gazette,* reproduced here just as they were printed and distributed at Oak Grove. Facing each sample page of *Grover's Gazette* are specific comments about some of the interesting elements or hints about techniques used by Bollero and her staff.

1

GROVER'S GAZETTE

Oak Grove School
Decatur, Illinois

EDITORS: Casey Custer
Sarah Winter

Adviser: Dolly R. Bollero

JAN #1 1987 4

2

S.N.A.C.

By: Jeff Kelly

The meeting started at 4 P.M. with about twenty- five students from different grade schools in Decatur. We had to sign a book for attendance. Then we had a snack of carrots, celery, and cucumbers. It was good!

3

After that was over, a man showed us some ways you can make some things out of vegetables for a platter. He made flowers, tulips, and potato roses. He made a snowman out of turnips and carrots, with arms out of toothpicks. Then he made a lily out of carrots and thin sliced potatoes. They were called garnishes.

At my second SNAC meeting, we had a tour to show us where they make food and send it to the schools in Decatur.

After we were done with that, we made cookies and decorated them with candy dots and icing. I made two cookies; one for my mom and one for my dad. They said they were good. Mine was good too !

MOM DAD Good

Mail For Tots

by Sarah Winter

Room 4 has been writing to a girl named Donna Trudeau. Donna is eleven years old and has leukemia. She lives in Middlebury, Vermont. The people at Mail For Tots sent a list of ill children and adults asking for you to send mail to them. The whole class sends a letter to Donna. We will also send her cards and signs made with Print Shop.

5

ANNOUNCING A NEW BABY !

By Beth Spitzer

Mrs.Platt is taking about 20 school days off because she is adopting a newborn baby girl! Her name is Jennifer Elizabeth Platt. She was born on January 10, 1987.

6

Mrs. Platt is really excited. The baby has dark hair. Mrs. Platt does not have dark hair but her husband does so that will work out really well. The baby weighed seven pounds nine and one-half ounces. Mrs. Platt and her husband wanted a girl and they got their wish!

Mrs. Ward will be our substitute while Mrs. Platt is gone.

Needle Point

Written by Bobbie Jo Perkins

Picture drawn by Pinky Desai

7

Mrs. Platt's class did needle point. The yarn we used was different colors : dark brown, white, yellow, and orange.

When we first started, Mrs. Platt passed hers around and everyone got to do a stitch in it. I got mine done the day after I started. I think needle point is fun. You should try it too.

1 The banner is so packed with text and graphics that it's hard to read. Even though the name of the newspaper is prominently displayed in large serif type, it's almost lost among the other, smaller text. A quick fix would be to remove the names of the editors and advisor and find a place inside the issue for a staff box, where all the reporters and editors names could be listed.

2 The art is a combination of images taken from the DINING1 and DINING2 files on the *Clip Art Collection, Volume* 2 disk. The cook was flipped to face inward. If the art had been cropped a bit lower, however, text would not have wrapped back to the far left side. The single line of copy (*celery, and cucumbers. It was good!*) at the bottom is slightly distracting.

3 The story's first sentence provides three of a news story's lead paragraph five W's—Who? (25 students), What? (the meeting), and When? (4 p.m.). Overall, the story is informative and well-written. One important fact left out, however, is what S.N.A.C stands for. It's unlikely every reader knows the meaning of that term.

4 The month and year are conveniently placed in the graphic where they can be changed without disturbing the art. Although this picture looks like it was built from two separate pieces of clip art, it's actually taken from the file RODENTS3 on the *Clip Art Disk*. Notice the #*1* inserted into the body of the squirrel. The name of the newspaper, *Grover's Gazette*, is clever and shows imagination. *Grover's* is a play on the name of the school and *Gazette* is a traditional news name.

5 This full-panel graphic was created in several steps. The carriage and baby are two separate images from KIDS3 on the *Clip Art Collection, Volume 1* disk which had to be pieced together. The circle was drawn, and the bricklike fill pattern was laid down with the Graphics Tools.

6 The body copy in *Grover's Gazette* is very readable because extra space is inserted between paragraphs. Two spaces are used between sentences. Since they're marked by space above and below, there's no need to indent paragraphs.

7 The dual byline lists the person who wrote the story and the one who drew the illustration. Bylines are an easy way to recognize a writer's or an artist's contribution to the newspaper.

1

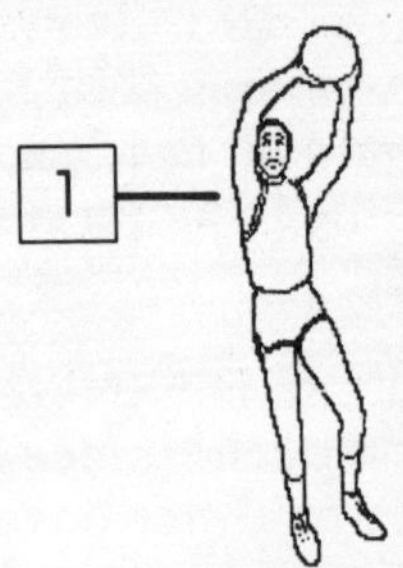

BASKETBALL NEWS

by Todd Harrison

We lost two more times, to French and to Harris. We're getting better though. Our passing, shooting, and defense are really improving.

Probably the reason we lost the last two were because the other teams were outside shooters. We're used to guarding each other and we're inside shooters.

We finally won a game. We beat Pershing 29 to 18. Scott Phillips became our first player to make two free throws.

2

Dress your craziest on Mismatch Day, February 13.

3

SPACE CAMP

by: Troy Spencer
Grade 5, Room 4

This summer I am going to go to Space Camp for a week. It is going to cost $525. They have a mock-up of a space shuttle. They also have something called a navigator and they do a simulated launch. You even eat frozen food!

The U.S. Space Camp is in Huntsville, Alabama, which is where I'll be.

4

THE GREAT BEAN CONTEST

The cafeteria people sponsored a contest to see who could guess how many soybeans were in a dispenser. ERIC LOSIER in the sixth grade was the winner with a guess of 2550. The actual number was 2586. He gets the dispenser but not the soybeans! Another close guess was 2300 by Corey French. The next closest guesses were made by Jamie Miller, Jeanna Skelley, Erica Ross, Cheri Fenton, Shantell Scott, and Ronnie Blankenship.

5

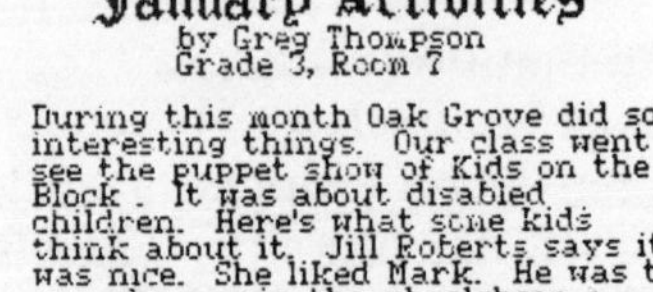

January Activities

by Greg Thompson
Grade 3, Room 7

During this month Oak Grove did some interesting things. Our class went to see the puppet show of Kids on the Block. It was about disabled children. Here's what some kids think about it. Jill Roberts says it was nice. She liked Mark. He was the one who was in the wheelchair. Angela Pane also says it was nice and she liked Mark too. Jami Hawkins says it's funny. Trudie Skelley says, "It was great!" I liked Randy.

On Fifties Day everyone had to dress up like they did in the 50's. That was fun!

6

On Martin Luther King's birthday our class had a film about Martin Luther King.

To end my story I would like to tell you about the play Jeremy Creek. This selfish little boy wants all the toys Santa has but at the end he was giving everything away.

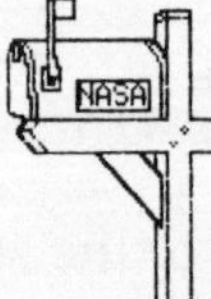

Shuttle Name

by Sarah Winter
Grade 5
Room 4

Fifth graders wrote to the Challenger 7 Fund suggesting names for the new shuttle they are planning on building.

7

President Reagan and Congress are thinking about passing a law that would require NASA to pick the new shuttle name from children's suggestions.

Most kids in our room picked Starship for the new shuttle name. Some kids picked Destination and Teacher 7. What will the new shuttle name be?

Remember your sweetie on Valentine's Day!

8

1 A good example of a school sports story. Facts are included (teams which beat Oak Grove's), an opinion or analysis is given (why the team lost), and sports celebrity names are mentioned (Scott Phillips, the boy who made the team's first two free throws). The clip art on the left came from the *Clip Art Collection, Volume 3* disk.

2 Because of the text size and its unusual border, this box really stands out. This news tidbit was created in the Photo Lab work area and then placed in the panel. The white space below the box makes it even more prominent.

3 The dotted line separates two news stories. Without it, readers would have been confused when they reached the headline *The Great Bean Contest*. There's not enough white space between the two articles, and the second head's small type size might have made some readers think it was only a subsection of the Space Camp story.

4 The small size type used for this headline tells readers that the story isn't as important as others on the page. To use a normal headline (large type), part of the story would have to be cut or it would have to be extended to the next column.

5 The art accompanying the story *January Activities* is made up of dozens of snowflakes taken from the file MISC7 on the *Newsroom Clip Art* disk. The snowflakes are grabbed from the file and repeatedly placed in the Photo Lab work area. The completed graphic is then cropped (probably across the width of the work space) and saved to disk. Finally, the photo is loaded into the Copy Desk work space, and the text is added.

6 This wrap-up of the month's activities, as seen through a third grader's eyes, makes for an interesting story. A good example of what even young children can do with *Newsroom* (one of Dolly Bollero's fifth graders undoubtedly typed it in, however).

7 This story includes an excellent lead paragraph and is a good example of news written in an inverted pyramid style. The lead answers the questions Who? (fifth graders), What? (wrote to the Challenger 7 Fund), Where? (Oak Grove is implied), and Why? (for the new shuttle being built). The story has the most important facts in the first paragraph (students suggested names) and the least important facts in the last paragraph (some of the names suggested).

8 This boxed news brief catches every reader's eye. Short news items like this are easy to create in the Photo Lab work area.

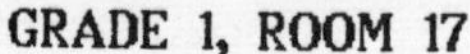

GRADE 1, ROOM 17

IF I COULD BE A
BEAR, I WOULD . . .

get away from the bees
and get honey.
1 by Tarone Woods

sit under a tree and
rest !
by Mindy Cambruzzi

dress nicely for a party.
by Jaylyn Nicole

try to get honey and
get stung by bees !
by Andy Paine

2 

sleep in my cave !
by Michael Roque

play in the sandbox.
by Jenny Key
be in a circus.
by Jennifer Sodko

talk to people.
by
Jamale
Howard

3 

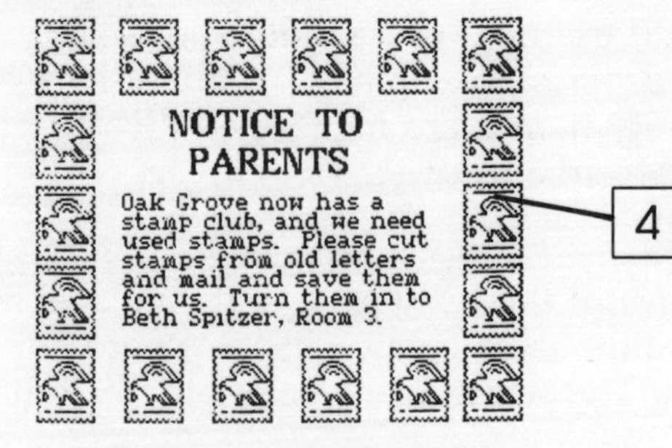 4

NOTICE TO
PARENTS

Oak Grove now has a stamp club, and we need used stamps. Please cut stamps from old letters and mail and save them for us. Turn them in to Beth Spitzer, Room 3.

Jump Rope For Heart

Oak Grove will be sponsoring our third JUMP ROPE FOR HEART day, April 4. Oak Grove earned over $2700 in 1984 and over $ 4700 in 1985 for the American Heart Association. Over 100 students participated each year. Let's make this year our biggest and best effort. 5

ALL Oak Grove students (K-6) are encouraged to participate. The event is not an individual jump rope marathon but a team event. Each student will jump rope for 2 - 3 minutes and then another team member continues. Teams will consist of six students.

The entire JUMP ROPE FOR HEART event will last from 9-12 (3 hours). Each student will be asked to get sponsors for each minute their team jumps.

All money benefits the Heart association. Students will be able to earn prizes (T-shirts, jump ropes, hooded sweatshirts, AM/FM headphone radios, satin jackets). All students participating and collecting pledges will receive a JUMP ROPE FOR HEART pen.

It's not too late to sign up. See Miss Reed (Room 16) for details.

Room 11 kindergarten will be going to Decatur Memorial Hospital for a Health Awareness Program on April 7. 6

1 *Grover's Gazette* uses large type whenever the story is written by or will be read by kindergarten and first grade students. Large type makes the story easier to read and is also suitable since the children's writings are quite short. The serif font is the most readable of the three large sizes.

2 A graphic created by combining the bear picture and three copies of the flying insect. Simple modifications like this are easy to do, especially when you have several clip art disks available.

3 Captions like the *Hi there!* in this graphic can quickly be added in the Photo Lab with lines and text. Comic strip-style balloons can be used instead. Create your own with circles or boxes, or use those in the file BALLOONS on the *Clip Art Collection, Volume* 2 disk.

4 A small stamp graphic creates the border for this full-panel special announcement. Found in the file MISC3 on the *Clip Art Collection, Volume 1* disk, the stamp was grabbed and set down several times to form the border. Careful placement made the stamps line up. Text was entered in the Photo Lab work area before the photo was cropped, saved to disk, and loaded into the Copy Desk.

5 Yet another example of a good lead paragraph. Although the news story is about an event in the future, the lead includes answers to such important reader questions as Who? (Oak Grove), What? (sponsoring a "Jump Rope for Heart" day), When? (April 4), Where? (Oak Grove implied), and Why? (for the American Heart Association). The event's name is printed in uppercase letters—that makes the event stand out from the rest of the story's copy.

6 Large type is used because the story is about a kindergarten class's field trip. The type size also makes the story appear more important.

ROOM 11 KINDERGARTENERS
MISS PETERSON

MY FISH
by Tricia Snell, Age 5

I got a fish from the store. It cost $4.00. I got the money to pay for it from my money bank.

1 My fish has black stripes on it. It is a catfish. It swims in a bowl. I keep the bowl in my living room. I call my fish Christi.

Christi likes to swim around. When I come by she hits the bowl. I think she says, "Hi!"

2 

MY FISH
by Kimberly Jackson, Age 6

I got three fish from my mom and dad. One fish is golden. I call it Number because he's a number fish. One is a blue gill. I call it Snowy. The third fish is a black one with red stripes. Its name is Color.

I put my fish in a fish bowl with a plant in it. The bowl is in the living room.

My fish like to swim. They do a trick. They swim around the plant.

MY FISH
by Brett Stenger, Age 5

I got a minnow and a goldfish at Raintree Garden. They cost $1.00. I used my allowance to pay for them.

I put them in an aquarium. The aquarium had blue rocks in the bottom. The minnow is blue and white. The goldfish is yellow. The minnow's name is Myra. I call the goldfish Skittles.

My fish like to swim.

1 This page was *not* produced only with *Newsroom*. It's reproduced here to demonstrate what other kinds of things you can include in your school newspaper. The text was typed in and printed with *Magic Slate;* notice how much more readable this type face and size is when compared with long sections of large type in *Newsroom*. *Magic Slate* also puts more space between each line of text for even better readability, something you can't really do with *Newsroom*.

2 The graphics *were* done with *Newsroom*. They were grabbed from various clip art files, modified, and saved to disk as photo files. The photo files were then printed out—directly, without putting them in panels and in a page layout—and the art manually cut and pasted or taped to the *Magic Slate*–produced paper.

CHAPTER 10

News from Clubs

Newsroom is perfectly suited to publishing newspapers, newsletters, and bulletins for any club, organization, fraternal order, or group you might belong to. Whatever a club's focus—public service, a hobby, politics, UFOs—*Newsroom* can help keep its members up to date on the latest group news.

It may be easy to get new members into your club, but keeping them is always a problem. People lose touch and lose interest. The organization loses members and loses dues. This losing spiral can be broken with an interesting and entertaining newsletter that regularly reaches every member.

Because *Newsroom* is so easy to learn, you can talk almost any member into helping to write, edit, lay out, or print the newsletter. Teaching time is minimal. And because *Newsroom* is so flexible, you can use it to produce newsletters for all kinds of clubs with all kinds of members.

Your club's newsletter can be 20 pages or 2. You can write everything and do it all or simply supervise a herd of reporters who send in stories by mail or modem. *Newsroom* lets you create the newsletter every member wants to see—something fun to read and full of news.

The *Alpha Iota Chapter News*

Alpha Phi Omega is a coeducational national service organization based on the ideals of the scouting movement. More like a community service club than a true fraternity (though its name sounds fraternal), Alpha Phi Omega has chapters across the country. One is on the campus of the Ohio State University in Columbus, Ohio. That chapter, Alpha Iota, is the sponsor of the newsletter *Alpha Iota Chapter News.*

The newsletter's audience is not just the active members of the chapter. It reaches scouting leaders and people in other areas of the Alpha Phi Omega organization and is a tool for communicating with potential members, current members, and even past members.

That alone makes it stand out from most club newsletters. But even more important, especially to *Newsroom* users, is the high quality of the publication. Not only is it packed with news and information the chapter's members find interesting and useful, but that news is presented in a well-written and attractively printed package.

Meet the Editor

Daniel Roberts, now a third-year law student, created *Alpha Iota Chapter News* and saw it through its first few years. When he began editing the newsletter, he used a simple word processor (*Bank Street Writer*), a graphics program (*Print Shop*), and paper clip art to generate text and graphics. Those printed words and pictures were hand pasted together and photocopied and then distributed to the chapter's current membership during the school summer break.

But the process was slow and clumsy. "Anything we pasted up by hand always managed to get a smudge on it," Roberts said. He was working in a computer software store at the time, and in mid-1985 he noticed *Newsroom*. He immediately bought the program. "Biggest thing that attracted us, just from reading the outside of the package, was the ability to do all the pasteup electronically," he said. That was its selling point, and its biggest advantage over more traditional newsletter publishing methods. "[Its best feature is] just being able to put everything together in one piece and then print out something that's camera ready."

Using an Apple IIe, an Apple IIc with an external drive, two printers (a C. Itoh 7500 and a C. Itoh 8510), and a mouse, Roberts and his staff put together a five or six-page newsletter four times a year. The result, some samples of which you'll find at the end of this chapter, are impressive. Roberts has since bowed out of the editor's position, leaving it to others. "The membership of the chapter had grown enough to supply more qualified people than jobs," Roberts said.

As you've found out, one of the trademarks of *Newsroom* is its ease-of-use. Roberts and the members of Alpha Iota discovered that, too, and claim it was one of the reasons why *Alpha Iota Chapter News* is so successful. Teaching others how to use *Newsroom*, Roberts said, was much simpler than it would have been with more complicated, feature-packed desktop publishing programs. And because it was so simple to learn and use, more members contributed not just stories, but gave of their time as well. That meant less work for the editor and more creativity expressed on the newletter's pages.

Making the *Chapter News*

Gathering news and writing the stories for *Alpha Iota Chapter News* was straightforward and probably typical of many newsletters. In some issues, Roberts wrote and edited everything. In other issues, he wrote only 20 percent of the newsletter, though he always edited everything. His workload depended on how many other chapter members were available and willing to write stories, lay them out, and help with printing. Generally, three or four people helped with each issue—all of them writing with the Copy Desk, most of them working on their own stories.

As time went by, though, things changed. "It was like a learning curve," Roberts said. "The longer the project (the newsletter) went on, the less the material was mine."

Creating an issue of *Alpha Iota Chapter News* usually went like this.

- Roberts and the other contributors would make a list of the story ideas they wanted to include in the issue.
- After volunteering for stories, each writer would look at the story title or description and go searching for an appropriate piece of clip art (they had all three volumes of the *Clip Art Collection* from Springboard).
- Occasionally, the art would be modified with the Graphics Tools in the Photo Lab work area. (At no time was original, non–clip art graphics used, according to Roberts.)
- The art would be added to a panel.
- Finally, the one- or two-panel story would be written at the keyboard using *Newsroom*'s Copy Desk.
- Layout was next, where the staff would make up the pages. The new banner file was positioned on the front page (more on this a bit later).
- A proof copy of each page was printed and used to check spelling, search for typographical errors, and make sure things looked good visually.
- Mistakes were corrected in each panel, and Layout was used again.
- When each page was satisfactory, a final master was printed.

Two-Color Printing

With a circulation of 200–250, it was impossible to print each copy on the computer's printer. And though Roberts had photocopied the early versions of *Alpha Iota Chapter News*, he went a different route not long after buying *Newsroom*.

The page masters were taken to a local print shop, where plates were made and placed on an offset press. What came off that press was a two-color newsletter.

The newsletter's standard banner was positioned and printed in blue on one side of 11 × 17–inch paper. On what would become the back page of the newsletter, a mailing return address was printed, also in blue. The rest of each sheet was left blank. To lower the costs of printing this stock, hundreds of copies were printed and stored at the printer's (in fact, the newsletter is still drawing from that first printing of its stock paper).

When an issue was printed with *Newsroom*, the masters were given to the printer. He took the masters and, shooting two 8½ × 11–inch pages at a time to save money, created the press plates. The printer was also responsible for making sure the pages were registered properly—in other words, insuring that the material wouldn't overlap what was already printed on the stock.

The preprinted stock, with some elements in blue, was run through the press again, this time printing with black ink.

The benefits of using a print shop, and of going with a two-color newsletter, were important to Roberts and Alpha Iota.

"It improves the impact of the issue in the mailbox," Roberts said. "It also helps establish some continuity for the newsletter format. And the single

11 × 17–inch sheet can be folded and mailed much more easily than the multiple-sheet approach we used before, which required collating, [had] more folding and stapling problems, [and used more] envelopes."

All this didn't cost the chapter any more money than if the newsletter had been photocopied. Once the preprinted stock was paid for (admittedly, a major expense), it cost about $20.00 an issue for printing. That works out to about 8¢ an issue (with 250 copies), or 2¢ per page (since one 11 × 17–inch sheet held four pages). That's well under most photocopying costs.

One of the few disadvantages was the time involved. "It required an additional three to eight days of lead time," Roberts said. But with a quarterly newsletter with less-pressing deadlines, that wasn't much of a problem. And when the newsletter ran longer than four pages or when late-breaking news developed, Roberts and his staff would prepare another page. That fifth page was printed or photocopied and slipped into the folded 11 × 17–inch paper as an insert.

If the late news wouldn't fit on a normal sheet of paper, they'd use the 8½ × 14–inch format in *Newsroom*'s Layout; then they'd reduce the page on a photocopier to fit on 8½ × 11–inch paper.

It's in the Mail

Many organizations have members scattered across several towns, counties, and states. Since the purpose of a newsletter is to keep all those members informed, you'll have to get the publication to them somehow.

The mail is the most efficient and cheapest way to do that. Check with your local post office for information on the best way to mail your newsletter and the least-expensive postal rate that you're allowed.

If, like Alpha Iota, your organization or club is a nonprofit group (most are), consider getting a nonprofit permit. The *Alpha Iota Chapter News* is mailed with that kind of permit, and according to Roberts, the cost was 7.3¢ per issue.

For a unique effect, you might want to use special stamps and cancellations. The *Alpha Iota Chapter News* did this twice. Once they use the new International Youth Year (IYY) stamps issued by the U.S. Postal Service and had them sent through the First Day Cover System. All the newsletter subscribers got an official first day cover of one of the stamps. Another time, they mailed the newsletter through the United Nations Postal Administration using the UN's IYY stamps with a New York City / United Nations cancel on the stamps.

Contact your local post office for more details on how to do special mailings like this. In Robert's experience, the Postal Service was more than happy to help. In fact, all he had to do was send the newsletters in a package to the correct address (New York City in the case of the UN cancellation) and everything else was taken care of.

Wish List

Even though *Newsroom* has simplified the newsletter publishing process, it's not a perfect program. Daniel Roberts notes three areas where he'd like to see *Newsroom* change.

Since Roberts uses the Apple version of *Newsroom*, the first modification would be to put *Newsroom* on a ProDOS-based disk and change the program so that it could save and load files from a ProDOS file structure. ProDOS, the more recent of the two most-common disk operating systems for Apple II computers (the other is what the *Newsroom* disk comes with—DOS 3.3), lets you create *subdirectories*. Like a folder, they let you organize files; you can place files within subdirectories, and those subdirectories within other subdirectories. ProDOS is most important when you have large storage space, like a hard disk or a 3½-inch microfloppy disk drive (such as the UniDisk).

The second request is a frequent one among *Newsroom* users of all kinds—the ability to see the entire page on the screen at one time. This full-screen view would make it easier to see how changes affected the page as a whole, not just one panel or banner.

The third suggestion would be to take advantage of the Apple IIGS's enhanced graphics capabilities and additional memory by adding new features (like the full-screen view). Roberts just recently bought an Apple IIGS, and like many owners, wants to see IIGS-specific software, not simply Apple IIe–like programs.

Springboard released their Apple IIGS update in May, 1987. If you have an Apple IIGS, send in your *Newsroom* Master disk and Springboard will return an updated version of the program. The update, however, is minor and doesn't add any IIGS-only features. The sole change is to the printing routines—the update lets you print *Newsroom* publications through the IIGS's printer port rather than requiring you to buy a separate card. If you want to use the Wire Service work area, though, you still must have a card of some sort installed (or an Apple IIe–compatible internal modem). The update will not let you use the IIGS's modem port.

Chapter News Bits and Pieces

Keep each issue on separate disks, Roberts suggests. One issue's worth of files (banner, panels, photos, and page files) would fill up an entire disk. It worked out best when *a single* issue was kept on *a single* data disk.

Being able to exchange material with other newsletters is an added bonus of *Newsroom*. Though he didn't get a chance to try it out before he left the editor's position, the sectional office for Alpha Phi Omega is now using *Newsroom*. "They liked what we were doing," said Roberts, "so they went out and bought it. [It] enables some file trading."

Typing too fast often made the Copy Desk work area wrap words incorrectly. "It (the Copy Desk) would just split a word where you didn't want it split." The solution? "Just don't type so fast."

You only need *Newsroom*, Roberts said. He and his staff used the program and the three volumes of clip art to do everything. They considered a *Print Shop*-to-*Newsroom* graphics conversion program called *ClipCapture*, but didn't buy it. (See Chapter 4 for information on *ClipCapture* and other *Newsroom*-related conversion programs.)

Serving Its Members Since 1985

The *Alpha Iota Chapter News* is a good demonstration of what *Newsroom* and some non-*Newsroom* publishing techniques can do. Typical of a club newsletter in the news it contains and in the writing experience of its staff, *Chapter News* stands out because of the way it's printed and the two-color format it uses.

It also illustrates an important part of newsletter production—involving the group's members in its creation. Take a look at the four sample pages which end this chapter and you'll see that several people—not just the editor—wrote news stories and selected graphics. Your newsletter should try to do the same. A one-person staff may work for small publications, but sharing the work does much to make sure the newsletter stays alive and well.

Roberts and his staff created a newsletter with a voice and look that its readers were comfortable with. That's just as important as the information it contained.

Four pages of *Alpha Iota Chapter News* are offered here for your viewing. Reproduced as they were created by Daniel Roberts and his staff at Alpha Iota, the figures include references to comments on the facing page. These comments point out some of the interesting and important page elements or techniques you may want to try.

Alpha Phi Omega National Service Fraternity

3 Columbus,Ohio | New Series V3 #2 | Spring 1986

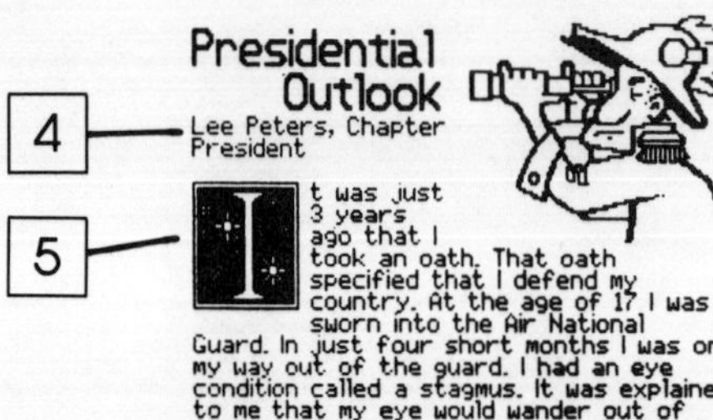

Presidential Outlook

4 Lee Peters, Chapter President

5 It was just 3 years ago that I took an oath. That oath specified that I defend my country. At the age of 17 I was sworn into the Air National Guard. In just four short months I was on my way out of the guard. I had an eye condition called a stagmus. It was explained to me that my eye would wander out of focus then jerk back to focus again only to repeat the process. Last summer I went through an operation so that my eyes would not wander so far off focus.

6 I feel that a similar situation has developed in the Alpha Iota Chapter. We have wandered off our focus then had to jerk back in to focus. We must remember our three principles of Friendship, Leadership, and Service. Service is an important part of our Fraternity but we must not forget the other two key aspects of Leadership and Friendship. We need an equal balance of these three things in order to be successful. Thus, my theme for the quarter is "BACK TO FOCUS"

I now challenge this chapter and its members to set out and accomplish several goals. First, to build membership. Second, to attend the Section Conference at The Bowling Green State University in Bowling Green, Ohio. Third, Plan on attending the Chapter Program Planning Conference in May. Fourth, extend your hand in Leadership, Friendship, and Service. If all these goals **are met** by all **brothers we** will indeed be

BACK ON FOCUS

Mini-Kool is Coming!!!

Mini-Kool

Hey Folks!!!, Plan NOW on helping with MINI-KOOL Fridge Pick-ups during the last week of the quarter. This is THE ONLY FUNDRAISER Alpha Iota does for its own benefit all year. You can start lifting weights now to get into shape or just carry your fridge up and down a nearby staircase. Remember, We need all the help we can get so check in with meetings or the office if you can help. Note: If you can't lift we can still use your help with cleaning and writing.

ELECTION REPORT

8

The Alpha Iota Chapter is happy to report the election of new officers for the coming three quarters. The next elections will be at the end of Winter Quarter 1986.
Lee Peters, past Service Vice-President was elected Chapter President.
Manny Flowers, Banana Split Chairman was elected Membership Vice-President.
Larry Ellis was elected Service Vice-President.
David Ward was elected Treasurer.
Chuck Shuey, Past Treasurer was elected Chapter Secretary.
Congratulations and Good Luck to All.
Mr. Banana Says: "Be There May 13 Y'all"

ELECTION REPORT

Operation Feed

The Foodbank is the central Warehouse for Operation Feed. It supplies food pantries with food for the needy. Hilary Godard, Manny Flowers, Lee Peters, and Chelsie Rhodes made the trip over to 25th avenue to sort and box massive **amounts** of crackers and other food. In addition to providing service for a worthy cause all of the members who participated had a really good time.

1 The banner was one of the two elements preprinted on the stock. Except for the location, volume, and date information, the entire banner is printed in blue. The art was edited by turning the left-hand character's original frown into a smile. The line which begins *Alpha Phi Omega...* is set in small sans serif, probably because it wouldn't fit if serif type had been used (it's 43 characters long).

2 The small piece of art in the middle of the banner is an emblem of the Alpha Phi Omega fraternity. It's not *Newsroom* clip art, but was originally drawn on paper. This was pasted in manually by the printer. "There are some things you just can't get electronically," said Roberts.

3 This information line is part of a banner file which each issue shares. The date, volume, and number changes with every issue. This line is at the bottom of the Banner work space screen—the space above it is left blank to account for the preprinted banner on the stock. "Using the banner for page 1 allowed us to be more careful about laying out a sheet that wasn't too big, one that would fit," said Roberts.

4 Notice that many of the stories in *Alpha Iota Chapter News* contain a *byline*, or author's name and title, beneath the headline. This is just one way to give recognition to your writers.

5 The *inset cap* is clip art from the file LETTERS 1 on the *Clip Art Collection, Volume 1* disk. Saved as a photo file, it was added to this panel. The graphic must have been cropped close to its right side since the type isn't far away.

6 To break up the large areas of text, additional spaces have been inserted between paragraphs.

7 This large graphic doesn't leave much room for the text at the right. The remaining space is so narrow that the copy beside the graphic looks strange. It would have been better to either drop the art entirely or crop it so that text wouldn't wrap around (and thus lengthen the story beyond the third panel). This art also "looks out" of the page, for the figure is facing to the left. Flip it so that the reader's eyes are kept on the page.

8 At first glance it seems that there are two stories titled *Election Report*. However, the headlines are only being used to frame the story. Less confusing would have been a text-filled box created in the Photo Lab; a similar but simpler method would have been to insert two horizontal rules at the top and bottom of the panel.

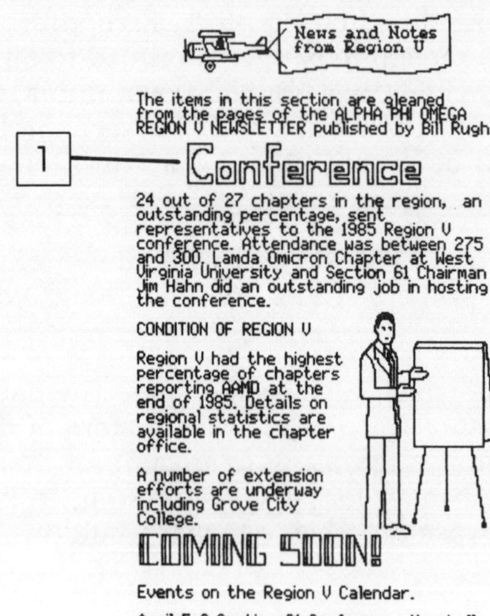

The items in this section are gleaned from the pages of the ALPHA PHI OMEGA REGION V NEWSLETTER published by Bill Rugh.

Conference

24 out of 27 chapters in the region, an outstanding percentage, sent representatives to the 1985 Region V conference. Attendance was between 275 and 300. Lamda Omicron Chapter at West Virginia University and Section 61 Chairman Jim Hahn did an outstanding job in hosting the conference.

CONDITION OF REGION V

Region V had the highest percentage of chapters reporting AAMD at the end of 1985. Details on regional statistics are available in the chapter office.

A number of extension efforts are underway including Grove City College.

COMING SOON!

Events on the Region V Calendar.

April 5-6 Section 61 Conference Marshall University Huntington, West Virginia

April 11-13 Section 57 Conference Bowling Green State University BG, OHIO

(late Summer) Region V staff retreat

National Capital Campaign

The National Fraternity has launched a new capital campaign to raise funds to buy our own National Headquarters building.

The current situation in the Waltower building is at best unstable. We are on a month to month lease. The building will be sold in the very near future. A subsequent increase in rent is likely. It is even possible that the new owner could ask us to vacate the building.

There is a need to acquire our own building and endow it. Now, more & more of our regular income goes toward the operation of the office & less & less for programs and services. Our own, properly endowed, building will enable the fraternity to better focus on programs & services.

What will it take to do this? We have set a goal of $1 million. We are not asking undergraduates to contribute money. (naturally we will accept any!!); We plan to raise the money over the next three years from Alumni. Contact any Chapter President for details on how you can help.

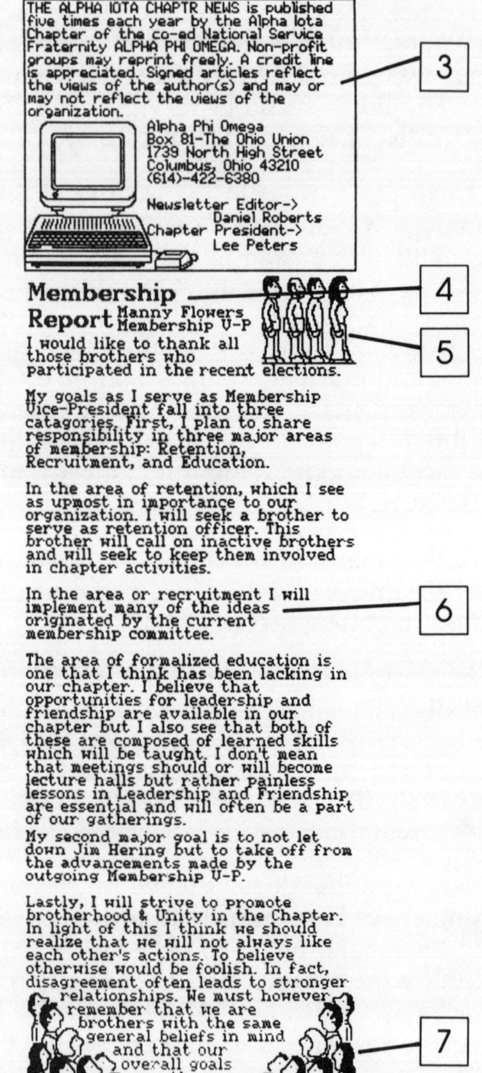

THE ALPHA IOTA CHAPTR NEWS is published five times each year by the Alpha Iota Chapter of the co-ed National Service Fraternity ALPHA PHI OMEGA. Non-profit groups may reprint freely. A credit line is appreciated. Signed articles reflect the views of the author(s) and may or may not reflect the views of the organization.

Alpha Phi Omega
Box 81-The Ohio Union
1739 North High Street
Columbus, Ohio 43210
(614)-422-6380

Newsletter Editor-> Daniel Roberts
Chapter President-> Lee Peters

Membership Report

Manny Flowers
Membership V-P

I would like to thank all those brothers who participated in the recent elections.

My goals as I serve as Membership Vice-President fall into three catagories. First, I plan to share responsibility in three major areas of membership: Retention, Recruitment, and Education.

In the area of retention, which I see as upmost in importance to our organization. I will seek a brother to serve as retention officer. This brother will call on inactive brothers and will seek to keep them involved in chapter activities.

In the area or recruitment I will implement many of the ideas originated by the current membership committee.

The area of formalized education is one that I think has been lacking in our chapter. I believe that opportunities for leadership and friendship are available in our chapter but I also see that both of these are composed of learned skills which will be taught. I don't mean that meetings should or will become lecture halls but rather painless lessons in Leadership and Friendship are essential and will often be a part of our gatherings.

My second major goal is to not let down Jim Hering but to take off from the advancements made by the outgoing Membership V-P.

Lastly, I will strive to promote brotherhood & Unity in the Chapter. In light of this I think we should realize that we will not always like each other's actions. To believe otherwise would be foolish. In fact, disagreement often leads to stronger relationships. We must however remember that we are brothers with the same general beliefs in mind and that our overall goals are the same.

1 This unusual headline looks hand-drawn, but it's actually a piece of clip art from the *Clip Art Collection, Volume 2* disk. Since it's so different from the normal headlines, it calls the reader's attention. Overuse of such display headlines, however, weakens their impact and only confuses the reader. Two on one page (as is the case here) is one too many.

2 A very effective combination graphic and headline is used for this news item. This is probably the first thing a reader will look at on this page. Note that the same typeface is used for the headline as is used for the body copy. This is a common occurrence in *Alpha Iota Chapter News,* as is a mixing of sans serif and serif typefaces for both headlines and body copy. This page uses sans serif for the left column, serif (mostly) for the right. The lack of consistency detracts from the newsletter's appearance and readability.

3 The *Alpha Iota Chapter News* staff box is a standard panel file transferred to each issue's data disk. Unlike most staff boxes, which simply list the people who put together the publication, this includes a short description of the newsletter as well as its address.

4 Headlines and bylines could have been separated with some white space for easier reading and clarity.

5 Although this graphic "faces" out of the page, the effect only slightly disrupts the design. That's because this is page 2 of an issue—*Alpha Iota Chapter News* is printed on 11 × 17–inch paper and so has facing pages inside. Many reader's will thus look at this graphic and then at the next (facing) page 3.

6 Some of the words in this paragraph should have been manually hyphenated in the Copy Desk work space so that the unsightly gap in the text was removed.

7 This unusual graphic nicely frames the story's text. The way the text appears close to the art and unevenly aligned indicates it was created in the Photo Lab. The art was selected (PEOPLE 3 from the *Clip Art Collections, Volume 2* disk) and placed in both bottom corners of the Photo Lab work space. One copy was flipped. The text (or at the least all the text from the line *relationships. We must however . . .* on down) was entered in the Photo Lab. The entire graphic was then inserted into a panel.

1

Things to Do

Please Note-This Schedule is not complete. Other events will be added later. All Regular Meetings are Tuesday at 6pm in the Ohio Union.

APRIL

SUN	MON	TUE	WED	THU	FRI	SAT
		1lr	2	3r	4	5sf
6	7	8lr	9	10	11 bg	12 bg
13 bg	14	15l	16	17	18	19
20	21	22l	23	24	25	26s
27s	28	29l	30	l=meeting f=social s=service		

r=rush activity bg=sectionals

2

APRIL

1st -Rush Event and Big Training
3rd -Rush Event
5th -Foxfire Skills Day-Lazarus
-Operation Feed Collection Project
-Section 61 Conf. Marshall Univ.
6th -Section 61 Conf. Marshall Univ.
8th -Regular Meeting
-Pledge Ceremony
-Officer Inductions
11th -Section 57 Conf. BGSU
-WWW Spring Fellowship-Lazarus
12th -Section 57 Conf. BGSU
-WWW Spring Fellowship-Lazarus
13th -Section 57 Conf. BGSU
-WWW Spring Fellowship-Lazarus
14th -Exploring Recognition Dinner
15th -Regular Chapter Meeting
16th -BSLBT #1-Westerville
18th -Law School Talent Show-Ohio Union
19th -Challange Adventure-Lazarus
22nd -Regular Chapter Meeting
23rd -BSLBT #2-Westerville
26th -WBNS-OPERATION FEED project
-Explorer Road Rally
-Cub-O-Rama-Fairgrounds
27th -March of Dimes Walkathon
29th -Regular Chaptr Meting
30th -Last Day of Spring Semester class
-BSLBT #3-W'ville

3

MAY

SUN	MON	TUE	WED	THU	FRI	SAT
				1	2	3
4	5	6l	7	8	9	10
11	12	13ss ssss	14	15	16	17
18	19	20l	21	22	23	24
25	26	27l	28	29	30	31

4

MAY

6th -Regular Meeting
7th -Spring Semester Finals Begin
-BSLBT #4-Westerville
8th -Anniversary of the Founding of the Alpha Iota Chapter
9th -WWW Ordeal-Brotherhood Lazarus
11th -MOTHERS' DAY
13th -BANANA SPLIT!!!!!!!!!!!!!!!!!!!!!!!!
14TH -BSLBT #5-Westrville
16th -Spring Semester Finals End
-EC6A Conclave at Lazarus
17th -OSU Alumni Day
-EC6A Conclave at Lazarus
20th -Regular Meeting
21st -BSLBT Make Up Session
25th -Hands Across America
26th -MEMORIAL DAY-No Classes
27th -Regular Meeting
31st -WWW Ordeal-Brotherhood-Lazarus

JUNE

SUN	MON	TUE	WED	THU	FRI	SAT
1	2	3l	4	5	6	7
8	9	10	11	12	13	14

JUNE

3rd -Regular Meeting
4th -Pre Outdoor Experience Meeting for BSLBT

5

6th -Spring Quarter Classes End
7th -BSLBT Weekend Starts
9th -Spring Quarter Finals Start
12th -Spring Quarter Finals End
13th -Spring Quarter Commencement
15th -Tenative Release of V3 #3 of the Alpha Iota Chapter News
20th -WEST VIRGINIA DAY
23rd -Summer Quarter Classes Start
-Summer Term 1 Classes Start

JULY

10th -Woodbadge Troop Meeting-Lazarus
18th -WWW Ordeal-Brotherhood-Lazarus
23rd -Last Day Summer Term 1 Classes
24th -Summer Term 1 Finals
25th -Summer Term 1 Finals
28th -Summer Term 2 Classes Start

AUGUST 1st -Tenative Release Date for V3 #4 of the Alpha Iota Chapter News.
AUGUST 9th -16th Woodbage-Camp Buckeye
AUGUST 26th -Last Day Summer Classes
AUGUST 27th -Fall Semester Classes Start
SEPTEMBER 24th -Fall Quarter Classes
OCTOBER 1st -Tenative Release of V3 #5
OCTOBER 5th -Musical Chairty
NOVEMBER 1st -APHIO National Service Day
DECEMBER 27th-30th -National Alpha Phi Omega Conference = Houston, Texas

HANDS ACROSS AMERICA

Hands Across America is Coming Sunday May 25th. For more information call (614)-228-HAND or the Chapter Office.

6

Swim for Diabetes

Dave Ward completed 50 laps in the Swimathon APHIO sponsered Dave at $1 a lap. Congrats to Dave for his efforts.

WOODBADGE

The Central Ohio Council, BSA is hosting Woodbadge course EC-323 August 9-16, 1986 at Camp Buckeye. Adult leaders in the scouting program are invited to take advantage of this outstanding training opportunity. For more information contact Dan Roberts at 5462 Blue Ash Rd. Columbus, Ohio 43229 (614) 294-8731 or the COC.

1 This page was an insert into the normal four-page newsletter, printed on a single 8½ × 11–inch sheet and slipped between pages 2 and 3. Since most of the page is schedule information and since the headline *Things to Do* is a good one, this page would have been a perfect place to use a two-column head (see Chapter 6 for details on how to create one).

2 The calendar is clip art from *Clip Art Collection, Volume 1*. The name of the month is another graphic found in the same file (TIME 1). Dates must be placed in the boxes with one of the small type sizes while in the Photo Lab. Unnecessary boxes (before and after the month's starting date, for instance) can be erased with the Eraser from the Graphics Tools menu. Note the key at the bottom right of this calendar—it indicates what the letter codes on various dates stand for.

3 More detailed explanations of the month's activities are listed here. Even though this was entered in the Copy Desk, it's hard to spot any column alignment problems. A clearer headline for this information would have helped considerably. At present, the head (APRIL) is below and to the right of the calendar. It's lost among all the other type of the same size and face.

4 Another calendar, but with fewer letter codes. Such codes are a good idea, since only eight characters, counting the date, can be squeezed into each box. The pattern-filled boxes at the top right of the calendar only confuse the reader.

5 The page's third calendar. Note that four of the six weeks on the original clip art have been erased. If you don't have *Clip Art Collection, Volume 1*, you can create something similar with small boxes drawn in the Photo Lab. Aligning them isn't a problem. Once you've made a standard calendar, save it with a memorable name like *CALENDAR*.

6 This graphics and text was created entirely within the Photo Lab. Once the map was placed on the screen, text in small and large sizes was entered across it. The shaking hands clip art was taken from another disk (*Volume* 2) and positioned, probably before the text was typed in.

1

Boy Scout Art Auction

The First Annual Boy Scout Art Auction of the Central Ohio Council was a success. Besides becoming cultured APHIO brothers were kept busy unloading, setting up, tearing down, and generally helping out with the leg work for the auction itself. We recieved a thank you note from Charlie Largent of the Central Ohio Council complimenting us on a doing a fine job. Six people came out for this project including a potential pledge. Thanks to everybody for a job well done.

2

CPL BOOK SALE

The Public Library of Columbus and Franklin County recieved our help for a special book sale. We even had too much help at several times, more brothers willing to help than there was work for, but everything went well. Our job was to restock tables during the sale. The Friends of the Library raised close to One Thousand, five hundred dollars with our help. That money will be used for different programs that directly benefit the community by improvements in the public library system of Columbus and Franklin County. Thanks Gang!!!!

Assorted Notes from.... THE NEWSROOM

Thanks to the foldin' and mailin' crews that helped out with the last two issues of the Newsletter.

Special Thanks this issue go to Lee Peters and all the officers, past and present, who submitted articles for this issue. Lee was especially helpful by submitting drafts of a number of the unsigned articles in this issue.

7

Lets get rolling for Sectionals at BG. No doubt this will be a highlight of your time in APHIO. All past BG-APHIO activities we've attended have been great!!!

Our new Advisors reported in the last issue have been duly installed. The Party at the installation was a good time for almost all who were there. If that comment seems cryptic to you you should attend more chapter activities.

The Surplus Duplicating Equipment that has been stashed in the office for several years has been donated to other groups who can make better use of it. The two smaller machines went to the Ohio State University Office of Forensics and the larger unit was donated to the Undergraduate Student Government.

Mr. Banana is safe from the Kidnappers and in hiding. HE URGES YOU to attend the 1986 ALPHA PHI OMEGA BANANA SPLIT May 13 in the Ohio Union West Ballroom. Be There!!!

3

Are you ready to go
BANANAS?? Annual Banana Split
for Charity $1.50
all you can eat. W. Ballroom. 7:30pm.

4

Alpha Iota Chapter
Alpha Phi Omega
Box 81-The Ohio Union
1739 North High Street
Columbus, Ohio 43210

Bulk Rate

6

5

1 This example of a headline set in English type shows how much harder it is to read than serif or sans serif. Readers can't just glance at the words; they must concentrate, perhaps read them more than once.

2 Even harder to read is this headline, which also uses the English typeface. The headline is in all uppercase characters, however, making it doubly difficult to read.

3 An ingenious advertisement. When the issue was put together, folded by thirds, and stapled for mailing, the ad appeared opposite the mailing label area. It's printed upside down so that when the second fold is made (right above the mailing label's rule), the ad is right-side up. The advertisement was built from parts of two pieces of clip art—the top of the sundae from DINING2 and the bottom two-thirds of the ladle (with the bowl of the ladle itself filled in with black) from DINING1—found on the *Clip Art Collections, Volume 2* disk. The graphics were positioned, and the text was added in the Banner work area. Once constructed, the banner was printed on a sheet of paper. That paper was then turned upside down and reinserted into the printer to print the rest of the page. When this page was created, only the top four panels were filled—the third row was left blank for the ad, and the fourth row remained blank to account for the mailing label already on the preprinted stock.

4 The mailing label area was the second part of each issue on the preprinted stock. Like the banner, this appears in blue. The text was entered in the Banner work area so that it would appear larger. A master was made and given to the printer.

5 Another Alpha Phi Omega emblem was pasted in by hand by the printer.

6 When the mailing label was created in the Banner work area, space was left here for the recipient's address. Notice that the term *Bulk Rate* is positioned so that it will appear directly below the stamp and cancellation.

7 An interesting feature, much like an editor's page in a magazine, this is written by the editor of *Alpha Iota Chapter News*. It keeps the members informed of any newsletter-related news. You may want to run something like this in your club's newsletter, since the publication is one of the most visible and perhaps one of the most important aspects of your organization. This column could also be used for club gossip, news tidbits too trivial to justify their own story, and other such things.

CHAPTER 11

News from Work

Newsroom can easily and quickly produce newsletters for businesses of all sorts—new or established businesses, companies with one employee or scores. *Newsroom* can help you reach the people you work with or reach your customers. And since it's so simple to use, almost anyone in your organization can learn how to create an impressive publication.

Your newsletter may take one of many forms. It may be quite simple, perhaps just one page a month. Or it may be longer and appear more often. You may want to stick to traditional *Newsroom* design, or you may want to try one of the techniques you've read about in this book. Maybe you'll insert dazzling graphics, or clip art, or even digitized photos. It's all up to you.

Craigmont Planetarium Skylights

In many ways, the Craigmont Planetarium of Memphis, Tennessee is run like any business. It offers a service, competes for customers, and gauges its success on how well it satisfies those customers. But in other ways, the planetarium is different. First of all, it's financed and run by the Memphis City School District and housed in Craigmont High School. Secondly, its customers are mainly school-aged children. And third, it seeks to educate as well as entertain its audiences.

That's not to say the planetarium doesn't have a businesslike air. Its director, Duncan R. Teague, is a knowledgeable and professional astronomer. His employees (actually unpaid student interns from Craigmont Senior High) are enthusiastic about their jobs. And the monthly newsletter, the *Craigmont Planetarium Skylights*, is a well-written and well-designed publication that communicates effectively with its readers.

A Veteran *Newsroom* Publisher

Teague and the Craigmont Planetarium have been using *Newsroom* since the fall of 1985. Before that, any news the planetarium wanted to share went out in a monthly bulletin prepared by the school district. A change at the district office—only letter-quality print was accepted since an optical character reader was used to enter information—forced Teague into a decision. He already had an Apple IIe and a dot-matrix printer. Why not use the computer to publish the planetarium's own newsletter? "*Newsroom* was the first of the desktop publishing programs," Teague said, and so he began using the program to write, edit, lay out, and print a one-page monthly newsletter.

It began as *The Comet Halley Flyer*, which was full of news and information about comets in general and Comet Halley in particular. It was so well received that when interest in Comet Halley faded, he kept the newsletter. It changed to become the *Craigmont Planetarium Skylights*, the planetarium's general newsletter.

With an Apple IIe, two disk drives, an ImageWriter II printer, and a mouse, Teague and his interns (during the 1986–87 school year, they were Robert Buice, Jennifer Merritt, Malinda White, and John Williams) put together a six-panel page once a month. Teague doesn't get involved in much of the actual production. Although he's a veteran *Newsroom* user, the four student interns do almost all of the writing, editing, and proofreading, as well as selecting or creating graphics, laying out the page, and generating a master copy for the printer.

One of the great things about *Newsroom* is that it's so easy to use. Simple enough, for instance, that employees who have no previous journalism experience can learn how to build a paper from scratch. That's the experience of the four student interns at the planetarium—they're astronomy students, not writers. But they have no trouble using *Newsroom*.

Putting Things Together

The *Craigmont Planetarium Skylights* is produced like many business newsletters. The staff—in this case the four interns—suggest story ideas to Teague, the editor. Sometimes the story is based on something they've read in an astronomy magazine; other times ideas are staff originals. The whole process is pretty informal. Story ideas are discussed among the staff and then each intern picks a story to pursue. At this point, Teague may have to make some editorial decisions about which stories should run and how long each should be. Since there are four interns but six panels to fill, some stories will be longer, and thus have more importance in the issue.

The interns do their research, sometimes going to Teague who makes sure they understand the material. A rough draft, done with paper and pen, is the result. Only then are the stories entered in the Copy Desk. Headlines are typed in, followed by the body copy. The last step before saving to disk is to insert graphics or clip art in the panel (the art is preselected).

Once each intern has her or his story typed in, Layout is used to build the page. The one-page newsletter requires a banner, which hasn't changed since its inception; the same banner file is used issue after issue. The only thing that's altered is the publication date.

Everything's ready for printing when the files are arranged in Layout. Printing masters takes time and patience, primarily because the ribbons the planetarium uses in its ImageWriter II often print light, especially in extremely dark areas of a graphic. Five or six masters may have to be printed before an acceptable one comes out. With a print run of over 400, it's more economical to print the newsletter than to photocopy it. Teague uses a local quick-print shop to produce the newsletter in final form. The result is a more attractive newsletter. It's also less expensive. *Skylights* costs about $12.00 an issue to print, or about 3¢ a copy.

It takes about one day—from writing to printing—to put out one issue of *Skylights*. And though it's primarily an intern-created paper, Teague acts as a publisher as well as an editor, for he says, "I'm ultimately responsible for the accuracy of anything the planetarium distributes."

Great Graphics the Easy Way

Newsroom isn't known for its specialized graphics. By necessity, *Newsroom*'s clip art must fit many kinds of stories. There's not much business-specific clip art on the disk which comes with the program. There's certainly not much clip art appropriate for a planetarium.

And graphics are very important to the *Skylights* newsletter, according to Teague. In fact, two of his interns, Malinda White and Jennifer Merritt, considered the clip art and the program's general graphics abilities to be one of its strong points. Yet, producing graphics appropriate to their stories takes time. "One of the more time-consuming aspects of *Newsroom* is using the Graphics Tools to produce your own artwork," says Teague.

Teague and his staff use a variety of techniques to create great graphics. Some clip art, of course, can be used as is, such as the rocket and space-shuttle shapes from Volume 1 of the *Clip Art Collection*. Others can be adapted—with some effort—and made into pictures which tell a better story. "A lot of times we use something from *Newsroom*, and then we change things, or improvise, make it better," Teague says. In other cases, graphics are hand-drawn. If they're simple shapes, they can easily be drawn with boxes, lines, and circles. If they're more complicated (and *Skylights* has published some very complex pictures), they're often painstakingly drawn, pixel by pixel.

But the most interesting way that *Skylights* generates and prints graphics is to use a little-known feature of the Apple version of *Newsroom*. Here's how Teague and his interns do it.

Note: The following procedure is only possible with the Apple version of Newsroom.

- Using another Apple program (one that's on a DOS 3.3–formatted disk), an interesting graphic is placed on the screen. The program must generate its screens in high resolution, not double high resolution. Teague uses astronomy programs like *Halley's Universe* and *Traveling Through the Solar System* for other teaching purposes at the planetarium and also to create high-quality graphics for *Skylights*.
- When the screen shows the desired graphic, press the Control and Reset keys at the same time. *Don't turn the computer off.* Most programs will return to BASIC. The screen may look like it's filled with random characters, but the] prompt should appear somewhere near the bottom of the screen.

- Place a DOS 3.3–formatted disk in the drive (it can be a *Newsroom* data disk, but make sure it has plenty of empty space on it).
- Type **BSAVE** ***filename*****,A$2000,L$2000** and hit Return. Don't forget the commas. You've just saved the high-resolution screen to disk under the name *filename*.
- Load *Newsroom*, enter the Photo Lab work area, and choose the Disk icon.
- Select the *Convert picture* option and put the disk with the saved screen in the disk drive. Type in the name of the file you saved to disk and press Return. The drive will whir for a bit. (If you're forgotten the name, press Control-C for a list of all the files on the disk.)
- Select *OK* on the next screen.
- Move the rectangle with the arrow keys until it frames the part of the graphic you want to convert. The rectangle is the same size as the Photo Lab work space. Press the select key.
- The part of the graphic which you placed within the frame should now be on the screen. You can modify it with the Graphics Tools, add other pieces of clip art to it, and crop it with the Camera.
- Once you crop it, you can save this converted graphic as a photo file. When it's on disk, treat it as you would any photo file. Place it in a panel to include it in a page-layout file.

You can use this same process with non-*Newsroom* software that's on ProDOS-formatted disks, but you'll have to copy the hi-res screen file (what you have on disk after the BSAVE command) to a DOS 3.3 disk at some point. Use the *ProDOS Systems Utilities* disk which came with your Apple computer to copy files from ProDOS format to DOS 3.3 format.

One of the things that *Skylights* must create is ellipses, necessary to show orbits of things like comets and unruly planets like Pluto. *Newsroom*'s Graphics Tools don't allow for anything but nearly perfect circles. Teague and his staff either use the method described above to capture ellipses from astronomy software or carefully draw them a pixel at a time.

Other artistic creations, from crossword puzzles to a portrait of Edmond Halley, find their way onto the single-page *Skylights* through hand-drawn methods.

Drawing a crossword puzzle, for instance, can be done from the Graphics Tools menu with boxes and the black fill pattern. More complex art, such as the Halley portrait, must be drawn almost a pixel at a time. Teague has access to artists at Craigmont High School, artists with enough time to create something extremely detailed. (It took a student artist a week and a half working an hour a day to draw the Halley portrait, for instance.)

Wish List

Like a lot of *Newsroom* users, Teague and his interns can see some room for improvement in the program.

The most important enhancement would be a preview mode of some sort. *Newsroom* doesn't let you see what things will look like until a page is actually printed (as you learned in Chapter 6). It's hard to visualize what the page will look like, the *Skylights* staff said, especially when graphics are concerned. At times, a finished page doesn't look right, perhaps because two pictures are atop one other.

The *Skylights* staff doesn't plan their publication's page by creating layout dummies, so time is wasted when they're forced to reload a panel, change things, and then save it out again before printing another version of the page. A preview mode in *Newsroom*—which would show the entire page on the screen—would be very valuable to the people who produce *Skylights*, even if the preview was a miniature reproduction of the page.

Another desired change to *Newsroom* would be to the way text is entered. *Newsroom*'s panels, which can artificially separate a news story into individual blocks, force Teague and his staff to pad stories with more words when a panel is too short or to cut out some things to fit. *Newsroom Pro*, which Teague has seen demonstrated, uses a column-based format instead of panels. In Teague's opinion, it's a much more logical way to write. Rather than splitting a page into six to ten panels, *Newsroom Pro* uses only left and right columns, and it even allows for copying text from one column to another. With this process, it's "much more likely that you can write as you think," Teague said.

Other, more minor additions to *Newsroom* would include the ability to print graphics in color, something possible only with a color printer. (*Skylights* uses an ImageWriter II printer, which is able to print in color with the proper ribbon and software.)

Skylights Odds and Ends

The biggest problem with *Newsroom*, according to one of the *Skylights* staffers, is the cursor jumping off the work space and onto the icon selection area when working in the Copy Desk, Photo Lab, or Banner sections of the program.

The Copy Desk's text editor is great, said another intern. "I like it a lot better [than word processors like the one found in *AppleWorks*]," she said. With *AppleWorks*, "I didn't know what I was doing." The interns like *Newsroom*'s Copy Desk because it's simple to learn and simple to use.

A good news story is one that *Skylights*' audience will find interesting. "We try to encourage the public . . . to go out and look at the stars," a staffer said.

Printing on colored paper is a good way to create a different look, and *Skylights* has used that technique several times. But if you think others will photocopy your newspaper for even wider distribution, don't use dark shades of paper. When *Skylights* was printed on orange paper, for instance, photocopies came out too dark.

Shooting for the Stars

Skylights has a lot of things going for it. Because the writers are interested in what they're writing about, that interest is transferred to the stories. The newsletter is fun to read. Don't underestimate the importance of making your own company's newsletter interesting and entertaining. Your readers are much more likely to remain readers if you combine those two elements.

The design of *Skylights* is clean and consistent. For instance, one typeface is used throughout for the body copy. Graphics are used extensively, but in most cases they're not overused. All these things give *Skylights* a professional look, obviously something important to a business when the newsletter is read by people outside the company. Less obvious, however, is that this same professional appearance is just as important when only employees read the newsletter. A newsletter is, after all, a way to project the image of a company to your customers, workers, or both. A shoddy-looking newsletter gives the impression that the company is equally shoddy.

In many ways, *Skylights* is a typical business newsletter. Written and composed by several people who share a common interest, it has a narrow focus. It presents news stories, graphics, and even some entertainment features, such as the crossword and word puzzles. Overall, it's an excellent example of what *Newsroom* can do.

The rest of this chapter presents several pages of *Skylights*, each page as it was printed by Duncan Teague and his staff. As in the previous three chapters, comments are included to point out the important and interesting page elements.

News from Work

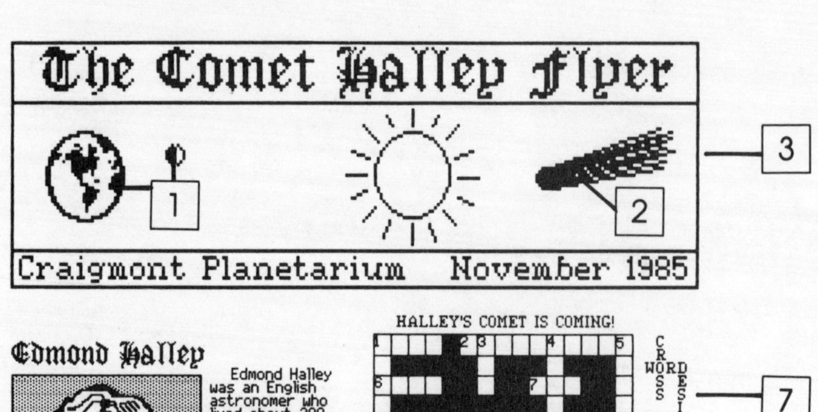

The Comet Halley Flyer

Craigmont Planetarium November 1985

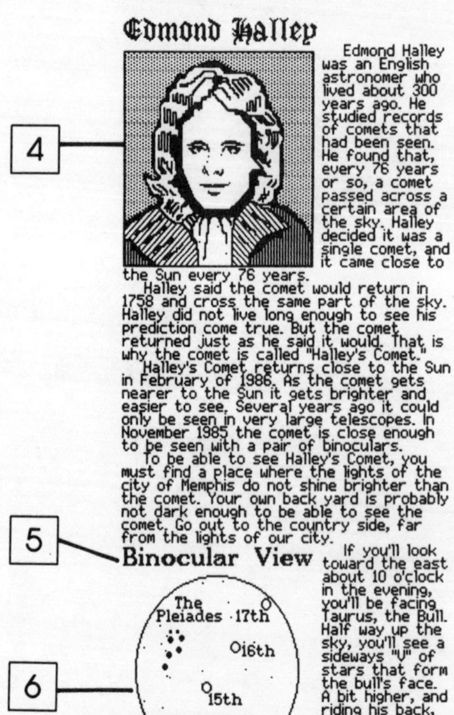

Edmond Halley

Edmond Halley was an English astronomer who lived about 300 years ago. He studied records of comets that had been seen. He found that, every 76 years or so, a comet passed across a certain area of the sky. Halley decided it was a single comet, and it came close to the Sun every 76 years.

Halley said the comet would return in 1758 and cross the same part of the sky. Halley did not live long enough to see his prediction come true. But the comet returned just as he said it would. That is why the comet is called "Halley's Comet."

Halley's Comet returns close to the Sun in February of 1986. As the comet gets nearer to the Sun it gets brighter and easier to see. Several years ago it could only be seen in very large telescopes. In November 1985 the comet is close enough to be seen with a pair of binoculars.

To be able to see Halley's Comet, you must find a place where the lights of the city of Memphis do not shine brighter than the comet. Your own back yard is probably not dark enough to be able to see the comet. Go out to the country side, far from the lights of our city.

Binocular View

November 1985

If you'll look toward the east about 10 o'clock in the evening, you'll be facing Taurus, the Bull. Half way up the sky, you'll see a sideways "V" of stars that form the bull's face. A bit higher, and riding his back, is a tiny cluster of stars called "the Pleiades." Halley's Comet will be near the Pleiades around the middle of the month. Refer to the map for the exact position of Halley's Comet.

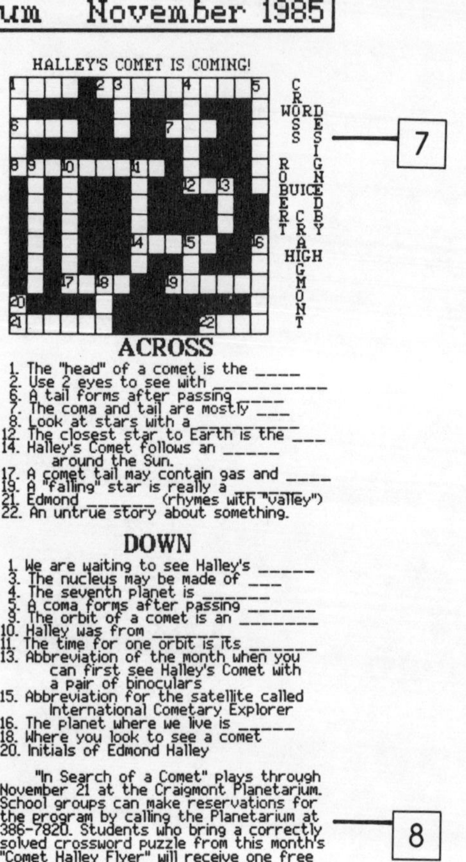

HALLEY'S COMET IS COMING!

ACROSS

1. The "head" of a comet is the ____
2. Use 2 eyes to see with __________
6. A tail forms after passing ____
7. The coma and tail are mostly ____
8. Look at stars with a ________
12. The closest star to Earth is the ___
14. Halley's Comet follows an ______ around the Sun.
17. A comet tail may contain gas and ____
19. A "falling" star is really a ________
21. Edmond _______ (rhymes with "valley")
22. An untrue story about something.

DOWN

1. We are waiting to see Halley's _____
3. The nucleus may be made of ___
4. The seventh planet is _______
5. A coma forms after passing ______
9. The orbit of a comet is an _______
10. Halley was from _______
11. The time for one orbit is its _______
13. Abbreviation of the month when you can first see Halley's Comet with a pair of binoculars
15. Abbreviation for the satellite called International Cometary Explorer
16. The planet where we live is _____
18. Where you look to see a comet
20. Initials of Edmond Halley

"In Search of a Comet" plays through November 21 at the Craigmont Planetarium. School groups can make reservations for the program by calling the Planetarium at 386-7820. Students who bring a correctly solved crossword puzzle from this month's "Comet Halley Flyer" will receive one free admission to "In Search of a Comet" at any Thursday evening star show at 7:30.

1 The banner uses several pieces of clip art, including this slightly modified picture of Earth and a half moon. The earth graphic is found in ALIENS 3 on the *Newsroom* Clip Art Directory disk, and the moon is a simple circle with its left half filled in black.

2 Another banner graphic is this comet, hand created with the Graphics Tools. A small circle was drawn, then filled with black. The comet's tail was created by drawing a number of lines from the circle and to the right.

3 Notice how clean the banner looks. Much of that stems from the rules which separate the name, the graphics, and the date. Extensive use of white space in the middle also contributes to the banner's appearance. The banner is completely boxed, which separates it from the rest of the newsletter.

4 This portrait of Edmond Halley was drawn with the Graphics Tools of *Newsroom*, sometimes on a pixel-by-pixel basis. A student artist spent approximately eight hours creating this impressive picture.

5 Although this looks like a story headline, it's actually a caption split above and below the graphic *(Binocular View* and *November 1985).* The large type size could confuse some readers, who may expect to find a story about using binoculars to stargaze. It would have been clearer if another caption style was used, perhaps with small type boxed and placed at the bottom of the picture.

6 An informative skymap showing the position of Halley's Comet in mid-November was created with the Graphics Tools. Circles and text make this graphic an effective page element. Note how the story copy refers readers to the graphic for more information.

7 The crossword puzzle was built with boxes and fills using the Graphics Tools. It takes up an entire panel.

8 This notice of a current star show is almost lost among the crossword puzzle clues that stretch down much of the right column. Many readers probably missed this. Since it's part of the last panel in the column, it would have been impractical to surround it with a box from within the Photo Lab work area. However, a rule could easily have been used to separate the notice from the text above it.

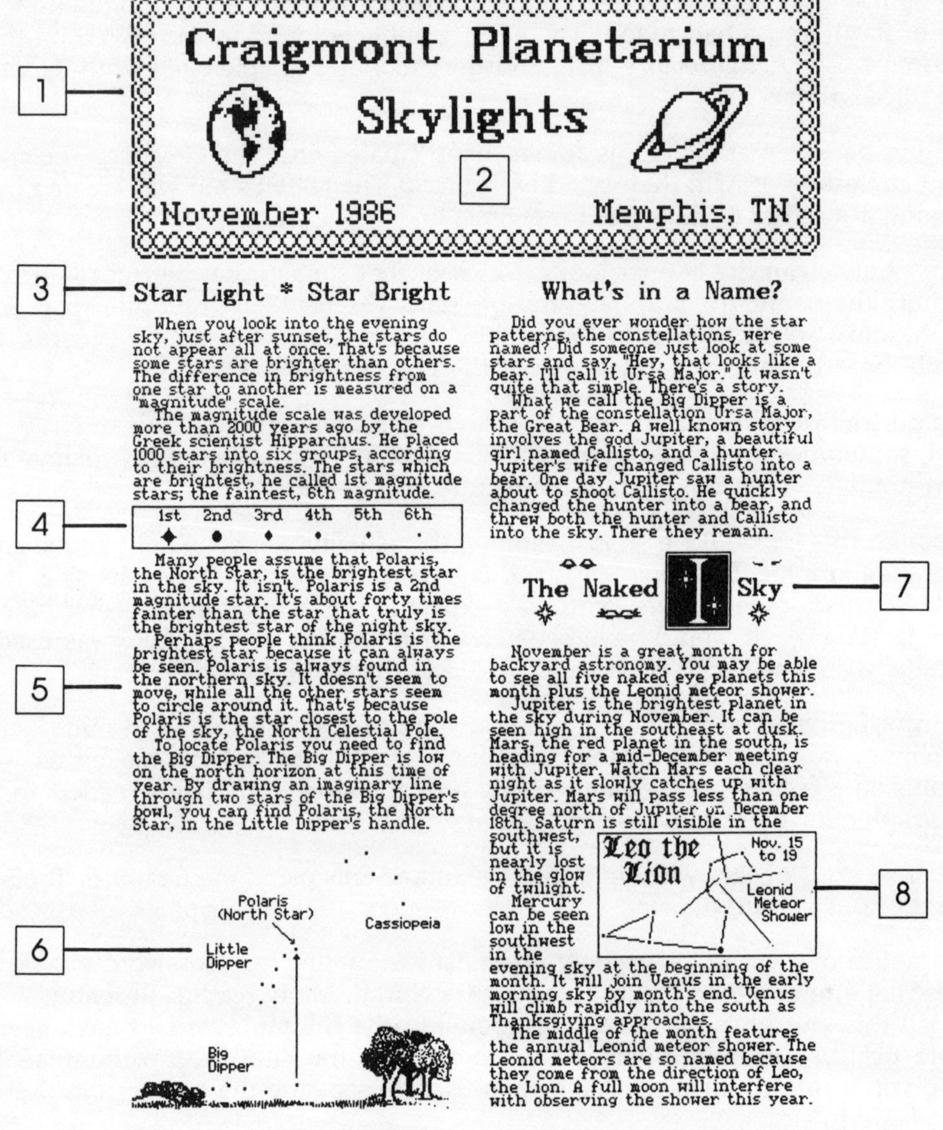

Craigmont Planetarium Skylights

November 1986 Memphis, TN

Star Light * Star Bright

When you look into the evening sky, just after sunset, the stars do not appear all at once. That's because some stars are brighter than others. The difference in brightness from one star to another is measured on a "magnitude" scale.

The magnitude scale was developed more than 2000 years ago by the Greek scientist Hipparchus. He placed 1000 stars into six groups, according to their brightness. The stars which are brightest, he called 1st magnitude stars; the faintest, 6th magnitude.

1st	2nd	3rd	4th	5th	6th

Many people assume that Polaris, the North Star, is the brightest star in the sky. It isn't. Polaris is a 2nd magnitude star. It's about forty times fainter than the star that truly is the brightest star of the night sky.

Perhaps people think Polaris is the brightest star because it can always be seen. Polaris is always found in the northern sky. It doesn't seem to move, while all the other stars seem to circle around it. That's because Polaris is the star closest to the pole of the sky, the North Celestial Pole.

To locate Polaris you need to find the Big Dipper. The Big Dipper is low on the north horizon at this time of year. By drawing an imaginary line through two stars of the Big Dipper's bowl, you can find Polaris, the North Star, in the Little Dipper's handle.

What's in a Name?

Did you ever wonder how the star patterns, the constellations, were named? Did someone just look at some stars and say, "Hey, that looks like a bear. I'll call it Ursa Major." It wasn't quite that simple. There's a story.

What we call the Big Dipper is a part of the constellation Ursa Major, the Great Bear. A well known story involves the god Jupiter, a beautiful girl named Callisto, and a hunter. Jupiter's wife changed Callisto into a bear. One day Jupiter saw a hunter about to shoot Callisto. He quickly changed the hunter into a bear, and threw both the hunter and Callisto into the sky. There they remain.

The Naked I Sky

November is a great month for backyard astronomy. You may be able to see all five naked eye planets this month plus the Leonid meteor shower.

Jupiter is the brightest planet in the sky during November. It can be seen high in the southeast at dusk. Mars, the red planet in the south, is heading for a mid-December meeting with Jupiter. Watch Mars each clear night as it slowly catches up with Jupiter. Mars will pass less than one degree north of Jupiter on December 18th. Saturn is still visible in the southwest, but it is nearly lost in the glow of twilight.

Mercury can be seen low in the southwest in the evening sky at the beginning of the month. It will join Venus in the early morning sky by month's end. Venus will climb rapidly into the south as Thanksgiving approaches.

The middle of the month features the annual Leonid meteor shower. The Leonid meteors are so named because they come from the direction of Leo, the Lion. A full moon will interfere with observing the shower this year.

1 Compare this banner with the one on the previous sample page. The typeface is different, the border is taken from the *Clip Art Collection, Volume 1* disk, and all its elements—name, graphics, and date—are grouped together within that border.

2 The Earth graphic was also used in the banner for *The Comet Halley Flyer*. Overall, the banner makes good use of the available space without crowding the different elements. The name of the newsletter, *Craigmont Planetarium Skylights*, identifies the business (the planetarium) and its subject *(Skylights)*. A clever and effective name for the newsletter.

3 The typeface and size of the headlines in this newsletter are consistent. In this issue, headline placement is also consistent—each headline is centered in the panel with what appears to be a single empty space (large size type) between the head and the body copy.

4 This figure was created with the Graphics Tools and boxed to set it off from the copy. It is placed immediately after the text which describes its subject.

5 One of the newsletter's few problems is its crowded look, brought on by large chunks of uninterrupted text. Though much of that problem is unavoidable with *Newsroom* (because of the small space between lines of text), the newsletter would look better if space was added between each paragraph. That, however, would mean the *Skylights'* staffers could get less news in their one-page newsletter.

6 This graphic was created by combining several small elements from the SCENERY 1 file on the *Clip Art Collection, Volume 1* disk. The trees, grass, and hill were pieced together; then the stars, text, and arrows were drawn. Taking up an entire panel, this picture shows the position of the North Star better than the text can describe. The large amount of white space in the graphic makes it stand out.

7 This unique headline (*The Naked "I" Sky*) was largely created in the Photo Lab. Parts from several files on the *Clip Art Collection, Volume 1* disk were combined with text. White space above and below the headline sets it off from the body copy.

8 Another hand-drawn graphic, this figure of the Leo constellation and the Leonid meteor shower was made with lines and a framing box in the Graphics Tools. The switch in typeface (to English) is slightly jarring, however. A ruled border was necessary since the graphic butted up against the text above and below.

1

Craigmont Planetarium Skylights

January 1987 Memphis, TN

2

Venus

Saturn

Morning Sky

Jan. 31

Jan. 1

Mars

Jupiter

Evening Sky

Cold Clear Skies Show Off Planets

The cold clear skies of January will provide sky watchers with an excellent view of the brightest of the planets. Both the closest and the most distant naked eye planets are in the morning sky. You will have to get up before dawn to see Venus and Saturn. Venus is at its brightest. The week of January 24 - 31 Venus and Saturn will be close together in the early morning sky.

Jupiter and Mars will be moving farther apart during January. At the beginning of the month they are only about 8 degrees apart. By the end of the month the two planets will be nearly three times farther apart. Look for Mars and Jupiter in the southwestern sky, just after sunset.

Late in the month Mercury will appear low in the southwest sky, below and to the right of Jupiter and Mars.

If you enjoy winter skywatching, the month of January will give you an opportunity to find the planets in its cool clear skies.

3

Futures: Things to Come

"Futures" is a program about the future, but it begins in the past. The stars served as a guide for ancient navigators both on the sea and on the land. Ancient skywatchers followed the movements of the Sun, the Moon, and the planets.

By watching the regular motions of the objects in the sky, people could predict astronomical events. Their ability to do so lead them to believe they could predict human events as well. Astrology was born!

Psychics, prophets, inventors, and scientists have made predictions that have been either misleading or completely wrong. Today "futurists" still forecast "things to come."

The view through Galileo's telescope

5

Galileo and Jupiter 1610 - 1989

On January 7, 1610, Galileo was the first person to see Jupiter through a telescope. In 1989, 379 years later, a space probe named Galileo will make a 6 year journey to the giant planet.

6

The space craft will separate into two parts, an orbiter and an atmospheric probe. The probe will descend into the Jovian clouds. The orbiter will fly by Jupiter's four largest moons, Europa, Ganymede, Callisto, and Io.

Compare this close-up picture of Jupiter with the view Galileo had through his small telescope. The small dots of light Galileo saw have become real worlds for us. The space probe that enters Jupiter's atmosphere will show us more than the multicolored clouds photographed by Voyager.

7

Ancient Skywatchers

8

With the aid of polls, surveys, and computers, they offer a variety of predictions about future events.

"Futures" will show you what kind of "batting average" today's prophets have. Then the program will be so bold as to make its own predictions about the next thirty years of space exploration.

4

1 The same banner is used for each issue. The only change is the date in the lower left corner. Exact placement isn't necessary, since there's plenty of room between the date and the nearest graphic.

2 The large sans serif type makes this graphic part picture, part headline. Although the planets in the graphic are overwhelmed by the text, the overall effect would be less effective if the type was set smaller. The line at the bottom of the graphic *(Cold Clear Skies Show Off Planets)* is somewhat confusing—is it a headline or a caption?

3 This headline is in sans serif, even though prior issues of the newsletter used serif for heads. The headline would have been more effective as a two-level head (*Futures* and *Things to Come* on separate lines) with white space between it and the text above.

4 The story *Futures: Things to Come* is laid out horizontally across the bottom of the page. Unfortunately, there's no indication to the readers that they're to move from the bottom of the left column to the text directly under the graphic titled Ancient Skywatchers. Several techniques could have been used, from a rule to a two-column headline, to guide the reader's eyes.

5 Another headline in an inconsistent format, this looks more like a caption for the graphic than a head. A large-sized headline would have taken up much more room, however.

6 An example of a well-written news story. Though not written in a news lead format, the first sentence grabs the reader's attention. The rest of the story is to the point, clearly written, and informative.

7 This graphic was created by another Apple program. The *Skylights* staff then saved the hi-res screen with the BSAVE *filename*,A$2000,L$2000 statement. The screen was converted into a *Newsroom* photo in the Photo Lab and then placed in a panel used in the page layout.

8 This picture was built from two files on the *Clip Art Collection, Volume 1* disk. The scattered stars were added by hand. Note that two graphics are stacked atop one another. Since they don't refer to the same story, that could be confusing. The text and graphic could easily be switched.

Craigmont Planetarium

Skylights

April 1987 Memphis, TN

1 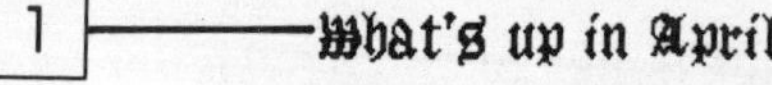

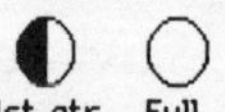

1st qtr	Full	3rd qtr	New
6th	13th	20th	27th

1st - Mars and the Moon are both near the Pleiades in constellation Taurus

2 13th - The Moon will pass through the outer portion of the Earth's shadow, a penumbral eclipse. Best time to look is 9:19 pm.

19th - The 1st Sunday following the full moon after the spring equinox determines the date for Easter. This means the earliest possible day for Easter could be March 23rd and the latest possible day is April 25th

22nd - The Lyrid meteor shower reaches peak activity tonight. From a dark area you can see about 15 to 20 meteors per hour.

25th - Venus is occulted by the Moon over much of North America. In the South, Venus will reappear from behind the Moon before sunrise.

Spring Ahead to DST Sunday, April 5th

3 April is the month when we set our clocks ahead one hour.
4 Daylight Savings Time formerly began on the last Sunday of April and lasted until the last Sunday of October. Recently Congress changed DST to begin on the first Sunday of April. When we are on Daylight Savings Time, sunset occurs one hour later than it does on Standard Time. This artificially allows us an extra hour of daylight for recreation, and it helps save energy.

Satellite Watching!

Mir 1, the Soviet space station, can be seen in April on certain dates and times. By using the chart below, you will know when and where to look for the satellite when it passes above the Memphis horizon.

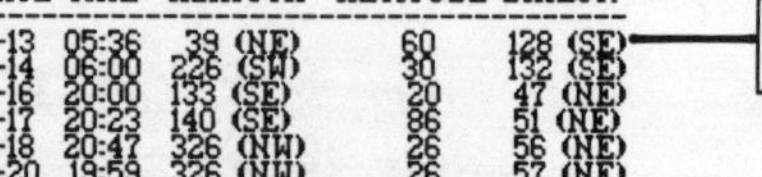

DATE	TIME	AZIMUTH	ALTITUDE	DIRECT.
4-13	05:36	39 (NE)	60	128 (SE) 5
4-14	06:00	226 (SW)	30	132 (SE)
4-16	20:00	133 (SE)	20	47 (NE)
4-17	20:23	140 (SE)	86	51 (NE)
4-18	20:47	326 (NW)	26	56 (NE)
4-20	19:59	326 (NW)	26	57 (NE)

A.M. times are hours from zero to twelve, and P.M. times are shown as hours greater than twelve.

Azimuth (direction) and altitude (elevation) help us to tell you more precisely than terms like north, south, east, and west where the satellite can be found in the sky.

Azimuth tells you what direction to face. Azimuth begins in the north at 0 degrees. It continues clockwise 6 until reaching 360 degrees. At this point you're back in the north again.

Altitude tells you how high in the sky to look. Altitude begins at the horizon at 0 degrees. It continues upwards until reaching 90 degrees. This is the zenith, the point in the sky directly above your head.

"Direct"(ion) is the azimuth toward which the satellite is moving. You'll see the satellite for several minutes.

The following diagrams illustrate the meanings of both these terms.

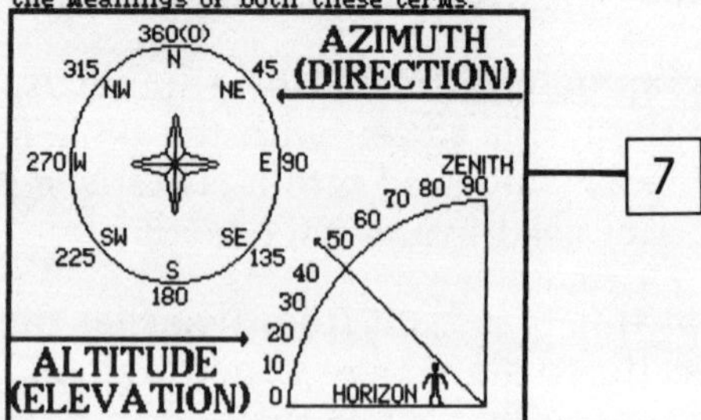

1 The headline for this story is set in the English typeface, which is difficult to read. Serif and sans serif typefaces make much more readable heads. The phases of the moon were created with the Circle tool and then filled with black. To fill only half the circle, draw a vertical line through the circle and fill one side. Erase any of the line outside the circle.

2 Notice that the text margin isn't perfectly straight. That's an unavoidable problem with *Newsroom*'s Copy Desk work area and has to do with the proportional type that the program uses. The only way to align columns exactly is in the Photo Lab, but the process takes more time. In this case, the misaligned text is only slightly noticeable.

3 *Spring Ahead to DST Sunday, April 5th* is a long, but effective headline. The clock graphic, found in the TIME 2 file on the *Clip Art Collection, Volume 1* disk, includes information that the story does not—the time to change to Daylight Savings Time is 2:00 a.m.

4 Although the wrap-around text is a useful technique in many instances, here the reader's eyes move first to the headline/graphic (because it's darker and larger) and then back to the text on the left. Guide readers to the text more naturally by placing the headline/graphic on the left and wrapping the text around the right side.

5 Satellite timetables are a recent feature of *Skylights*. Note again the slight misalignment of the columns. The imperfections are so minor that most readers won't even notice them.

6 This story, though somewhat technical and full of new terms, is an excellent example of a clearly written and informative article. Explanations of the table's headings and their meanings are needed—without them, most readers would be lost. The information is presented in such a way that the typical *Skylights* reader (school-aged children for the most part) can easily understand it.

7 The information-packed illustration does much to explain the terms and ideas found in the article. Without this graphic, the idea of *azimuth* and *altitude* would be harder to understand. This picture was created with the Graphics Tools, though the small figure at bottom left was pulled from the Clip Art Directory. The large type makes the labels stand out.

PART 3

Beyond the News

CHAPTER 12

Beyond the News at Home and School

Newsroom is a versatile program. By now, you'll agree that it's an amazingly powerful piece of software, especially considering its size and the outdated technology of the computers it uses. With your help, however, *Newsroom* can produce newspapers that read and look as professional or as homey as you want them to.

But restricting *Newsroom* to newspaper publishing is to waste part of the program's power. You can use *Newsroom* for a variety of other tasks, most of them totally unrelated to news or newspapers.

Considering the cost of computer software—rarely cheap—it's even more wasteful when you buy specialty software to do things *Newsroom* can handle. This chapter shows how to use *Newsroom* to create flyers, comic strips, calendars, and more—just some of the home and school projects you can tackle when you have *Newsroom*, some time, and your imagination.

Flyers

Flyers can advertise anything from a garage sale at home to a benefit concert at school. Advertising—letting people know you have something to sell, that you've lost something, that you're throwing a party—doesn't have to be strictly business.

Because they're advertisements, the first thing a flyer has to do is get people's attention. That's not hard if you remember these three guidelines.

Pictures. People notice flyers faster when they include pictures. The larger the picture, the better. It can't be a confusing drawing; it has to present an idea at one glance.

Hey you! The flyer's main message should be understandable in that same short glance. If you're selling something, for example, *For Sale* should appear in large letters. If you lost your dog, *REWARD FOR LOST DOG* gets the point across immediately.

Far away. A successful flyer should also be easily readable, if not from a distance, then at least from arm's length. Remember, you'll want to stick flyers on bulletin boards or stack them on a table or desk.

Let's put together an easy banner, one that you could post to sell your used car. During the process, you'll learn lots of tips for your own flyers.

Hot Car

One way to make your flyer jump out at the reader is to use large pictures and letters. The best way to create large graphics and text with *Newsroom* is in the Banner work area. Everything in a banner prints out double the size of a panel.

Another advantage of banners is that they reach completely across the page. There's no gutter between columns, so you don't have to worry about columns.

You can't lay out a page with more than one banner, of course, but that problem is easily solved. *Newsroom* doesn't automatically start printing at the top of a page, so you can manually set the place where things begin to print.

You'll use these two techniques—banners and manually positioning those banners when they print—when you create any flyer.

Start with what will appear at the top of the flyer, a picture of a car. It doesn't have to look exactly like your car (in fact, it may be best if it doesn't look *anything* like your car).

- Enter the Banner work area, select the Clip Art icon, put the *Clip Art Collection, Volume 1* disk in the drive, and choose AUTO2.
- Grab the car at the bottom left and position it in the middle of the work space.
- Choose the Disk icon and save the banner as FLYER1.

> Make sure any clip art you choose fits in a banner. You may be able to position large clip art so that it looks okay even when part of it is cut off. If you use small clip art, consider putting down more than one copy. Chapter 3 offers suggestions on selecting art for banners.

For Sale

The next step is to create words that scream out your message. Be as simple as you can—don't waste words being clever here.

You're trying to sell your car, so use *FOR SALE*. Not very original, true, but it gets the idea across.

- Erase what's in the Banner work space and put the *Clip Art* disk in the drive, side 2 facing up.
- Select WORDS2 and grab the FOR SALE graphic.
- It doesn't take up the entire banner, so you can lay down more than one copy. Position the graphics in the work space.
- You can add other clip art or go to the Graphics Tools menu to draw lines, boxes, or circles. Figure 12-1 shows one possible banner.

Figure 12-1. Sale, Sale, Sale

FOR SALE
FOR SALE
FOR SALE

≡ Save this banner as FLYER2.

Just the Facts

Now you want to list the car's selling points. Imagine you're writing a classified ad. What can you tell people that will make them buy the car?

Again, use the Banner work area to create this text. Characters will print twice as large in a Banner, making the details easily readable from several feet away.

≡ Clear the work space again and select the Crayon icon.
≡ Choose one of the two small typefaces and exit.
≡ Enter the work space and place the cursor about a fifth of the way in from the left edge. Press the select key to set the cursor.
≡ Type these seven lines, pressing Return at the end of each.

1983 Honda Accord, 4-door
Blue in and out
Runs great
42,000 miles
Sony stereo FM/tape w/ 4 speakers
Excellent gas mileage
Brand new radials

≡ Press the select key to free the cursor and then choose the Crayon icon again.
≡ Pick the Draw tool and the third pen from the left.
≡ In the work space, position the cursor (it's now a small black circle) to the left of the *1* in the first line. Press the select key. This will place a small *bullet* at the head of the line.
≡ Using small increments, move the cursor down until it's beside the *B* in the second line. Press the select key again. Repeat for each line.
≡ When this bullet list is complete, return to the Graphics Tools menu and pick the Box tool and the second pen from the left.
≡ Box the text in the work space so that it looks like Figure 12-2.
≡ Save the banner as FLYER3.

Figure 12-2. Selling Points

```
• 1983 Honda Accord, 4-door
• Blue in and out
• Runs great
• 42,000 miles
• Sony FM/tape w/ 4 speakers
• Excellent gas mileage
• Brand new radials
```

The Bottom Line

The final piece of this flyer is the most important—the price of the car and your telephone number. Most people will want to know these two things right away. That's why you'll use large type for the price and phone number.

- Erase the work space by selecting the Garbage Can icon.
- Choose the Crayon icon and pick one either serif or sans serif in the large size.
- Set the cursor in the work space just to the left of center.
- Type **$10,000** and press Return.
- Reset the cursor down and near the left edge.
- Type **Call 777-8888 after 5** and press Return.
- Save the banner as FLYER4 to the same disk as the other files.

Roll the Printer

Four is the maximum number of banners you can print on one 8½ × 11–inch sheet of paper.

If you want to put more information in the flyer, you could print on 8½ × 14–inch paper and then reduce it on a copier to fit on a normal-sized sheet. Five banners is the most you can print on 8½ × 14–inch paper.

If you have fewer than four banners, you can position them anywhere you want on the page, simply by rolling the paper in or out of the printer as each one finishes printing. This manual positioning of the paper lets you do things with *Newsroom* that aren't possible when you're dealing with page layout files.

Let's print the car flyer, and do just a bit of manual positioning.

- Go to the Press work area and choose *Print banner*. Put the disk containing the FLYER files in the drive and choose *OK*.
- Highlight FLYER1 and press the select key.
- Position the paper so that the top of the sheet is just above the print head.
- Select *OK* now on the screen.

- Wait until the banner is through printing the car on the paper. Roll the paper out of the printer half an inch.
- Choose *Print banner* again, this time selecting FLYER2.
- When the FOR SALE prints, roll the paper out of the printer another half inch.
- Print FLYER3
- Roll the paper out another half inch.
- Print FLYER4

The completed flyer should look like Figure 12-3.

Figure 12-3. Selling My Car

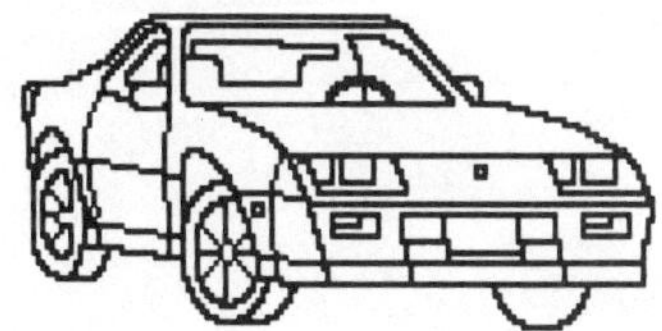

FOR SALE
FOR SALE
FOR SALE

- 1983 Honda Accord, 4-door
- Blue in and out
- Runs great
- 42,000 miles
- Sony FM/tape w/ 4 speakers
- Excellent gas mileage
- Brand new radials

$10,000

Call 777-8888 after 5

Of course, your own flyers will look different. With *Newsroom*'s banners and a bit of judicious printer-paper rolling, you can work miracles.

If your flyer includes information you expect people to write down—like your phone number—think about doing this.

At the bottom right, put several (five to eight) copies of the phone number. Enter them in small type, one above the other. The rightmost character of the number should be as close as possible to the edge of the work space.

Once you have the flyer printed, take scissors and cut the paper between each phone number. Readers of the flyer can then easily tear off the phone number and stick it in their pocket for later reference.

Figure 12-4. Tear-offs

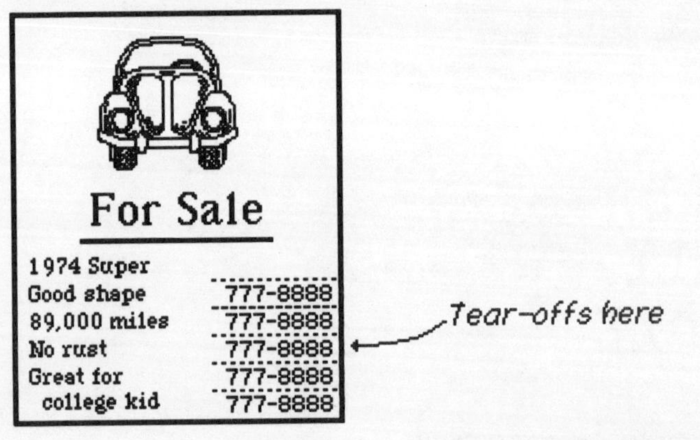

Flash Cards

Flash cards are the kind of thing that will be around schools forever. They're simple to use, great for drill and practice, and perfect for group learning.

In the best possible world, flash cards would fit your students' or children's needs exactly. And they'd be free. Unfortunately, neither is true.

Flash cards aren't always available for the exact lesson being taught. And you or your school can't afford to buy every set of cards you'd like to have. The solution is custom cards. To make your own flash cards, though, you need some drawing ability, for flash cards often show pictures—especially those aimed at younger children—and the letters need to be legible.

Use *Newsroom* instead of testing your artistic talent. With more than 600 pieces of clip art on the disk which comes with the program, and another 1800 pieces on the three *Clip Art Collection* disks, you have an amazing number of pictures at your disposal. And by planning ahead, you can create large, legible letters to label your new deck of flash cards.

From Across the Room

Flash cards are meant to be used at a distance. That's why the pictures and letters are so bold and readable. When a group of children are clustered around a teacher, each child has to be able to see the flash card. And they must be able to identify it almost immediately. (Why else are they called *flash* cards?)

You, too, must use large letters and graphics in your custom-designed flash cards. The only way to do that is in the Banner work area. There's one problem—most flash cards are taller than they are wide, just the opposite of the Banner work space's dimensions. Here's how to get around that inconvenience.

Let's say you're making a set of flash cards for preschoolers. The cards will have pictures and letters to teach them the alphabet.

Master FLASH

Enter the Banner work area and select the Crayon icon. Pick the Line tool and the smallest pen and then exit. Move the cursor so it's just a bit more than halfway across the work space; then draw a vertical line from top to bottom. Make sure both ends are clearly visible (you're going to erase this line later, and that's easier if you can see its entire length).

Save this banner as FLASH. It's your master flash-card banner file.

The line acts as a guide. Whenever you want to create a flash card, load the FLASH file and use it to position any graphics or text. As long as you don't let anything cross the line, all your flash cards will have the same maximum width.

A is for *Apple*

To demonstrate, let's make the first flash card in the series. Sticking to tradition, you want to put a picture of an apple on the top half of the card and both the lower and uppercase *A* on the bottom half.

- Load the FLASH banner file into the work space.
- Put the *Clip Art Collection, Volume 1,* side A, in the drive and select the Clip Art icon. Scroll down through list until FOOD1 is highlighted. Press the select key.
- Grab the apple on the screen.
- Position the apple on the far left of the work space. Lay down two more copies. Make sure that the rightmost apple doesn't extend over the line. At this point, the screen should look like Figure 12-5.

Figure 12-5. Three Apples

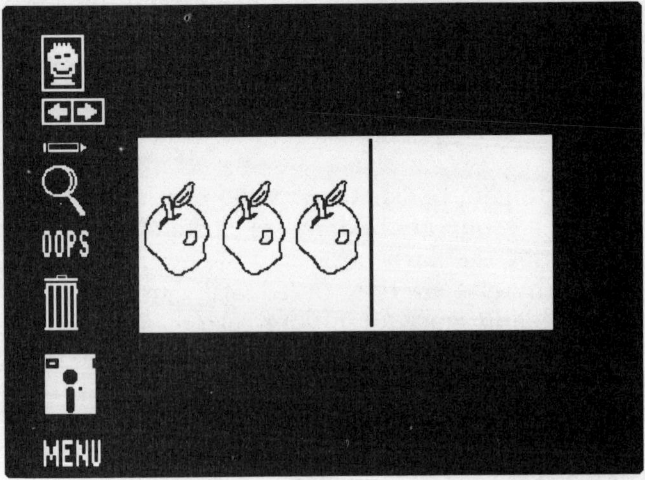

- Select the Crayon icon and pick the Eraser tool and the thickest pen.
- Erase the vertical guideline.
- Save this banner as LETTERA.

The top half of the flash card is done. Now for the rest of it.

- Select the Garbage Can icon to clear the work space and then load the FLASH banner file into the work space again.
- Choose the Crayon icon and pick the large serif type.
- Position the cursor and enter an uppercase *A*, a lowercase *a*, and the word *Apple* (refer to Figure 12-6 for approximate placement).
- You can add some additional graphics if you want, such as the lines you see in Figure 12-6.

Figure 12-6. Apples—The Bottom Half

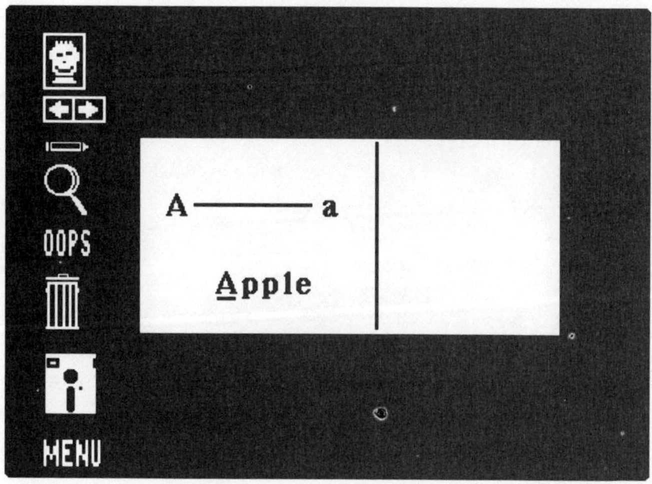

≡ Erase the guideline before saving the banner as LETTERA2

You've got both pieces of the flash card. All you have to do is put them together.

Tops and Bottoms

The Press work area is your flash-card glue. It's in the Press area where you'll combine the top and bottom halves of your flash cards. The process is laughably easy.

≡ Enter the Press work area.
≡ Assuming the setup is correct and that your printer is connected and turned on, select *Print banner* from the list.
≡ Put the disk containing the LETTER files in the drive and choose *OK*.
≡ Highlight LETTERA and press the select key.
≡ Position the paper and select *OK*.
≡ Wait for the apples to print. *Don't move the paper when printing is over.*
≡ Choose *Print banner* again, this time selecting LETTERA2.
≡ Print the bottom half of the flash card. When it's done, roll the paper out of the printer.

The completed card should look much like Figure 12-7.

Figure 12-7. Final Flash Card

A——— a

Apple

You have several options here. You can cut out the flash card and paste it on an index card. Color it with pencil, marker, crayon, or paint if you want (a good idea for this card, since it'll be used with preschoolers). Or you can cut out the flash card and then laminate it so it's stiff enough to use.

The process takes longer to explain than it does to do. Even if you're a bit rusty with *Newsroom*, it won't take you long to make an entire set of custom flash cards.

> Sometimes flash cards are two-sided. A good example is foreign language vocabulary drill cards. They commonly have the foreign language word on one side and the English translation on the other.
>
> You can create double-sided cards, too. Follow the steps already outlined (you may want to use just one banner file for each side). When you have both sides printed, simply glue one on each side of an index card. If you're laminating the cards, you can tape the two pieces of paper together back to back before running them through the lamination machine.

Comic Strips

With its panels and cartoon-like clip art, *Newsroom* seems tailor-made for creating comic strips. It's almost a comic-strip construction set.

Don't expect to create comic strips (or even entire comic books if you're really ambitious) that show off your artistic abilities. If you're an artist extraordinaire, you should look elsewhere—to sophisticated draw and paint software—if you want some tools to help you create a comic masterpiece.

But if you're like most people—in other words, drawing even the crudest sketches is more than you can bear—you'll love what *Newsroom* can do for comedy.

Note: This section of "Beyond the News at Home and School" doesn't try to teach you how to write comic strips or how to be funny. Being funny is your business, and no book is going to show you how. All this part of the chapter does is show you how to use *Newsroom* to do the mechanical parts of comic-strip creation.

Panels

Comic strips and books are divided into what's called *panels*. Each panel is a scene, with the strip or book made up of 3 to 30 (or more) scenes.

Within each panel, there are usually characters drawn by the artist and words written by the writer. Sometimes, like now, as you put together your own comic strip with *Newsroom*, the artist and writer are one and the same person.

Generally, a comic strip's panels build up to a conclusion, whether that's a joke's punch line or the climax of a comic book's plot. Though creating the panels in sequence isn't terribly important when you use *Newsroom*, it might be best if you wrote the strip in chronological order.

There are two common layouts for comic strips and comic books, as Figure 12-8 shows.

Figure 12-8. Comic Layout

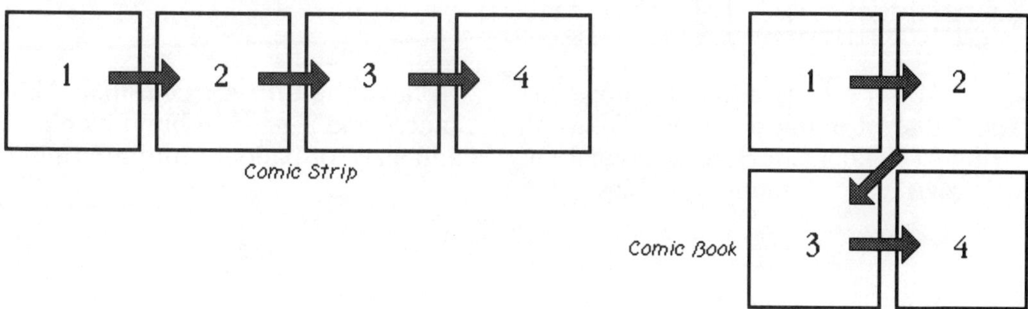

Either layout can accommodate more than four panels. Which layout you use depends on personal preference and the length of the strip. If you're making a three- or four-panel comic strip, the top layout in Figure 12-8 is probably best. But if you're creating a comic book-length project, you'll want to use the bottom layout.

Newsroom is perfectly suited to the second layout scheme. You can use one of *Newsroom*'s panels for each comic strip panel and then simply lay out the panels on a normal page. The first layout, though, takes some cutting and pasting.

Newsroom won't let you turn text and pictures sideways; if it did, you could use one half of an eight-panel page to create a four-panel strip. What you'll do, then, is lay out the completed panels, print them, and then cut them out. Later you'll paste or tape them into their proper order.

Words and Balloons

Dialog spoken by a character in a comic strip is usually placed in a *balloon*. This oval contains words, with a line, curved arrow, or bubbles to show which character said what, and whether it was spoken aloud or just thought.

You *can* make balloons from scratch with the Graphics Tools in *Newsroom*, but the results won't be the best. You can't draw ovals with the Tools, remember, so you'll be limited to rectangles and lines. With more work, you can use the Magnifying Glass icon and "round" the corners of a rectangle, as shown in Figure 12-9.

Figure 12-9. Faking Balloon Ovals

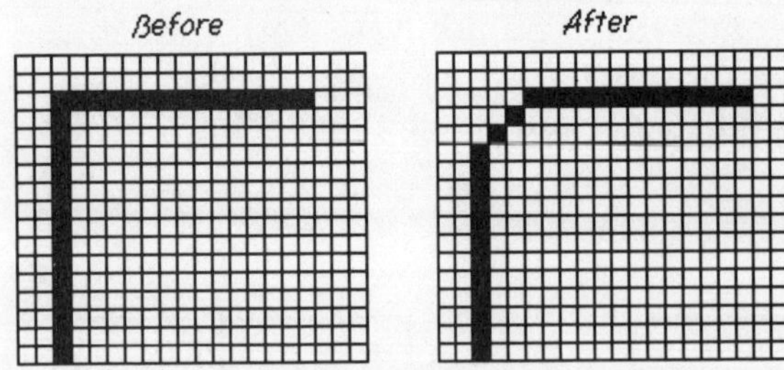

You'll get better results, however, if you have the *Clip Art Collection, Volume 2* disk. The file BALLOONS has all the pieces you'll need to build comic-strip text balloons, including several shapes and sizes of balloons and a number of arrows and "thinking" bubbles.

Figure 12-10. BALLOONS

Reprinted courtesy Springboard Software, Inc. Copyright 1985, 1986, Springboard Software, Inc.

Comics and the Photo Lab

The best place to create your comics is in the Photo Lab. There you can easily place clip art and draw balloons if you don't have *Volume* 2. Since most comic strips don't have lots of words, the text entry capabilities of the Photo Lab are fine.

Let's create a simple comic strip made up of three panels. You'll see the entire process from start to finish and pick up all the techniques you'll need to launch your own comedy publishing empire.

- Enter the Photo Lab work area, choose the Crayon icon, and pick Box and the second smallest pen.
- Draw a box which is almost as large as the Lab's work space. Leave about half an inch at the bottom of the work space, however. This helps later, when you're cutting out the panels.
- Crop the entire screen with the Camera and save the photo file as COMIC. This is your master comic-strip panel.

With the master file completed, you're ready to tackle the first panel in the strip. Have two clip art disks handy—*Clip Art* (it came with *Newsroom*) and *Clip Art Collection, Volume* 2. You can use any of the characters on any of the clip art disks, but the most cartoonlike are on the *Clip Art* disk.

- If it's not there already, load the photo file COMIC into the work space.
- After you've put the *Clip Art* disk in the drive (side B up), select the Clip Art icon and highlight the file WOMEN6. Press the select key.
- Grab the woman character in the upper left.
- Place her near the left side of the work space.
- Put the *Volume* 2 disk in the drive and choose the Clip Art icon again.

≡ Highlight the file BALLOONS and grab the balloon in the upper left.
≡ Position it in the upper right of the Lab's work space.
≡ Return to *Volume 2*'s clip art list, choose BALLOONS again, and grab the arrow in the bottom left.
≡ Place the arrow so that it comes out of the balloon.
≡ Choose the Magnifying Glass icon and clean up the junction of the arrow and balloon.

The panel is only lacking text. Figure 12-11 shows what should be on your screen by now.

Figure 12-11. Without Words

≡ Select the Crayon icon and pick the small sans serif type.
≡ Place the cursor in the balloon and type **My husband wanted a raise at work, so I said he should ask.** Remember that the Photo Lab doesn't automatically wrap text around and down—press Return when the cursor is close to the side of the balloon.
≡ Crop the entire work space with the Camera and save it to disk as COMIC1.

Figure 12-12 shows the finished comic-strip panel.

Figure 12-12. Panel Done

Many times, comic-strip characters and their positions don't change from panel to panel. You'll find this true with your comics as well. In fact, *Newsroom* saves you lots of work when characters remain the same. To make one panel into another often means changing only the text in the balloon.

- After choosing the Crayon icon, pick the Eraser tool and the large, square-shaped pen.
- Move the eraser into the balloon and erase the text that's left over from the first panel.
- Select the Crayon icon again and choose the small sans serif type.
- Place the cursor in the balloon and type **I said to him, "What's the worst that could happen?"** Just like with the first panel, you'll need to set and reset the cursor several times to fit all the words inside the balloon.
- Crop the entire work space and save the file as COMIC2.

Figure 12-13. Second Panel

Panel three uses some of the same graphics as the other two, so you'll save even more time and effort.

≡ Erase the text in the balloon.
≡ Pick the Hand from the Graphics Tools list and move the woman to the left.
≡ Put the *Clip Art* disk (side B up) in the drive and choose the Clip Art icon.
≡ Highlight the file MEN4 and grab the figure in the upper left of the screen (the one wearing the barrel).
≡ Put the man on the right side of the work space.
≡ Now, move the balloon and its arrow to the middle of the work space.
≡ Flip the arrow (you may have to insert *Volume 2*'s disk into the drive for a moment) and move it so that it seems to come from the man's mouth. You may have to move it up and then clean the inside of the balloon with the Magnifying Glass.
≡ With the Magnifying Glass option, change the woman's mouth so that it looks closed. Change the man's mouth so that it looks open.
≡ After choosing small sans serif from the Graphics Tools, set the cursor inside the balloon and type **At least they let me keep the barrel....** Set and reset the cursor as needed to fit the text inside the balloon.
≡ Crop the whole work space and save the file as COMIC3.

Figure 12-14. The Punch-Line Panel

Printing Comics

You can print your comic strips one of two ways.

The first, and fastest, is to print each panel as a photo file from the Press work area. This method works best if you're creating a short comic strip, say three to five panels. Since you'll be pasting them into a strip form by hand anyway, you don't need to place them in a *Newsroom* page layout file.

The second method takes more time, but it's best if you're creating a longer comic book and want to take advantage of *Newsroom*'s layout abilities.

Fast printing. To print your photo files, go to the Press work area and choose *Print photo*. Put the appropriate data disk in the drive and select the photo file you want to print. Only photo files will appear in the list.

To save paper, you can print up to four of the comic-strip panels on a page. If you wisely left some space at the bottom of each photo, there's no danger of one overprinting another, nor of accidentally destroying one when you take scissors to paper.

That's the next step. Cut out each panel—you want them in order left to right, not top to bottom. Arrange them on another sheet of paper and paste or tape them down.

You may want to photocopy the assembled comic strip at a reduced size. That way it will be closer in size to the comic strips you commonly see in the newspaper. You may also want to consider using this reduced comic strip in your own *Newsroom*-produced paper. You'll have to plan ahead—leave some blank space (perhaps the bottom two panels in a layout) for the strip—and paste them in by hand before photocopying or quick printing the newspaper.

The comic strip you created earlier would, in final form, look like this.

Figure 12-15. Completed Comics

Using Layout. To use *Newsroom*'s Layout work area, you need to go through two additional steps before printing.

Enter the Copy Desk work area and, one at a time, load the comic-strip photos into the work space. Save them to disk again, this time as panel files. You can use the same names as you assigned to the photo files if you want.

That done, enter the Layout work area and compose each page with the panels you've just created. Save the page file(s) to disk.

Finally, go to the Press work area and select *Print page*.

Calendars

Keeping yourself, your home, or your school organized isn't easy. A calendar—one with room for notes on appointments, meetings, special activities, and everything else that makes up modern life—can be a lifesaver. A customized calendar can keep everyone on schedule.

Strictly speaking, this calendar-creating project is most useful when its final product is included as part of a *Newsroom*-produced newspaper. This reduced calendar can easily be inserted in a *Newsroom* page-layout file and printed as part of the newspaper. Its small size makes it less practical as a stand-alone calendar.

Forget the Weekends

It's tough enough to squeeze five days across one panel in *Newsroom*, much less seven. The only solution is to toss out Saturday and Sunday.

That's no great loss for a school calendar—school activities on the weekend are rare. At home, though, it's more of a problem. Saturday and Sunday are often packed with things to do. If you can't do without the weekends listed in your calendar, read the box near the end of this chapter. It outlines how to create a calendar two panels wide.

Here's how to create your custom calendar.

- Enter the Photo Lab work area, select the Crayon icon, and pick the Lines tool and the smallest pen.
- In the work space, draw lines from the top left of the screen to the bottom, another across the bottom of the space, and a third back up to the top.
- Choose the Crayon icon again, but this time select the Line tool and the smallest pen.
- Divide the enclosed space into thirds vertically and into fifths horizontally. Use your best judgment on line placement, or put a ruler up to the screen and use that as a guide.

At this point, the screen should look like Figure 12-16.

Figure 12-16. Master Calendar

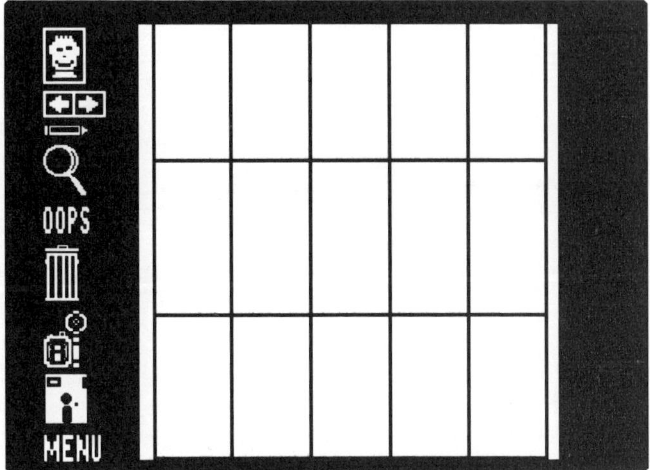

≡ Crop the entire work space and save the photo file as CALENDAR.

With that safely on disk, you can build a specific calendar. Here's how.

≡ Load CALENDAR into the Photo Lab work space.
≡ To create the top half of the calendar, choose the Crayon icon and pick the Eraser tool and the large, square pen.
≡ Erase the vertical lines in the top third of the work space.
≡ Return to the Graphics Tools menu and choose one of the large type sizes.
≡ Type in the name of the month across the top of the panel. Figure 12-17, the completed top half of the calendar, uses **February, 1988.**
≡ Position the cursor above the middle of each date column and type **M, Tu, W, Th,** and **F** for the days of the week. You'll probably have to set and reset the cursor several times to get them aligned and spaced correctly.
≡ Still with the same large type size, type in a date in the upper left corner of each box. Set the cursor separately for each number. If you use the space bar to move the cursor, lines are erased.
≡ Go to the Graphics Tools menu one last time and change to the small sans serif type. (Sans serif is slightly narrower than serif, so you may be able to get a bit more text in a date box.)
≡ Type notes in the appropriate date boxes.
≡ When you're through with the first two weeks of the month, crop the whole work space and save the file as CAL02A (CALendar file, 02 for February, and A for the top half).

Figure 12-17. The First Two Weeks of February

February 1988

M	Tu	W	Th	F
1 10:30 Emily's doctor appoint.	2	3 Take day off!!!	4	5 5:30 pm Leave for NYC
8	9 2:30 pm Back from NYC	10	11 4:00 pm Lori's work- shop	12 7:00 pm Becki & Neil for dinner

The bottom half is easier—there are no days of the week or name of the month to include. It's all dates and notes.

≡ Load the CALENDAR file into the Photo Lab work space.
≡ Using the same large type as you used in the top half, enter dates in the boxes.
≡ Call up the Graphics Tools by selecting the Crayon icon. Pick the small sans serif type.
≡ Type in any notes in the appropriate boxes.
≡ Crop the entire work space and save the file as CAL02B.

Figure 12-18. The Rest of the Month

15 7:30 pm P.E.O. meeting here	16	17	18 Call Ellen D.	19
22	23 7:00 am Break- fast with Selby	24 Lunch at Spring Garden Cafe	25	26 Leave for Silva at 4:00 pm
29 Extra day this year				

Printing the Calendar

Like the comic strips you read about earlier in this chapter, you can print the calendar in one of two ways.

For a stand-alone calendar that's not part of a *Newsroom* newspaper, just go to the Press work area and choose *Print photo*. Print the top half of the calendar. *Don't touch the paper.* Return to the Press menu list and select *Print photo* again, this time highlighting the bottom half of the calendar. When it prints, the bottom of the top half should perfectly merge with the top of the bottom half. (That's why the master file had a horizontal line across the *bottom* of the work space, but not the top.)

Printing the calendar as part of a newspaper is just slightly less simple. Load the two photo files into the Copy Desk work area and save them out as panels. As always, you can reuse their photo names. Place the panels in a page-layout file from within Layout and then print the page as you would any other. Again, the lines of the top and bottom halves of the calendar should meet exactly.

Here's what the February, 1988 calendar would look like in final form.

Figure 12-19. All 29 Days

February 1988

M	Tu	W	Th	F
1 10:30 Emily's doctor appoint	2	3 Take day off!!!	4	5 5:30 pm Leave for NYC
8	9 2:30 pm Back from NYC	10	11 4:00 pm Lori's work-shop	12 7:00 pm Becki & Neil for dinner
15 7:30 pm P.E.O. meeting here	16	17	18 Call Ellen D.	19
22	23 7:00 am Break-fast with Selby	24 Lunch at Spring Garden Cafe	25	26 Leave for Silva at 4:00 pm
29 Extra day this year				

If you can't do without Saturday and Sunday, try this less-than-elegant solution.

Instead of vertically dividing the master calendar file into fifths, divide it into fourths. Run the three horizontal lines all the way to both edges of the work space. Place the leftmost and rightmost vertical lines against the edges as well.

Use the two-panel headline technique discussed in Chapter 2 when placing the month and year at the top of the calendar. Break the head between the month and year.

When working on the right side of the calendar (top and bottom), erase the column of boxes at the far right. In other words, there will be only three columns (to add to the four in the left side of the calendar) in this file.

Printing must be done from a page-layout file. The photo files must be loaded and saved as panels. There will be a small gap (the gutter) between the fourth and fifth days of the week.

All other aspects of the calendar creation process are as explained earlier.

More Projects

As you play with *Newsroom*'s features and explore some of the nonnewspaper things you can do with the program, you'll undoubtedly find other projects it can handle.

For instance, *Newsroom* can help you write and print impressive-looking, two-column reports for school. Keep the cartoonlike clip art to a minimum and lay out bannerless pages for the best reports.

Or use it to generate worksheets for the classroom or for home teaching. The Graphics Tools of the Photo Lab make it simple to insert lines for fill-in-the-blank review and boxes for multiple-choice questions. The MAPS files on the *Clip Art* disk are especially useful for social studies and history classes, while the UMPIRE files on the *Clip Art Collection, Volume 3* disk are great for physical education classes (not to mention drilling a young football team on possible penalties).

Experiment with *Newsroom*'s hidden talents. You may discover some of your own.

CHAPTER 13

Beyond the News at Work

Newsroom isn't just for the home or classroom. It's a simple-to-use desktop publishing program that can produce high-quality newsletters for almost any business. That alone is worth its price.

But *Newsroom* can fill more jobs than just newsletter publishing. If your business is small or your budget tight, you probably think twice about spending money on high-priced business software. It doesn't mean you have to go without such things as computer-created forms or charts or letterhead, though.

This last chapter of *Using Newsroom at Home, School, and Work* shows how to use *Newsroom* to create custom forms, charts, stationery, and more for your business. With clear, step-by-step instructions, you'll see what *Newsroom* can do for the bottom line.

Forms

Business forms come in as many, well, forms, as there are businesses. Forms for recording sales, forms for new clients or patients, forms for work orders.

Your office or business may have dozens, even scores, of forms. Designing efficient forms and having them printed takes time—and money. You may be spending more than you want on the paper your workplace generates.

Don't think you'll use *Newsroom* to electronically store the information normally placed on your forms, however. That's impractical at best. *Newsroom* isn't a database or filing software. It doesn't pretend to be, and no matter how many things it can do other than publish newsletters, it will never be part of a computerized office record-keeping system.

What it can do, though, is help you create the paper forms every office uses every day. Not all businesses are completely computerized. Yours may be one. And even if it's full of personal computers, it probably still needs paper and forms to function.

Let's create a custom form for a small business. In this case, it's an invoice used by a small publishing company. The techniques can be applied to almost any form for almost any firm.

Logo

Depending on the form and how much information you need to pack on one sheet of paper, you can either use the Banner or Photo Lab work areas. The former creates larger type, and more importantly, lets you run text and graphics all the way across the page. The latter prints smaller type and so lets you put more on a page. But you have to contend with the gutter in the middle of the page. Of course, you may want to go with a combination of the two, though that may look strange because of the big difference in the type size.

Make your decision based on your requirements. Which is more important, more information on the page or the ability to use the entire width of the page?

You should stick with these two work areas of *Newsroom* and ignore the Copy Desk for form generation. The Copy Desk makes it too hard to use graphics, even simple ones like lines. And most forms need lines and boxes. Such graphics can be quickly created in the Banner or Photo Lab work areas.

The first thing you'll want to do is make this invoice distinctive. You want your forms to be recognized as coming from your company. The simplest way to identify the form as yours is to include your normal company or business logo at the top of the form.

If you already have a logo, you can duplicate it for use with *Newsroom* in one of several ways.

- Recreate it by hand with the Graphics Tools
- Copy it by tracing it with the Graphics Tools (see Chapter 3 for details)
- Digitize it with video or scanner and then convert it to *Newsroom* photo format (see Chapter 4 for details)

If you don't have a recognizable logo yet, your task is simpler. You can use the Graphic Tools in either the Banner or Photo Lab work areas to create one from scratch. Many times this is easier than reproducing an existing logo because you can plan to use tools such as Line, Box, and Circle—they're the most manageable of those in the Graphics Tools.

This invoice will use a banner-sized space for the logo and company name to make both elements more noticeable. How you create your own logo is up to you. Figure 13-1 shows the result of about 15 minutes of work with the Graphics Tools in the Banner work area. Take a look at it and its explanation—you may find some techniques you can try when you build your own form logo.

Figure 13-1. Form Logo

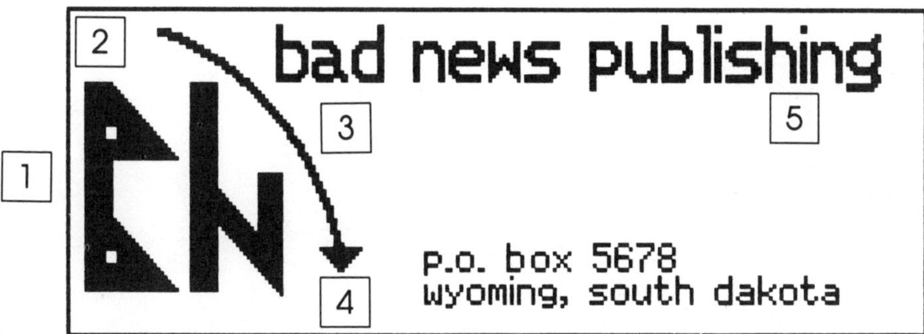

1 The abstract *B* and *N* were created with the Box and Lines tools and then filled with the black pattern.

2 The arrow was drawn by picking the Circles tool and the pen third from the left. Starting from the lower left corner of the banner work space, the circle was pulled to its present position.

3 The Eraser was used to erase parts of the circle; the result was this arc.

4 The head of the arrow was drawn pixel by pixel in the Magnifying Glass option.

5 Lowercase was used for the company name and address to make it less formal (this is a *really* small publishing company). The sans serif type contributed to this look as well. Just as importantly, though, only sans serif type would fit in the available space.

Note: The box around the banner was not part of the original design, but was added only to show the size of the banner when reproduced in this book.

Panel Forms

The rest of most forms will be made in the Photo Lab work area. Although a banner runs clear across the page, even the small type size is too large. You just can't pack enough information in a banner-based form.

Eventually, you'll transfer the photo files to the Copy Desk and its panels so that you can lay out and print the form as a unit. Panels present other problems, the most important being the gutter between the columns. You can't draw lines all the way across a page, for instance.

You can get around this with several solutions. One is to put the form's information into imaginary boxes which correspond to panels.

Figure 13-2. Little Boxes

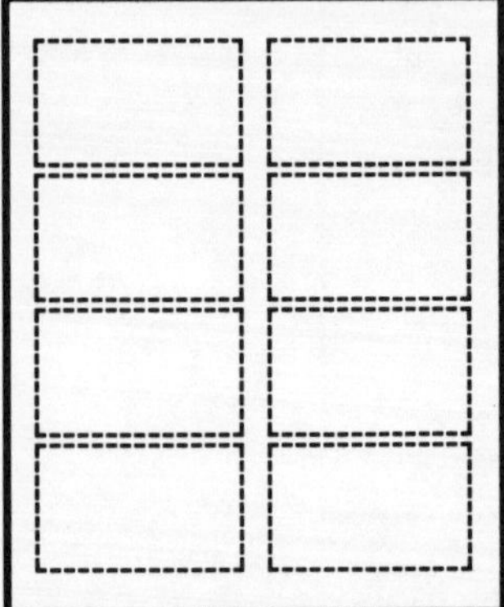

You'll compartmentalize your form's information in these imaginary boxes. For example, if you were making an order form, you might put the customer's name in one box, the item(s) and prices in another box, total sales plus tax in another, and such things as delivery date, method of payment, and delivery location in yet another box. Each section is self-contained.

A second solution to the panel/gutter problem is to carefully align the information in neighboring panels. This is harder, but the results are worth it. Let's try it with the invoice from bad news publishing.

- Enter the Photo Lab work area, select the Crayon icon and pick the Line tool and the smallest pen.
- Position the cursor at the top left corner of the screen. Press the cursor or arrow key once to move down. Press the select key and move across the screen. Press the select key again at the other side to draw a line.
- For evenly spaced lines, press the down-arrow or -cursor key one time; then hit the select key. Draw another line across the work space. Continue until the entire screen is filled with horizontal lines.
- Crop the whole screen and save the photo as FORM.

Figure 13-3. Master Form Panel

≡ Pick the large serif type from the Graphics Tools menu and type **book name** and **author** above the top line. To align both equally, position the large cursor so that its bottom edge is immediately above the top line.

≡ Using the Line tool and smallest pen again, draw a vertical line to create the two columns (see Figure 13-4 for its approximate position). Draw the line from the top horizontal line all the way to the bottom of the work space.

≡ Type in the book name and author information with the small sans serif type.

This will be the left side of the form.

Figure 13-4. Book and Author

book name	author
managing the art of basket selling	arthur baskinson
growing greens at home	billy bob tucker
decorating chairs with wood burning	chuck babbit
refrigerator repair made easy	chuck babbit
tub 'o fun making bathtubs	eddy toode

- Crop and save it, perhaps with the name FORMUL (FORM, Upper Left).
- Return to the main menu, enter the Press work area, and print this photo file so you have it for reference.

To make the right side of the book-sales form, load the master file FORM back into the Photo Lab work area.

- In large serif, type **isbn, price, #,** and **total** on the top line. Align the column headings as you did before by placing the cursor right above the top line.
- Draw vertical lines to separate the columns (remember to draw them all the way down to the bottom of the work space).
- Enter the appropriate information in the first two columns.
- Crop and save this photo file as FORMUR (Upper Right).

Figure 13-5. Numbers and Money

isbn	price	#	total
123-1	$12.95		
123-2	$8.95		
123-3	$12.95		
123-4	$9.95		
123-5	$8.95		

If bad news publishing had more books to place on its form, you'd have to load FORMUL and FORMUR into the Photo Lab, erase the column heads, and then type the new information over the old. Such new files could be saved as FORMML and FORMMR for Middle Left and Middle Right, or FORMLL and FORMLR for Lower Left and Lower Right.

When creating the lower parts of the form, however, don't forget to extend the vertical lines into the top space (where the column heads once were).

Form Printing

Almost all forms will be printed as page-layout files, which means you must convert all the photo files (but not any banner files) to panel files from within the Copy Desk.

Proceed to Layout and assemble the form. In the case of the invoice from bad news publishing, the files would be placed in the order shown in Figure 13-6.

Figure 13-6. Form Layout

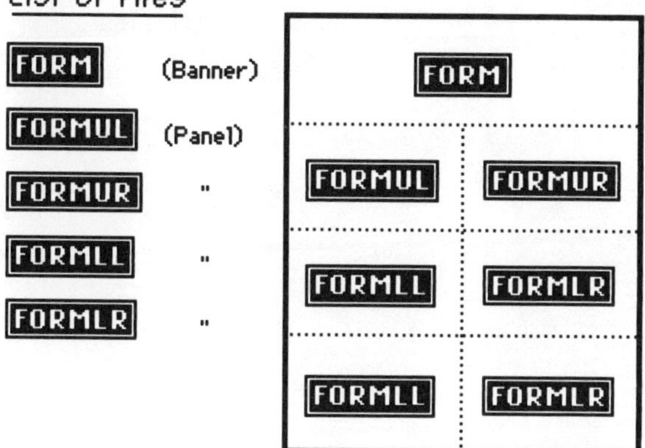

Print the form, make copies of it (photocopies, probably), and put it to use. The final printed bad news publishing form would look like Figure 13-7.

Figure 13-7. Final Form

book name	author	isbn	price	#	total
managing the art of basket selling	arthur baskinson	123-1	$12.95		
growing greens at home	billy bob tucker	123-2	$8.95		
decorating chairs with wood burning	chuck babbit	123-3	$12.95		
refrigerator repair made easy	chuck babbit	123-4	$9.95		
tub 'o fun making bathtubs	eddy toode	123-5	$8.95		

If you're using a more free-form form—banners perhaps, or a combination of banners and photos—you can manually roll the paper before printing each element. Chapter 12 has complete details on this method of printing multiple banners on one page.

Charts

Charts are an important part of business presentations, reports, proposals, and announcements. When you want to show your salespeople how they're doing, a bar chart or graph communicates the message faster than page after page of numbers. Describing a business's hierarchy takes much longer than a simple organizational tree chart. And a list of ideas or points in a proposed plan is much clearer when presented in a bullet chart.

Newsroom has chart-making powers that can enliven any company's way of doing business with its customers and with its employees.

Ready-Made Charts

The simplest way to create great charts in *Newsroom* is with *Clip Art Collection, Volume 2.* Three files on that disk contain pieces that you can combine to make a wide variety of charts.

Figure 13-8. *Volume 2* Chart Art

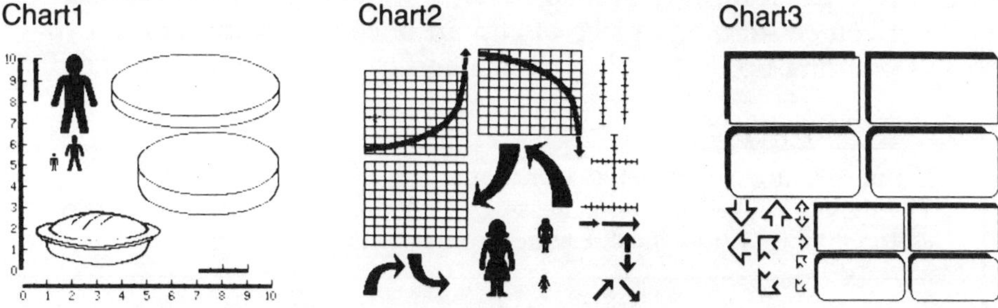

Reprinted courtesy Springboard Software, Inc. Copyright 1985, 1986, Springboard Software, Inc.

You can grab pieces from one or more of these files and put them together on the Photo Lab screen. Once there, the Graphics Tools can be used to change the charts, add legends and labels, or paint with fill patterns.

The graph axes (the rulerlike line) in CHART1, for instance, can be modified to represent sales by year with a few simple steps.

- Grab the short vertical axis. Position four copies of it on the left side of the screen.
- Grab the short horizontal axis and position four copies of it near the bottom (refer to Figure 13-9 for the finished chart).
- Select a small type size and type **5, 10, 15, 20, 25, 30, 35,** and **40** along the vertical axis; type **81, 82, 83, 84, 85, 86, 87,** and **88** along the horizontal axis.
- Draw rectangular boxes to represent each year's sales amount (the numbers along the vertical axis could indicate the sales in dollars or units, in increments of hundreds, thousands, tens of thousands, or whatever).
- Fill in the boxes with one or more fill patterns.
- Clean up and small mistakes with the Magnifying Glass.

Figure 13-9. Sales Chart

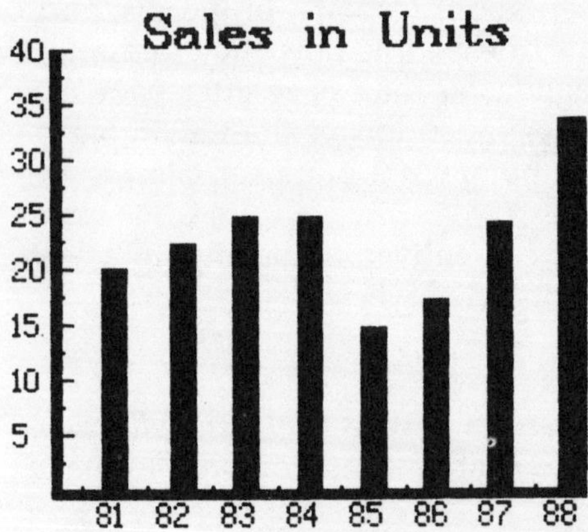

Pie charts, bar charts, graphs, organizational tables, and even project flow charts can be created quickly and easily with these chart components. Don't forget that you can flip any piece of clip art once it's on the Photo Lab screen—arrows pointing up and to the left can be flipped to point down and right.

If you're using *Newsroom* at work, buy *Clip Art Collection, Volume 2.* The disk is packed with business-oriented clip art, much of it far less cartoonlike than the clip art which comes with *Newsroom.*

But even if you don't have the *Volume 2* disk, you can still create attractive charts by hand with the Graphics Tools. The rest of this section shows you how to do that and more.

Bar Charts and Graphs

Bar charts and graphs usually have axes along the left and bottom edges to show the values (numbers or dates, normally) being charted.

Figure 13-10. Chart and Graph Axes

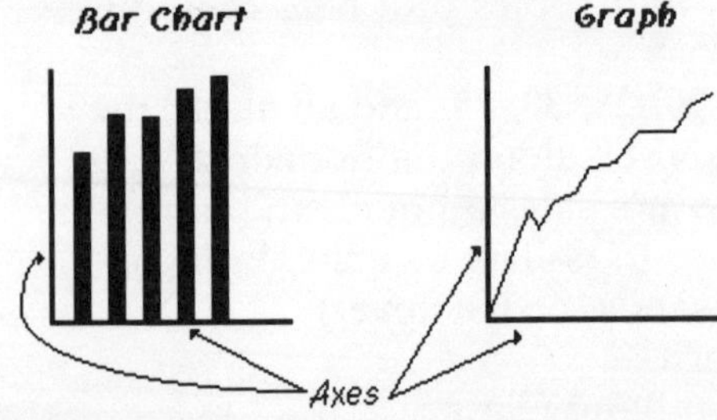

The hardest parts of a chart or graph to make by hand are the axes.

- ≡ Draw the axes themselves with the Line tool and the third pen from the left.
- ≡ You'll have to clean up the ends and junctions of the lines with the Magnifying Glass.
- ≡ Accurate increments within each axis are difficult to create. You can use the Magnifying Glass feature and count the number of pixels between each increment mark (a painfully slow and tedious process). A much faster (and usually very acceptable) method is to draw very short lines with the Line tool and the smallest pen. Simply "eyeball" the space between each increment. Clean up any noticeable mistakes with the Magnifying Glass.

Figure 13-11. Handmade Axes

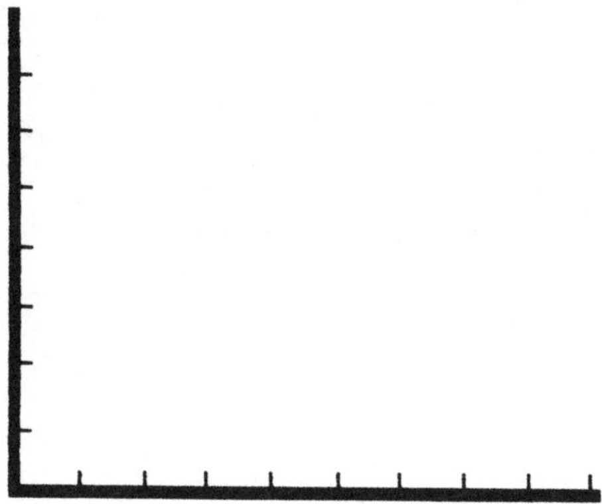

Once the axes are in place, building the rest of a bar chart or graph is simple.

- ≡ Enter any labels with one of the small type sizes. Abbreviate to make them fit within the increments.
- ≡ For a bar chart, draw a rectangular box of the proper length (with the Box tool and the smallest pen). Try to draw all the boxes the same width. Fill in the boxes with one or more of the fill patterns.

Figure 13-12. Handmade Bar Chart

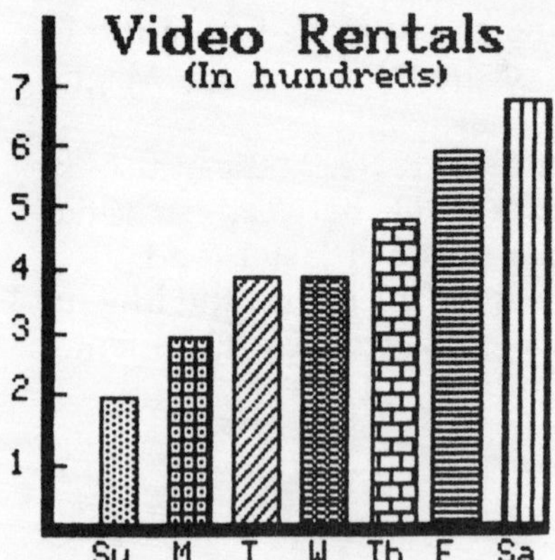

≡ For a graph, choose the Lines tool and one of the smaller pens (always select a smaller pen than that used to draw the axes). Starting at the junction of the axes, plot the graph by pressing the select key, moving the cursor, pressing the select key, and so on. You may want to close off the right edge of the graph and fill the space with a pattern.

Figure 13-13. Handmade Graph

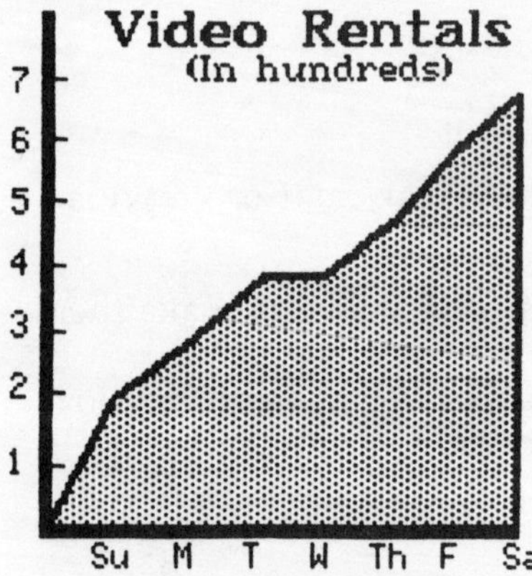

Organizational Charts

Plotting the organization of your business, whether it's for new employees or to show a restructured department, is important to a smoothly running office. Though you could describe the organization in words, you can get the message across much easier with a graphic representation.

Often called a *tree chart* because of its limb-and-trunk appearance, a clear graphic can provide information at a glance.

If you have *Clip Art Collection, Volume 2*, you can create such a chart from the pieces the CHART3 file. But if you're doing without that disk of clip art, it's pretty easy to make the pieces yourself.

The simplest tree chart consists of boxes and lines. The boxes are filled with names or titles, and lines connect the boxes to show who reports to whom. Boxes and lines can be drawn with the Graphics Tools within the Photo Lab work area.

Figure 13-14. Simple Tree Chart

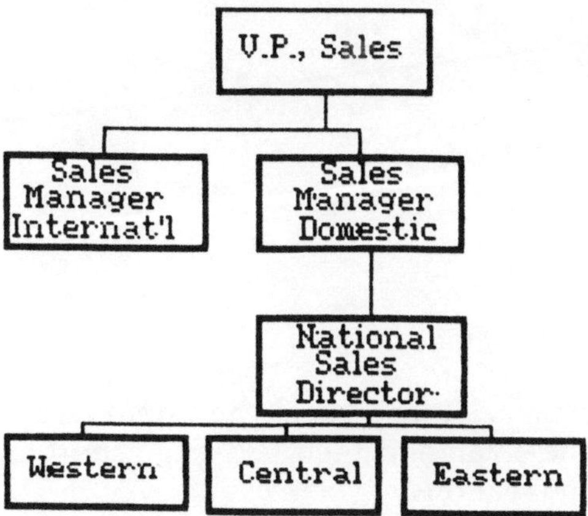

Here are a few notes on making a chart like this.

- It may be difficult to make the boxes the same size. The surest way is to use the cursor or arrow keys, and count the number of keypresses used to build the box. The fastest way is to draw the boxes by relying on your eye for size, dimension, and placement.
- Center the text within the boxes for best effect. Set and reset the cursor with the selection key if necessary, or set the cursor at the left edge of the box and use the spacebar to center it.
- Use a smaller pen for the lines than that used for the boxes.

More impressive-looking boxes can be drawn with shadows and three-dimensional edges. In fact, in just a few moments you can have boxes that look as good as the ones in CHART3.

- Choose the square pen and draw two lines, one for the top, another for the left side. Change to a smaller pen and draw a box atop the lines; the box should extend below and to the right of the black shadow (see Figure 13-15, top).
- Or use the left-facing diagonal pen (third from the right in the pen list) to draw the left and top sides. Change to a smaller pen and draw the bottom

and right sides. Clean up any mistakes with the Magnifying Glass (see Figure 13-15, bottom).

Figure 13-15. Handmade Shadow Boxes

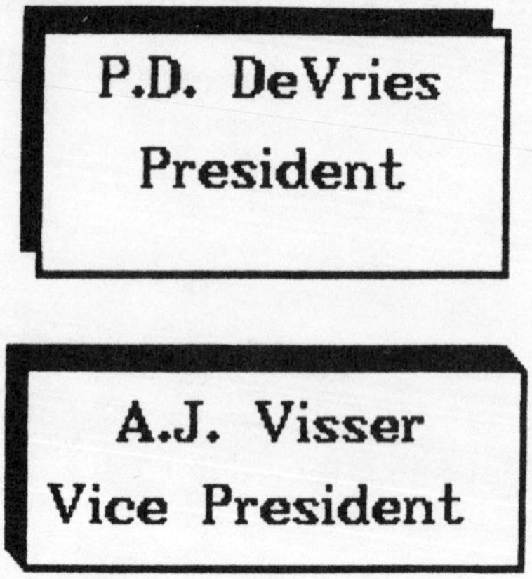

P.D. DeVries
President

A.J. Visser
Vice President

Bigger than a panel. You can't get much of a chart into the Photo Lab work space. Unless you make the boxes quite small and their text quite short, you're going to have to produce multiscreen creations.

The key to building a multiple photo file chart is to account for the connecting lines. Where a line exits in one photo should perfectly match where it enters in another.

It's easier if you don't try to create page-wide charts, but stick to those a panel wide and several panels deep. That way you don't have to worry about the gutter in the middle of the page. Remember, there's no intervening space between panels in the same column.

Draw the chart so that one box, or row of boxes, is very near the bottom of the work space. Position any lines exiting off the bottom edge with the cursor or arrow keys, not the joystick or mouse. Count the number of keypresses, in small or large increments, that it takes to reach the line from the left side of the work space. When you continue the chart in the next photo, place the lines by counting that same number of keypresses before hitting the select key.

Printing is straight-forward. As long as the chart is only one column wide, you can print it directly from the Press, no matter how many photo files are involved.

Figure 13-16. Large Tree Charts

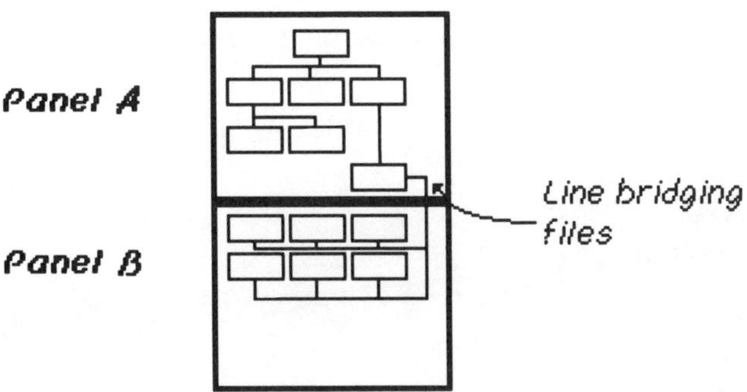

With a Bullet

Bullet lists—they're used throughout this book, even though they don't have standard typographical bullets, those small black circles (or dots when they're really small) so often used to

- Separate points in an argument.
- List items in a step-by-step fashion.
- Outline thoughts in a proposal.

Bullet lists are especially useful when you're making a presentation before a group. They clearly identify each element or point you're trying to make, quickly communicating the main parts of your report or proposal.

Armed with an overhead projector and clearly marked bullet lists on transparencies, you can impress and astound your superiors and subordinates with your organizational skills.

You don't need special software to create such bullet lists; you can throw away your markers and grease pencils, too. *Newsroom* makes it easy to generate short or long bullet lists which you can photocopy onto paper or transparencies. Here's how.

≡ For most bullet lists, use the Photo Lab work area. Some lists, however, may require larger type, in which case you'd want to use these same techniques in the Banner work area.

≡ In the Graphics Tools menu, choose one of the large type sizes for the text.

≡ With the large cursor's left edge against the left side of the work space, press the right-cursor or -arrow key once. Press the select key to set the start of text.

≡ Enter the bullet list's text, pressing Return or Enter twice between each item. Press Return or Enter only once to continue a multiline item (text doesn't automatically wrap in the Photo Lab).

≡ Go back to the Graphics Tools and choose Draw and the largest circular pen or the large square pen.

- Position the cursor beside each item and press the select key to lay down a black circle or square.
- Keep the bullets aligned by using the cursor or arrow keys (not joystick or mouse) to move down to the next item.

Figure 13-17. Bullet Lists

- **Write grant proposal**
- **Develop prototype**
- **Publish paper**
- **Show prototype to Dept. of Energy**
- **Get money**

Bullet lists can easily be made up of several photo files and can then be printed out one at a time. Once they're printed, you can photocopy the results to paper or a transparency.

> Photocopying to transparencies isn't hard. You can find blank transparencies—thin sheets of plastic, actually—at most office and art supply stores. Ask for the kind that will stand up to the heat of the photocopying process. Put the transparency in the copier's paper cartridge or tray and run a copy normally.

Letterhead

Don't underestimate the importance of your company's letterhead. Unless your business has a large advertising budget, your letterhead is one of the first things you use to create your image.

If your letterhead looks unprofessional, that's how people think your business is run. If it's unimaginative, then that's how potential customers see you. And worst of all, if you don't have customized stationery, people wonder if your business isn't just temporary. First impressions are never more important than in business, and your letterhead is often the first thing someone sees of you and your company.

Newsroom can create letterhead for your home or small business in a matter of moments.

Big and Bold

For big and brassy letterhead that shouts at the reader, use the Banner work area. With the entire width of the page at your disposal, you can create prominent letterhead that no one will ignore.

Use as much of the Banner work space as you want to create your letterhead. Just keep these things in mind as you design and build your letterhead.

- Banner text and graphics print twice as large as in the Copy Desk's panels or Photo Lab's photos. Small type will do in almost all situations.
- An unbalanced design has more impact than one that's perfectly centered or balanced. White space to one side adds to a letterhead's effectiveness.
- Most letterhead appears on the top of the paper. Consider printing the letterhead at the bottom of the page for an unusual look.
- Make sure you include the vital information in the letterhead. Company name, street address, city and state, zip code, and telephone number are the bare minimums.
- Simple graphics are more powerful than complicated art.
- Don't be afraid to modify clip art to suit your letterhead needs.
- Use rules to signal the end of the letterhead. This separates the letterhead from the body of the letter later typed on it.
- Print the finished banner and use that master for photocopying or offset printing.
- If you're using an Epson or Epson-compatible printer, leave extra blank room at the sides of Banner work space to account for the narrow margins that printer creates. (Ideally, you'll want an inch on either side of the final master; the typed letter will look better if the letterhead's margins are close to the letter's margin size.)
- Print the letterhead on high-quality paper. Consider taking the master to a quick-print shop for printing in a color other than black.

Figures 13-18 and 13-19 show two simple letterheads created in the Banner work area. Neither took more than five minutes to create. Note the large text used in Figure 13-19.

More Discreet

You may not want to overwhelm the letters you'll type on this letterhead. You don't want to scream your company's name and stamp your company's logo indelibly into the reader's mind. Something more subtle might be in order.

For a smaller, and so more discreet, letterhead, use the Photo Lab work area. The Photo Lab offers the same tools as the Banner work area, but in half the size.

The disadvantage, of course, is that you can't easily stretch the letterhead across the width of the page. The best that you can do is something a column wide.

Even with those restriction, you can produce effective and powerful letterhead that still presents the image you're after. Take a look at Figures 13-20, 13-21, and 13-22, which show several letterheads and their placement on the final page.

Figure 13-18. Big Letterhead

Figure 13-19. Even Bigger Letterhead

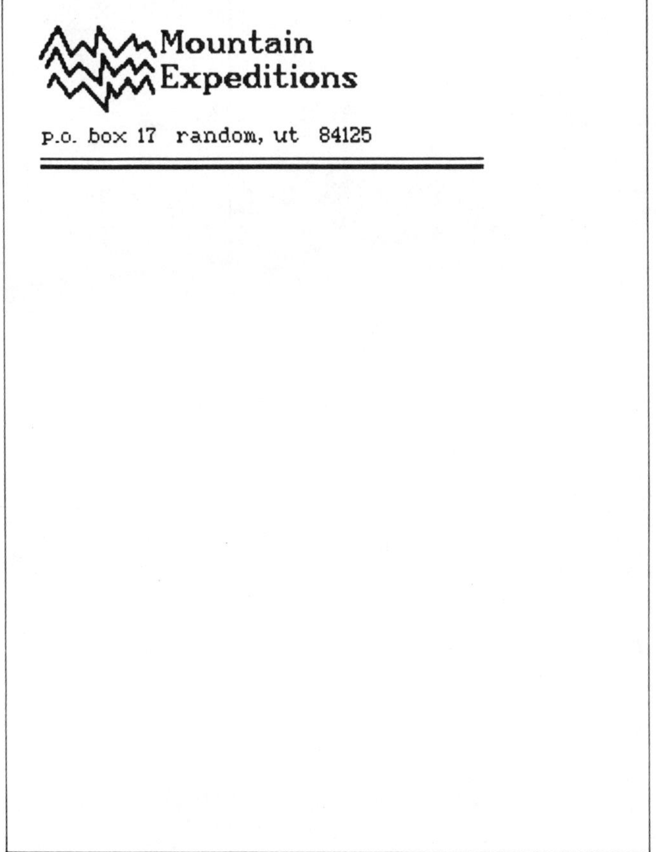

Figure 13-20. Wayne's Pork Products

Figure 13-21. Peter Larrs Studio

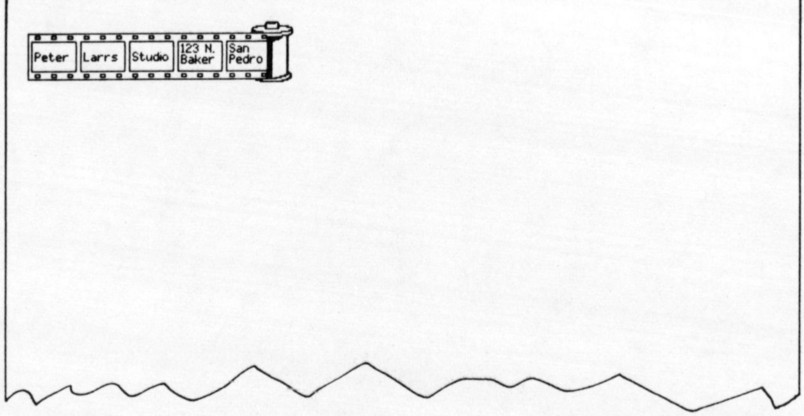

Figure 13-22. Philip Barnes, Inc.

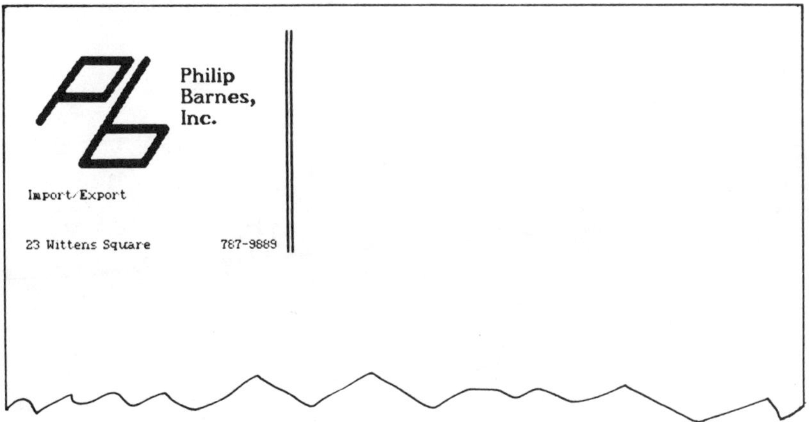

Keep these techniques in mind while you're making letterhead in the Photo Lab work area.

- If you want to position the letterhead on the right side of the page, load the photo in a panel within the Copy Desk work area and then use the Layout work area to create a page layout file.
- A rule to one side (as in Figure 13-22) separates the letterhead from the body of the letter.
- Perfectly centered letterhead is impossible with the Photo Lab approach. If you want this size letterhead, break it into left and right components, much like you did two-panel headlines (see Chapter 2).
- Flip clip art so that it "faces" into the page.
- Look for opportunities to change or combine existing clip art (see Figure 13-21).
- If the letterhead is followed by a rule, you can (with care) extend that line by hand with a fine-tipped black pen.

Split Letterhead

You can even create letterhead that has widely-separated elements. The company's logo can go at the top left, for instance, and the address at the bottom left when you use the Photo Lab, the Copy Desk, and Layout before printing.

Figure 13-23. Up and Down Letterhead

The first step in creating Figure 13-23 was to grab the clip art from *Volume 2*. The flower and hand were flipped, and the hand was then erased (with the Eraser first and then with the Magnifying Glass). The flower was saved as the photo file ROSE.

ROSE was loaded into the Copy Desk, where it was immediately saved back to disk as a panel using the same name. The text at the bottom of the page was entered in the Copy Desk and saved as panel ROSEBOT (for BOTtom).

The last step before printing was to enter the Layout work area and create a bannerless page-layout file with ROSE at the top left and ROSEBOT at the bottom left.

What Else?

The three nonpublishing business projects in this chapter are only the beginning of what *Newsroom* can do at work.

Flyers of all sorts can be made and printed with *Newsroom* to announce sales or specials if you're involved with the retail end of things. Whether you're a butcher pushing ground beef or a Realtor promoting a new listing, you can produce attractive and informative advertising with this program. (Chapter 12 outlines in considerable detail the process of creating flyers. The information there can be applied to any business flyer.)

Sales progress reports can be written and illustrated in *Newsroom*. With its two-column format and charts and graphs—either handmade or pulled from *Clip Art Collection, Volume 2*—*Newsroom*-produced reports get your boss's attention.

Put your imagination to work with *Newsroom* at work and you'll be astounded at the results.

The End

If you've moved through *Using Newsroom at Home, School, and Work* a chapter at a time, you've seen it all by now. How to use each of *Newsroom*'s six work areas to create better newspapers and newsletters. How real *Newsroom* publishers use the program to write, edit, and print great newspapers for the home, school, club, and office. And how to put *Newsroom* to work completing projects ranging from flash cards to business forms.

If you weren't a *Newsroom* pro when you started reading *Using Newsroom*, you probably are by now. And if you were a veteran publisher to begin with, you've undoubtedly picked up countless techniques and tricks you can use in your own newspaper.

But there are certainly things I've missed. Things you know about and want to share with other *Newsroom* users. If you have a favorite *Newsroom* tip, trick, technique, or just plain hint, let me know.

Send your *Newsroom* tidbit to:

Gregg Keizer
c/o COMPUTE! Books & *Newsroom*
P.O. Box 5406
Greensboro, NC 27403

APPENDIX

Printers Supported by *Newsroom*

APPENDIX

Printers Supported by *Newsroom*

These are the printers supported by the most current versions of *The Newsroom.*

Apple

Anadex 9000
Anadex 9001
Anadex 9500
Anadex 9501
Anadex 9620
Anadex 9625B
Apple DMP (normal)
Apple DMP (wide)
Apple ImageWriter (normal)
Apple ImageWriter (wide)
Apple Scribe (normal)
Apple Scribe (wide)
BMC BX-80
Citizen MSP-10
Citizen MSP-15
Citizen MSP-20
Citizen MSP-25
C. Itoh 7500 EP
C. Itoh 8510
Datasouth DS-180
Epson FX-80
Epson FX-100
Epson LQ-1500
Epson LX-80
Epson LX-100
Epson MX-70
Epson MX-80 with Graftrax Plus
Epson MX-80 with old Graftrax
Epson MX-100
Epson MX-100 (older versions)
Epson RX-80
Epson RX-100
Gorilla/Banana
IDS 440g
IDS 445
IDS 460g
IDS 480
IDS 560
Legend
Mannesmann-Tally Spirit 80
MPI 88g
MPI Printmate 99
MPI Printmate 150
MPI S Printer
MPI SX Printer
MPI X Printer
Okidata Microline 82
Okidata Microline 83
Okidata Microline 84
Okidata Microline 92
Okidata Microline 94
Panasonic
Printek 910
Printek 920
Printek 930
Prism 80
Prism 132
Prowriter
Prowriter 2
Riteman
Seikosha GP100
Seikosha GX100
Star Gemini

Commodore

BMC BX-80
Citizen MSP
C. Itoh 8510
Commodore MPS 801
Commodore MPS 803
Epson MX-70
Epson MX-80
Epson MX-80 (old)
Epson MX-100
Epson MX-100 (old)
Epson FX-80
Epson FX-100
Epson RX-80
Epson RX-100
Epson LX-80
Epson LX-100
Epson LQ-1500
Legend
Miscellensous printer 1
Miscellensous printer 2
Miscellensous printer 3
Miscellensous printer 4
Miscellensous printer 5
Miscellensous printer 6
Okidata type 1
Okidata type 2
Okidata type 3
Okimate 10
Panasonic
Prowriter
Prowriter 2
Riteman
Star Gemini SG10.15

IBM

Anadex 9000
Anadex 9001
Anadex 9500
Anadex 9501
Anadex 9620
Anadex 9625B
Citizen MSP-10
Citizen MSP-15
Citizen MSP-20
Citizen MSP-25
C. Itoh 7500 EP
C. Itoh 8510
Datasouth DS-180
Epson FX-80
Epson FX-100
Epson LQ-1500
Epson MX-70
Epson MX-80 with Graftrax
Epson MX-80 with old Graftrax
Epson MX-100
Epson MX-100 (older versions)
Epson RX-80
Epson RX-100
Gorilla/Banana
IDS 440g
IDS 445
IDS 460g
IDS 480
IDS 560
MPI 88g
MPI Printmate 99
MPI Printmate 150
MPI S Printer
MPI SX Printer
MPI X Printer
Okidata Microline 82
Okidata Microline 83
Okidata Microline 84
Okidata Microline 92
Okidata Microline 94
Panasonic
Prism 80
Prism 132
Prowriter
Prowriter 2
Riteman
Seikosha GP100
Seikosha GX100
Star Gemini
Tandy DMP-120
Tandy DMP-200
Tandy DMP-2100P

Index